UNDERSTANDING INTERNATIONAL POLITICAL ECONOMY

with readings for the fatigued

UNDERSTANDING INTERNATIONAL POLITICAL ECONOMY

with readings for the fatigued

Ralph Pettman

LYNNE RIENNER PUBLISHERS

BOULDER
LONDON

Grateful acknowledgment of previously published material is made for
David Bensusan-Butt, "Learning Economics 1976," in Heinz Arndt (ed.) *Our Economic Knowledge: A Sceptical Miscellany* (Australian National University Press, Canberra, 1980), pp. 65–76. Frédéric Bastiat, *Economic Sophisms*, translated by P. J. Stirling (T. Fisher Unwin Ltd, London, 1909), Chapter 7. David Lodge, "My First Job," which first appeared in *London Review of Books*, v. 2 no. 17, 4–17 September 1980, pp. 23–24, reprinted by permission of Curtis Brown on behalf of David Lodge, copyright © David Lodge 1980. Stephen Hymer, "Robinson Crusoe and the Secret of Primitive Accumulation," in *Monthly Review*, v. 23 no. 4, 1971, pp. 11–36, copyright © 1971 by Monthly Review Inc., reprinted by permission of Monthly Review Foundation. Cynthia Enloe, "Women in Banana Republics," in Cynthia Enloe, *Bananas, Beaches, and Bases: Making Feminist Sense of International Politics* (University of California Press, Berkeley, 1990), copyright © Cynthia Enloe 1989. Anthony Sampson, "The Barbecue," in Anthony Sampson, *The Sovereign State: The Secret History of ITT* (Hodder and Stoughton, London, 1973), pp. 15–21, reprinted by permission of The Peters, Fraser and Dunlop Group Ltd and of Hodder Headline PLC. Cheryl Payer, "The Lawyer's Typist: Variations on a Theme by Paul Samuelson," in *Monthly Review*, v. 25 no. 10, pp. 44–48, copyright © 1974 by Monthly Review Inc., reprinted by permission of Monthly Review Foundation. R. A. Radford, "The Economic Organization of a P.O.W. Camp," in *Economica, New Series*, v. 12 no. 48, November 1945, pp. 189–201. M. Atterbury, "Depression Hits Robinson Crusoe's Island," in Joyce Kornbluh (ed.) *Rebel Voices: An IWW Anthology* (University of Michigan Press, Ann Arbor, 1964), reprinted by permission of Charles Kerr Co., Chicago, IL. Jonathan Swift, "A Modest Proposal for Preventing the Children of Ireland from Being a Burden to Their Parents and Their Country," in Jonathan Swift, *Satires and Personal Writings* (1729), edited by W. A. Eddy (Oxford University Press, Oxford, 1932). Pura Velasco, "I Am a Global Commodity: Women Domestic Workers, Economic Restructuring and International Solidarity," in Cindy Duffy and Craig Benjamin (eds.) *The World Transformed: Gender, Work and Solidarity in the Era of Free Trade and Structural Adjustment* (RhiZone, P.O. Box 4927, Station E., Ottawa, Ontario, Canada K1S 5J1, 1995). E. F. Schumacher, "Buddhist Economics," in Herman E. Daly (ed.) *Toward a Steady-State Economy* (W. H. Freeman and Co., San Fransisco, 1973), reprinted by permission of Vreni Schumacher. Hinmatoo Yalkikt, Chief Joseph of the Nez Percé, "Surrender Speech" (1877), in T. McLuhan, *Touch the Earth: A Self-Portrait of Indian Existence* (Outerbridge and Dienstfrey, New York, 1971), p. 20. "Arthur and Dennis," in *Monty Python and the Holy Grail* (Eyre Methuen, London, 1974), pp. 10–12, reprinted by permission of Python Productions Ltd.

Published in the United States of America in 1996 by
Lynne Rienner Publishers, Inc.
1800 30th Street, Boulder, Colorado 80301

and in the United Kingdom by
Lynne Rienner Publishers, Inc.
3 Henrietta Street, Covent Garden, London WC2E 8LU

Library of Congress Cataloging-in-Publication Data
Pettman, Ralph.
    Understanding international political economy : with readings for the fatigued / Ralph Pettman.
        p.   cm.
    Includes bibliographical references and index.
    ISBN 1-55587-666-8 (alk. paper)
    ISBN 1-55587-677-3 (pbk. : alk. paper)
    1. International economic relations. 2. Competition,
International. I. Title.
HF1359.P486   1996
337—dc20   96-1321
                                                  CIP

British Cataloguing in Publication Data
A Cataloguing in Publication record for this book
is available from the British Library.

Printed and bound in the United States of America

The paper used in this publication meets the requirements
of the American National Standard for Permanence of
Paper for Printed Library Materials Z39.48-1984.

5 4 3 2 1

*laughter from the mountains
and appeals to reason from
the broad plains*

— Don DeLillo,
Americana

Contents

Preface

International political economy (IPE) is a serious subject, and it inspires serious prose. Understanding the intricacies of world production and trade; describing and explaining the patterns of capital accumulation and work; making clear the connections among state-making, international marketeering, and world development—these are hard tasks. And it shows.

Could patterns of human practice as complex as these be analyzed in any other way? Many scholarly accounts of IPE seem to be as difficult to understand as the subject itself. Max Weber is supposed to have said once that he saw no reason his books should be any easier to read than they had been to write. How many students of IPE harbor similar sentiments? The first paragraph above is reasonably representative in this regard. It would be easy to use it as the basis for a random jargon generator. List the technical terms it cites in three columns of similar length. Read across these columns in any order. Three-part, impressive-sounding concepts prize themselves off the page. Some of these concepts will actually mean something.

It is ultimately unjust, however, to complain that few analysts of IPE are great stylists when this is such a notable feature of social science analysis as a whole. Moreover, being hard to read does not in itself preclude the pursuit of "truth." Nor does being scintillating necessarily allow of superior insight. Which is why parodies, like random jargon generators, run the risk of confusing means and ends. After all, being boring doesn't mean that a piece of analytic prose can't serve a valid analytic purpose.

We want to know how IPE works not just because we are intellectually curious but because we *need* to know how it works. It is, after all, a basic dimension of world affairs. Unless we decide to surrender to the flow of current events and think no more about it, we will want to direct that flow as best we can toward a vision of the future. Unless we believe this to be the best of all possible worlds, in other words, we will want to change it. To change it we will have to have some idea of what we want to change it to, and how to get from here to there. And to do that we will in turn have to have some idea of how the world works.

Indicting scholars for being pretentious doesn't annul this purpose. Poking fun at jargon may make us a little more aware of the choice many analysts seem to make to objectify and to abstract, renewing at the same time our respect for plain English. It reminds us that being erudite means something more than being difficult to read. It does not mean we should stop trying to understand the international political economy.

The question is how well we are served by specialized vocabularies and by the objectifying mind-set such vocabularies serve. Standing back from the forest of human practices is supposed to allow us to appreciate better the patterns the trees make. Choosing words that are equally disengaged is supposed to make that standing-back step easier to take. Disinterested language and mental detachment are meant to make for less-partial judgments and greater value neutrality. Do they?

Detachment allows for nuanced and sober analysis. That is undeniable. Academic libraries abound with thoughtful books that discuss the issues and the institutions of the international political economy in self-consciously academic prose, and to variously informative effect. There is no end of detail about the key concepts that recur in disciplinary narratives, the major analytic languages used in making sense of those concepts, and subtle critiques of these self-same languages. There is shelf after shelf of intellectually challenging literature on world capitalism, the growth of the world market, the global patterns of production, the new international division of labor, transnational corporations, the main features of the world's trading and financial systems, and contemporary aspects of "development." Similar works also abound about important global industries like oil, transport, communications, tourism, armaments, drugs, and food. And all this is done in full accord with the conventions of scholarly discourse, conventions meant to reduce the immediacy of the human presence and the unwanted influence this presence is supposed to have upon our capacity to understand it.

Does this kind of writing and thinking work? Does it allow us to understand IPE as well as it might? There are now growing doubts that it does. Indeed, some would argue that such an approach only allows part of any analytic story, including that of IPE, to be told.

This whole question raises deep issues of epistemology (knowing) and ontology (being) that can't be covered in a short preface. They are not new issues, nor are they confined to IPE. We do need to note, however, that the whole Enlightenment project is now under scrutiny. By this I mean that the bid we have been making for the last couple of hundred years for universal, absolute, and eternal answers to everything has now itself become debatable. Many analysts, though raised in the Enlightenment tradition, now find it wanting, and I am one of them (Bernstein 1976; Lather 1991; Denzin and Lincoln 1994).

The point I want to make here is that "social analysis [and this includes analysis of international political economy] can be done—differently, but quite validly—either from up close or from a distance, either from within or from the outside" (Rosaldo 1989:188).

All too often "the ideal of detachment" leads in our discipline to "actual indifference" (Rosaldo 1989:7). And even when it doesn't, detachment leads to partiality of a particularly insidious kind. Textual traditions become realities instead of being used to represent realities. What is said is believed to reflect the world "as it is." A reading of the Western philosphical tradition in terms of rational logic and empirical procedure is said to make all meaning accessible to us, and in these terms alone.

I am not a romantic. To reject the claim that rationalism and empiricism provide exclusive access to truth is not of necessity to dive into the irrational or to celebrate the unknown. It is impossible, for example, to perform completely aseptic surgery. But that does not mean that we might as well operate in sewers. There may be limits to what the objective analysis of IPE can achieve; that doesn't mean we give up on analysis. It may mean, however, looking for other ways to analyze IPE that transcend those limits.

In practice, the search for alternatives means paying greater attention to emotive, subjective, unconventional accounts of the subject—though this has its limits, too. I'm very wary, as I've said, of how quickly the "self-absorbed Self" can lose sight of the "self-absorbed Other" (Rosaldo 1989:7). And I know, just as well as the next person, how emotions can cloud our judgments and our understanding. I'm very familiar, too, with the way passionate particulars are wont to rise up to overwhelm our attempts to find the patterns to human practice.

It is time, however, to take an interpretive turn. Simply put, this means making a bid for experiential as well as intellectual knowledge, that is, for understandings of a subjectifying as well as an objectifying sort.

It was some such sense—intuitive at first, but gradually gathering analytic shape over the years as I made it a matter for direct reflection—that prompted me to look for readings that dealt with IPE in other-than-academic and even downright nonacademic ways. Some of the readings I found have been used as the backbone of this book. Some strike me as ironic. Some are little narratives. Some are more-conventional academic analyses of less-conventional topics. None of them would normally be accepted as part of the orthodox disciplinary canon. All, to my mind, are arresting and revealing, and by giving them such prominence here I am making the structure of this book itself an argument for other ways of knowing about IPE.

In choosing to construct the book this way, my initial concern was to alleviate "reader fatigue." Pertinent material that enlivens as well as informs provides a happy alternative to the usual scholarly fare, and as far as I'm concerned, there can never be enough of it. My first plan, therefore, was simply to complement an orthodox attempt to survey IPE with less-conventional material. The literature on the subject is wide and wonderful, and some of the unconventional bits, I've found, can be every bit as enlightening as those of the more conventional kind.

Indeed, rather than using readings to complement a more conventional analysis, I began to consider replacing such an analysis altogether with a selection of evocative essays by various authors that seemed to me to provide a richer experience of IPE than my survey did, or even could. This plan fell through, mostly because publishers considered it commercially nonviable. The whole process left me convinced, however, that readings of the kind provided here do illustrate how serious and substantial points can be made about IPE, despite an unfamiliar focus or informal prose. Making those points this way can be just as, and even more effective than, the orthodox alternatives. Indeed, I now believe that to further our understanding of IPE we have to look somewhere other than the work of conventional scholars. We have to look from other than conventional scholarly points of view.

Why is it that objectifying analyses of subjects like IPE never seem to explain enough? Is it that we haven't yet got it right? Or does the answer lie not in what we study but in how we choose to study it? As social scientists, we objectify. We choose to know our subject intellectually, that is, by means of rationalistic concepts, mental models, and empirical research. We are taught and we learn to privilege what we are pleased to call "the light of the mind." If we subjectify, on the other hand, we are said to be opting for analytic chaos. We are said to be moving away from the "truth," not toward it. Is this so? After all, there is more than one truth. Indeed, IPE is characterized by highly competitive analytic languages that present us with very different "truths." What's more, knowing is not only an intellectual process. We "know" much by nonintellectual means. To privilege the intellect is to marginalize our emotions, for example, and the other ways of knowing that feeling-states provide. It is to assume that nothing *but* the intellect can inform us, and in making that assumption, it is actively to forgo what else the mind can do.

The light of the intellect not only illuminates, it also blinds. When we privilege detachment we marginalize much that actually goes on in the world—indeed, much that happens becomes literally incomprehensible to us. So much of IPE is about human emotions and wishes, visions and dreams. We can talk about these things in objectifying terms, but what do we "know" when we talk this way? What do we "know" when we talk about production or finance or trade in detached terms? We know how people think about these things—or how they say they think. We know about their feelings. But is knowing about such things the same as knowing these things themselves? Surely, if we are to understand other people and why they do what they do, we must try to understand them subjectively as well. Surely, at the very least, we should address their own writings about what they feel and why they behave the way they do, even when these writings are of a subjectifying sort. Indeed, might it not be these sorts of writings that are the most revealing in this regard?

What we are told by such readings remains of necessity within the confines of linear print. Writing is writing after all. It is not a year in Somalia or in the bowels of IBM. Even the most unconventional readings can only suggest other ways of knowing about IPE. They can only show us vicariously what other understandings might be. How often, however, are we encouraged to venture even this far? Very seldom, in my experience. "Objectivity," "neutrality," "impartiality"—words like these get used every day in our discipline. They refer to the "subject positions" with the greatest "institutional authority," and the discipline's paradigm police work overtime to keep them there. And yet these positions are "arguably neither more nor less valid than those of more engaged, yet equally perceptive, knowledgeable social actors" (Rosaldo 1989:21). Or so I wish to argue here.

It seems to me that responsible research is a matter of standing back from IPE to look at it, while standing close to listen as well. At the very least, we ought to "work from one position and try to imagine (or consult with others who occupy) the other [or the others]" (Rosaldo 1989:189). But what if these others are muddled by false consciousness? What, heaven forbid, if we are too? Don't we need to stand back again to look from a distance? Yes, we do, so we objectify again, and our descriptions and explanations start missing the point again, and, oh dear, shouldn't we then stand close and listen again? Once more what we hear seems to be distorted by "their" understandings or our "own," however, and so we step back to look, and so on.

The circle we tread is a spiral one. Having listened in subjectifying ways, that is, we find ourselves objectifying differently when we come to do so again. We see more or we find that we no longer see in the same old way. Does the spiral go up or down, sideways or back on itself? I don't know. There are few alternatives, though. There is madness and there is revelation and there is postmodern pastiche, and that's about it. The first two are not viable options for the academic student of IPE. The last has limits of its own.

In this book I move continuously around the spiral just described. I stand back to reflect on what each reading has to say, making much of the competing analytic languages in which such reflections are made, and then I return to the readings again. Rather than create a dialog or a hybrid between rational-objective and nonacademic points of view, however, I've tried to construct a kind of double helix of experience and analysis. Understanding IPE requires no less, since experience and analysis are inextricable.

This book has been long in the making. In its original form, as I've said, it never saw the light of day. In its stead is this one, a less bold but a much more measured attempt to address the limits that rationalism places upon the study of IPE.

That it appears at all is due in no small part to Stewart Letford, who, much earlier in my life, shared with me his own intuition that seriousness of purpose and lightness of touch are entirely compatible. Much more recently, however, I would like to acknowledge the help of Setsuko Miike, who, when asked to show me where her mind is, as most Japanese would, immediately pointed to her heart. Only after that did she think to point to her head.

—*Ralph Pettman*

1

What Is
International Political Economy?

❖ David Bensusan-Butt (1980) "Learning Economics . . . "

I

Let us imagine a youth who is entering a university—any university, anywhere—and choosing a subject for study. He [sic] has more than a meal ticket in mind, and he does not particularly plan an academic career. But he has the intention of remaining interested in later years, as more than a hobby, in the subject of his choice . . . he has been hearing about the *Wealth of Nations* and economics seems a possibility. But he is not at all sure what has happened to the subject over two centuries or how he will find it treated in his university. He consults an ancient of his acquaintance who came to the subject . . . since Marshall was allowed to establish a separate Economics tripos in Cambridge—the word went round that "it is time that Alfred had a little hell of his own"—and who, after watching recent developments has recently abandoned it for gardening and regrets. It is a case of *si jeunesse savait, si vieillesse pouvait.* As is proper in such cases they discuss the matter at length. The outcome is an oration from the young man to his future teachers, delivered with all the brashness nowadays expected of the young.
    It runs much as follows:

II

"*Gentlemen:* Not knowing what you teach as economics here or how you teach it, I venture to tell you what I want to start learning. I will first, briefly, define the subject as I wish to find it, in the broadest possible terms, and then, at greater length but still in generalities, explain what I hope to find within its main subdivisions.
    "*Definition:* I am told that two views of the scope of the subject persist among present-day teachers. Some following the older tradition take it to cover men's lives in which money and markets play an important role, and also public policies of all kinds that impinge upon those activities. Others, in a more recent tradition, regard it as the scientific study of the rationale of intelligent choice when means are scarce and ends numerous. When I first heard this it struck me that—since for one thing everything takes time and time is certainly scarce for each of us—the second definition would prove

too wide for my capacities. But after it had been explained to me that the proponents of Scientific Economics use language in ways different from those of other people, it seems to me too narrow.

"Apparently they do not mean by 'scientific' what most of us would expect: the cool impartial collection of any kind of fact, hard or soft, relevant to the matters to be discussed. They only admit hard 'objective' facts of an overtly quantitative, measurable kind. Hence they exclude all observation of the conscious psychology, private or social, of economic agents. Further they do not mean (as others do) by 'rational behaviour' the kind of decision-making entailed in first distinguishing and comparing the expected outcomes of all relevant possible actions and selecting that which, by some accepted and pre-examined criterion, is the best. It would be necessary, if they did that, to admit that most of our decisions are *not* rational and then their science would *either* have to be confined to the tiny fragment of our behaviour which is rational (and be prefaced by identifying this fragment), *or* it would degenerate into speculation about imaginary, though maybe ideal, modes of behaviour. They escape this dilemma, I learn with alarm, by the trick of asserting it as an axiom, not to be debated, that all behaviour is rational, though sometimes ill-informed, and proclaiming the science of 'revealed preference'. By this semantic jugglery they can construct a fake psychology that is implied by actions and employs language also used in real psychology; they can apply it to any topic for which a supply of statistics can be concocted, and they can, and I am told do, trumpet like anything about the superiority of a mindless economics over one in which the mind is observed.

"Gentlemen, if there be Scientific Economists among you I must go elsewhere, for two reasons. First, I wish to learn about economic psychology for its own sake, and as a necessary foundation for both positive and normative economics. And, second I do not trust myself (or if I may say even you either) not to get into a welter of muddle and delusion in a group where some are arguing from real mind to action and others from action to artificial imaginary minds, and where such basic terms as science and rationality are being simultaneously used in diverse and contradictory senses.

"Permit me to assume that your views of the scope and method of the subject lie within the limits of the older traditions of the subject. Then I have still some observations to make about the contents of the different parts of economics and the balance between them as I wish to find them here. The subject shall, of course, have two main divisions, positive and normative, and I start with the principal sub-divisions of the first . . .

III

"*Descriptive:* Naturally I am alarmed, as well as excited, by the prodigious variety of hard and soft facts encompassed by economics (and the breadth of the gradation between the economic and the non-economic). Naturally I wish to generalise, and to have theory derived from generalisations which, when applied, will impose a recognisable order upon the chaos of economic events, past, present and future. Nevertheless I must from the very outset of my career learn facts, lots and lots of them, and my interest and delight in them must be fostered by the integrity, skill and taste with which you (who have been among them so much longer than I) bring them before me during the years in which my appetite is liveliest, my learning capacity at its best, and I am most easily cheated by fanatics and doctrinaires.

"I must have a great deal of *economic history*. In my little scramble from the cradle to the grave the world will change about me, for good or ill. I cannot begin to understand the trends of events about me unless I see them in the context of a long evolution. Besides, I cannot properly rejoice in my luck or find consolation for my misfortune in being here for this one brief spell among all others unless I can vividly picture what went before. Now is the time for me to acquire that sense of distance and that appreciation of the littleness of any direct experience that I can have, which mark out educated men.

"Needless to say I must have much about *contemporary affairs* also. But one little patch of these will be always around me, and my own eyes and ears will show it to me unaided. Hence what I want especially will be an account of the larger social framework, the aggregates and the structure too large to see for myself, and information about parts of my own country's economy and about other economies that I am unlikely ever to see at close quarters. I wish to learn the extent to which what I see familiarly will differ from what I do not see and to avoid judging the world by the affairs of my parish.

"When I say information naturally I do not mean only statistics: though I must of course so swat at them as to develop an "instinctive" sense of orders of magnitude. I do not want to load my mind with numbers, and will be entirely content to learn how to look them up. What I especially seek is a knowledge of the range and variety of the ways men take economic decisions, individually and within organisations. I must get, too, some appreciation of the place economic affairs have *vis-à-vis* the non-economic in the lives of my contemporaries near and far in space and time. Obviously this is elusive, prismatic, indefinite, literary stuff all too conveniently apt for sociological waffling and hazy generalisation. But please make it as concrete for me as you can by letting me inspect detailed accounts of particular people and places as vivid as can be found. And may I, please, see as much as I can for myself. Visit factories, stay with families outside my circle, be helped to take temporary vacation jobs outside the likely scope of my adult life, share in surveys, attend board meetings, sit in parliamentary galleries, supplement book-learning in every way you can manage for me. I do not wish to become a pedant peering out at reality from libraries and classrooms.

IV

"Theory: I have been assured that you will certainly not raise any objection in principle to assisting me towards this descriptive knowledge but that you may intend to treat it as something merely consequential and subsidiary to economic theory, pure and applied. These branches of positive economics, I have been warned, may be so swollen as to occupy the great bulk of your students' time. Lest there be any misunderstanding between us I must explain to you the place I intend to give them in my studies.

"Like everyone else luckily—or unluckily—endowed with the intellectual energy that takes them to universities I long, not only to know, but to understand; to discover how to explain, to predict, to see the actual, past, present and to be, as the exemplification of General Laws. (And like them I impatiently refuse to resolve the contradiction between this conviction of Determinism and their other conviction of Free Will which I also share.) But just because I delight in the (relatively) simple processes of knowing, am self-conscious about my own experience, and curious to observe and sympathise with that of my fellow-humans, I am shy of this second stage of generalisation, systematisation, classification, abstraction, rationalisation, explanation, prediction, scientification, polysyllabilisation. What multitudinous masses (or clouds) of economic phenomena, hard, soft, diaphanous and even gassy, there are to explain and predict! And how mixed up they are with equally hard, soft, diaphanous and gassy non-economic events! What a sea of words I must plunge into and how thick it is with the detritus of a million forgotten books and articles! Before I slide in, dressed in your second-best wet-suit and your spare oxygen cylinder, I want to be confident that you will lead me to those beds of pearls that I would delight to rifle.

"If you can credibly assure me that you have found them, I will joyfully follow you even if the journey be so long and arduous that I should postpone some of my 'descriptive' studies. (Equipped with your pearls as touchstones the later collection of factual truth and the discarding of delusions would be greatly accelerated.) But have you found them? This is what worries me. I have been listening to the most distressing tales about your activities.

"They say that theory has become exceedingly rigorous and mathematical and that, though economics is not yet entirely closed to those who come to it without a mathematical training, the rest have to spend much of their time in universities acquiring that training, simply in order to understand Modern Theory.

"The great bulk of this theory, they tell me, consists of the analysis of rational, well-informed, selfish decision-making, assumed to extend over the whole range of economic behaviour (the extent of which in the totality of human action is undiscussed but tacitly supposed very wide, including everything measured in the GNP). Most of it, I am told, abstracts from the passage of time and deals, with the greatest elaboration, with moments in which millions of these anthropomorphic computers acting independently dismiss myriads of alternatives in a flash and find a single optimal Equilibrium Solution. But a part, vast in itself, minutely scrutinises another class of dream worlds in which there are almost never more than two kinds of factor making one or two kinds of commodity in conditions so rigged that everything grows, to eternity, at constant rates either from the arbitrarily described starting point or after a little settling down.

"These scholastic fantasies are, they say, regarded as the apogee of two centuries of theoretical endeavour. They lie at the frontiers of knowledge and the little titivations, the translations into more sophisticated brands of mathematics, the little 'generalisations' from one set of crazy postulates to another believed infinitesimally less so, upon which the leaders of theory spend their time, are presented as the triumphs of intellectual progress. I am warned that it will be your pride to take me to this frontier, and keep me apprised, when I am advanced enough, of these latest little nibbles being made at hitherto unimagined tracts of Cloud-Cuckoo Land beyond.

"I have protested that this *must* be wrong, that in a world of sane men things cannot *be*. But it has been argued that they *are*, for reasons that sound plausible. Modern economic theory, it has been explained to me, arose in mid-Victorian times, when analogies with the mechanical and exact sciences were all the rage in the dawn of the social sciences, and mathematics accordingly had a high prestige. It was founded by an English metallurgist who had little mathematics and no psychology (Jevons), a French *doctrinaire* in the same case, a dear obsolete silly-billy of the first water (Walras), and an aristocratic Italian railway engineer of brilliant intellect and racing temper deeply contemptuous of the entire human race (Pareto). Between them they concocted a great web of abstract reasoning with the grandest pretensions. Its psychological foundations were appallingly weak, a crude Benthamism borrowed without scrutiny, and its mathematical structure was still incomplete. But it is easier to elaborate a superstructure than to dig in a boggy subsoil, and in the next generation, the progress of specialisation and the rise of pedagogics caused the foundations to be forgotten while university careers in economics came to be made, and pupils dazzled, by the endless polishing of the unearthly superstructure by men who knew theory but left themselves no time to know anything else. That at least is the tale I am told.

"If these transparently false and artificial pearls be all that you can offer me why should I so labour to follow you down to them? And if you have come sincerely to believe them the real thing, then, gentlemen, you must all be suffering from the bends.

"If I am to understand, explain and predict as well as know, and to use conditional predictions in my efforts to improve the world about me, I *must* have theory. The world is too complex for unaided common-sense. That theory must be spun out of simplifications I grant in advance. But they must be good simplifications, not leaving many big things out, and I must be

taught what it is that they leave out. I forgive the founding fathers for missing out too much and not fully recognising what it was that they overlooked:
what is progress in such a subject as this but a widening, deepening and
thickening of basic theories boldly advanced in times of relative ignorance
and in a much simpler world than that now around us? I can have no time for
a version of classical theorising which has been narrowed, shallowed, and
thinned out, in the name of rigour, into a patently preposterous mythology.

"If this is what you offer me I must have permission to neglect your
theory classes and get on with such theory as I find relevant in the older
classics and the work of those who remain in their tradition and my own
cultivated sense of observation. . . .

VI

"*Normative Economics:* Being young I am a prig. I wish the economics I
learn here to be not only interesting but useful to me all my days. I wish it to
improve not only the quality of my private economic decisions as an individual, but also the quality of my contributions to public policy as an active
citizen, and to be correctly believed to know more of economic affairs than
those not trained in the subject, and accordingly to be trusted by my friends.
If you allow me enough descriptive economics I hope the wisdom of my
private life will be increased—at least I shall lose the temptation to believe
myself rational and well-informed and acquire some sympathetic understanding of other people's economic experience—but leave that to me. Here,
I have only some remarks to make about what I hope that you will teach me
about public policy.

"You shall, of course, not tell me what policies I should espouse. Any
stance on policy involves moral attitudes, and these are my private affair. It
involves too a view on what is politically practicable and what the consequences of advocacy and activity will be to the advocacies and activities of
others, and you are not political scientists. Besides I will only achieve
political weight in years to come and you know the future no more than I.
You must be cool about social issues: there is plenty of heat outside.

"I say that with hesitation and apology. But I cannot help noticing that
some professors sign manifestos at elections giving their university addresses
and I have heard of promotion quarrels in which assertions of political creed
are claimed to be relevant. And I have been told by one who has read Professor Harcourt's lively surveys of the disputes of pure theorists that they
even accuse each other of choosing between two-sector models in the idiot
conviction that such toys can have a tendency to justify *laissez-faire* capitalism or socialism. If I find such tomfooleries here it will be the last straw.

"Nevertheless there is much that you can help me with. I have the
inevitable inexperience and innocence of youth in all political matters; there

is a din of fanaticism and flap doodle all around me, and economic issues, I am told, underlie most of the mass murder and misery I read of daily. Help me towards a sense of reality! I want in the descriptive part of my reading and lectures details of past and present legislation and its administration an awareness of what it means in the practice of daily life in more than my own type of economy, warts and all. I want some of the politics of political economy: how do pressure groups operate in practice? And since I keep hearing about the splendours of revolutions, what are these like to those who live through them? If there be such things (other than in the creed of the Marxist religion), tell me about theories of the determination of economic policy—and let them not depress me by being altogether deterministic. Though, as I say, I do not want your moral or other verdicts, assist me at least to the detailed analysis of the concrete significance and practical interpretations of the large ideals I hear so much of, equality, freedom, etc.

VII

"To sum up I want you to lead me into economics as one of the moral sciences, dealing with the feelings and aspirations of ordinary mortals in one large tract of their daily lives, one indissolubly linked and only arbitrarily distinguishable from the rest. It must therefore be (still) a largely literary study, much concerned with the subjective aspects of life that only words can approach. If that means it is not a science, so much the worse for science.

"That some measurable objective entities exist in it is, as I understand it, most fortunate. It gives its students an *occasional* opportunity to retreat into something like the simpler world of the natural sciences, and *occasional* relief from the task of human sympathy and understanding, *occasional*, if remote, analogies with mechanics and an *occasional* excuse for mathematics. But of course to linger too long in these little corners of the subject, contemplating cobwebs, would be disastrous to my education. They have their place—in the corners.

"That gentlemen, is how I see economics and the pattern of education in it that I seek. Please tell me whether you agree. If you do not, please try to persuade me that what you offer is a superior article. And if you do not succeed, forgive me if I slink sadly away. I may remain interested in the subject as I interpret it, but I will be an amateur and you will be professionals. We need not meet again."

VIII

Here, at last, the young man shuts up. An embarrassed silence certainly follows. But then?

THE OLDER TRADITION

Bensusan-Butt's arrogant young man has come to a university, perhaps to study "economics." What he really wants to do, however, is study "international political economics," which is the "older tradition" he refers to early in his harangue. To him, "economics" is one of the "moral" sciences, not one of the "natural" sciences that most contemporary economists would have it be.

We are told that after laying down the law at some length, the impertinent student finally shuts up. He is met with an "embarrassed silence," however, and the author asks, "What then?"

What follows is an attempt to answer this question. There is a brief discussion of the older tradition of international political economy, a discussion cast in the context of the study of world affairs as a whole. I highlight some key concepts that recur in the study of international political economy, and I then outline the major analytic languages that have been developed over time to account for IPE in general terms, namely, mercantilism, liberalism, and Marxism.

What, then, is international political economy?

WORLD AFFAIRS IN THREE DIMENSIONS

International political economy is the study of the wealth-making dimension of world affairs.

World affairs are most simply characterized in terms of their three major dimensions, namely, state making, wealth making, and mind making. "International political economy" refers to the second of these dimensions. Though it has a lot to do, on the one hand with how states and the state system are made and maintained (the first dimension), and on the other hand with how people are coached to think and feel about the world (the third dimension), the issues and institutions currently associated with the concept of an international political economy allow a study of their own.

The first dimension of world affairs is colloquially called "high politics," and it is the domain of diplomats and military personnel. It is the world of foreign ministries and foreign policies, of defense budgets and strategic might, of the balance of power and war. It is the stuff of the study of international relations (or IR for short).

The second dimension of world affairs is colloquially called "low politics," and it is the domain of entrepreneurs and those who sell their labor for a wage. It is the world of ministries of trade and central banks, of international firms and financing, of the balance of productivity and global "development." It is the stuff of the study of international political economy (or IPE for short).

The third dimension of world affairs—only dimly recognized as such by the scholars and practitioners of our day—lies somewhere beyond low politics. It is the domain of ideologists and social movements. It is the world of education ministries and the media, of school curricula and cultural formations, of the balance of ideologies and the battle for the world mind. It is the stuff of the study of international political culture (or IPC for short).

Each dimension of world affairs clearly implicates the others. I've separated them out like this largely for analytic convenience, though each does have a life of its own, and they do reflect important differences in how world affairs work. There are scholars, however, who wouldn't accept this tripartite distinction. They would see the attempt to make and sustain such distinctions as being part of an attempt to get world affairs to work that way, and they refuse to be party to such a project. The assumptions it makes are simply not ones they would share. While this is an important argument and one I'll consider as we proceed, I do give enough credence to the common practice to want to start with it, and that means identifying the particular issues and institutions currently considered most characteristic of IPE.

The focus of international political economy typically falls upon world capitalism. More specifically, it falls upon the growth process in world markets; patterns of global production—primary, secondary, and tertiary; changes in the international division of labor; changes in the international labor market; trade and its commodity composition (such as the world trade in manufactured goods, technology, services, and natural resources, as well as the cause and effect of such international associations as the World Trade Organisation); international money flows and global financial and investment practices (particularly the post–World War II ones instituted by the International Monetary Fund [IMF] and the World Bank); intensifying regionalism (as evident in the European Union, the North American Free Trade Association, and the Asia Pacific Economic Community); the story of global "development" and "underdevelopment"; and the question as to whether the human practices involved are sustainable or not—socially and ecologically.

A SHORT HISTORY OF IPE

International political economy has only recently become a professional discipline. Indeed, scholars of international relations, which is a relatively recent profession itself, were openly dismissive of IPE until the last few years. It was not until the global effects of the oil price rises of the 1970s began to be felt worldwide, a shock to the system that culminated in a global debt crisis in the 1980s and global recession in the 1990s, that more than a handful of IR scholars began to take notice of the material dimension to their own discipline. This was well after ministries of foreign affairs had begun renaming themselves ministries of foreign affairs and trade.

In historical terms, however, an interest in international poltical economy is not new. The recent concern for wealth making in world affairs is something of a return, in fact, to the eighteenth century and beyond, and its reinstatement has meant rediscovering ways of looking at the world that later academic specialisms had supposedly made redundant.

The term *political economy* was first used by the English administrative reformer Sir William Petty, in the year 1671 or so. In a work on Ireland he talked about "Political Oeconomies" (Hull 1899:181). He did so, what's more, in notably "modern" ways. He showed, for example, a distinct preference for quantitative methods. He wanted to make a "Par and Equation" between "Lands and Labour" so that he could express the "value of anything by either alone" (Hull 1899: 181). He wanted his political economy available in what he called a "Political A-llrithmetic" form, since as far as he was concerned mere intellectual arguments didn't have the same strength. Numerical ones were quantitative ones and as such, he believed, they had "visible Foundations in Nature."

As for the "Minds, Opinions, Appetites, and Passions of particular Men"—well, you were just as well off, Petty believed, trying to predict "the cast of a Dye" (Hull 1899:244).

The seventeenth century was the Age of Reason in Europe. It was the century of Descartes and Galileo, of Bacon and the "new philosophy" of objective science and research, and true to the spirit of his age, Petty was a most rational man. He was a charter member of the council of the Royal Society for Improving of Rational Knowledge and he clearly embodied the spirit of his place and time. He played an active part in an intellectual revolution that was eventually to revolutionize the whole of human society.

Petty's preference for numbers, not words, was prophetic. Many faced with a similar challenge today come to the same conclusion Petty did three hundred years ago, and Bensusan-Butt parodies this preference.

Petty's preference for numbers was a radical one, and he knew it. He realized that it was "not yet very usual" to solve the problem of how best to deal with feelings, intentions, and beliefs by ignoring them. He sensed, too, the authority of the statistic, and though he had few figures to work with, and he personally appreciated the need to generate more, he loved the precision they brought to his subject.

As Bensusan-Butt argues, however, arithmetic can mislead. Precision can become an end in itself, and a surrogate for objectivity. It is all too easy to suppose that conclusions are "accurate" because their form is "definite." Thus: "mathematical presentations of industrial facts, both symbolic and graphic, have by their definiteness," Petty's editor, Hull (1899:lxviii), concluded, "encouraged many an investigator in the false conceit that he now knew what he sought, whereas he had at most a neat name for what he sought to know."

Early political economists were not so misled, the most telling example in this regard being the Scottish moral philosopher, Adam Smith. In 1776, a century after Petty, Smith wrote what was to become one of the classics of international political economy, *The Wealth of Nations*—a book, by the way, that uses a great many words and very little arithmetic.

Smith was the first to explore in detail the commonsense idea that greater productive power depends upon more-complex divisions of labor, as well as the less than commonsense idea that to promote personal gain is to promote the common good.

Smith began by wondering how the most humble commodity in his immediate environment could possibly have come to be. Think, he said, of the "woolen coat" that "covers the day-labourer." Then think of the "joint labour of the great multitude of workmen" that went into making this single, seemingly simple garment: "the shepherd, the sorter of the wool, the wool-comber or carder, the dyer, the scribbler, the spinner, the weaver, the fuller, the dresser," not to mention the "merchants and carriers . . . ship-builders, sailors, sailmakers, rope-makers," and so on (Smith 1892:9). In primary school social science courses children still list in similar vein what they had for breakfast and where everything came from.

Smith's musings highlighted the seemingly miraculous way in which people's material needs get met from one moment to the next with no "conscious direction . . . guiding State . . . [or] planning instruments, only a market and competition" (Harris 1983:9). It's as if some "hidden hand"—to use Smith's most famous phrase—was at work, meshing the myriad pieces of a vast planetary mechanism that makes goods and services, prosperity and peace. "Were we to examine, in the same manner, all the different parts of . . . dress and household furniture," Smith concluded, "we would soon realise that without the assistance and cooperation of many thousands, the very meanest person in a civilized country could not be provided." Indeed, he compares civilized life most favorably, in this respect, with the life of an "African King." Even as "absolute master of the lives and liberties of ten thousand naked savages," Smith (1892: 9–10) says, an African king is worse off than a European peasant.

What is it that makes all this possible? How do the "civilized persons" in Smith's industrious world pull off their amazing feat of production and supply?

First, there is the way in which complex divisions of labor make for much greater output. While the technological amateur, Smith (1892:4) says, can only make one pin a day, ten men, who divide the eighteen distinct parts of the pin-making process between them, can make forty-eight thousand pins a day. "It is [in other words] the great multiplication of the productions of all the different arts, in consequence of the division of labour," says Smith, "which occasions, in a well-governed society, that universal opulence which extends itself to the lowest ranks of the people."

> Every workman has a great quantity of his own work to dispose of beyond what he himself has occasion for; and every other workman being exactly in the same situation, he is enabled to exchange a great quantity of his own goods for a great quantity, or, what comes to the same thing, for the price of a great quantity of theirs. He supplies them abundantly with what they have occasion for, and they accommodate him as amply with what he has occasion for, and a general plenty diffuses itself through all the different ranks of the society (Smith 1892:8–9).

Note the simplicity of the math. Note also that the precondition is a "well-governed society."

The second explanation for planetary production and supply is the way the division of labor works between countries as well as within them. This is called "comparative advantage," a concept associated most closely with one of Smith's heirs, the nineteenth-century political economist David Ricardo, but one that Smith himself refers to. The "natural advantages which one country has over another in producing commodities," Smith says, are sometimes "so great" that it is acknowledged by all the world to be "in vain to struggle with them." He cites here as example the fact that "by means of glasses, hotbeds, and hot-walls, very good grapes can be raised in Scotland, and very good wine, too, can be made of them at about thirty times the expense for which at least equally good can be brought from foreign countries. Would it be a reasonable law to prohibit the importation of all foreign wines merely to encourage the making of claret and burgundy in Scotland?" (Smith 1892:347).

Clearly not. Comparative advantage is a more efficient choice, and one that works for acquired advantages (like giving advice on political economy) just as well as for natural advantages (like a wine industry).

Note once more the simplicity of the math and the way the argument is addressed, first and foremost, to state-making legislators.

The third explanation for the workings of the world political economy is the coincidence of personal and social interest. Smith (1892:343) argued that "every individual is continually exerting himself to find out the most advantageous employment for whatever capital he can command. It is his own advantage, indeed, and not that of the society, which he has in view. But the study of his own advantage, naturally, or rather necessarily, leads him to prefer that employment which is most advantageous to the society." Greed is good, in other words, and it is good not only for the self but happily and coincidentally for society as a whole.

The picture is not all as happy as Smith is wont to suggest, of course. What, one might ask, of the men and women who lose their jobs in one part of the world because of some event they know nothing about many thousands of miles away? What of the children who starve in a Peruvian fishing village "because news of the harvest of soya beans arriving in Chicago has depressed the price of their fathers' anchovy catch" (Harris 1983:9)? Here we get a glimpse of another, much darker, and much less desirable side to comparative advantage. While market practices like this do sustain more people today than this planet has ever carried before, and for many of them at a standard of living once enjoyed by only very few, this does not mean the market is beneficial for all. We don't, for example, see or hear the suffering that makes some or even much of world production possible. "The spoonful of tea you pop in the pot," for example, "does not cry out because the Tamil fingers that plucked the leaf in Sri Lanka were weak with malnutrition. Fortunately, commodities are mute" (Smith 1892:9–10). Examples like these are legion since the "liberal reward of labour" is a mixed one at best.

Market-induced misery was apparent long ago to another great international political economist, Karl Marx. A century after Smith (but still more than a century short of our own) we find another classic of international political economy, the Communist Manifesto. This was a direct attack on the system Smith so admired; a system that by the nineteenth century had "pitilessly torn asunder the motley feudal ties that bound man to his 'natural superiors'" to leave "no other nexus between man and man than naked self-interest, than callous 'cash payment.'" This was a system that had "drowned," Marx said, "the most heavenly ecstacies of religious fervour, of chivalrous enthusiasm, of philistine sentimentalism, in the icy water of egotistical calculation." It had resolved "personal worth into exchange value" and in place of the "numberless indefeasible chartered freedoms" it had set up "that single unconscionable freedom—Free Trade" (Marx and Engels 1942:207–208).

Marx had no doubt about what was to blame. The problem was the market system itself. This was not a system, as Smith had claimed, that ran itself. The system was capitalist and was run by capitalists, that is, those who owned and managed the means of production. Marx called the class of capitalists the "bourgeoisie." Those with no means of production of their own, who were reduced to selling their labor power in order to live, he called the "proletariat." All history, he said, was a history of class struggle, and our own history was no different. It was characterized by class struggle between the bourgoisie and the proletariat—a struggle Marx believed the bourgeoisie were going to lose.

In their time the bourgeoisie had been revolutionaries. "The bourgoisie cannot exist," Marx argued, "without constantly revolutionising the instruments of production, and thereby the relations of production, and with them the whole relations of society."

> Constant revolutionising of production, uninterrupted disturbance of all social conditions, everlasting uncertainty and agitation distinguish the bourgeois epoch from all earlier ones. All fixed, fast frozen relations, with their train of ancient and venerable prejudices and opinions, are swept away, all new-formed ones become antiquated before they can ossify. All that is solid melts into air, all that is holy is profaned (Marx and Engels 1942:208–209).

What drove the bourgeoisie on so? Comparative advantage? For Marx it was more as if, having roused a sleeping giant, having filled him with terrible resolve, the bourgeoisie no longer had a choice. It was as if having conjured up a means of production so profound, "like the sorcerer who is no longer able to control the power of the nether world whom he has called by his spells" (Marx and Engels 1942:211), they had to see the whole process through to the end. The end, of course, being a revolutionary one as befitted revolutionary times; one where the expropriators were expropriated, as Marx put it, and it was the proletariat that prevailed.

A century on from Smith, Marx was deeply impressed by the extraordinary changes going on around him. A "constantly expanding market for its products" was chasing the bourgeoisie all over the globe to "nestle everywhere, settle everywhere, establish connections everywhere" (Marx and Engels 1942:209). "Old-established national industries" were being destroyed by "new industries" whose introduction was becoming a "life and death question for all civilised nations . . . industries that no longer work[ed] up indigenous raw material" but drew those materials from the "remotest zones"; industries whose products were consumed "not only at home, but in every quarter of the globe. In place of the old wants, satisfied by the production of the country," the bourgeoisie found "new wants, requiring for their satisfaction the products of distant lands and climes. In place of the old local and national seclusion and self-sufficiency," they found "intercourse in every direction, universal interdependence" (Marx and Engels 1942:209).

Marx's logic was relentless. With the "rapid improvement of all instruments of production [and with] immensely facilitated means of communication," he could not see that any country would be able to resist. The highest walls of national seclusion would be battered down by cheaply priced commodities—the "heavy artillery" of the new order; the big guns, as it were, that would compel "all nations," on "pain of extinction," to adopt the "bourgeois mode of production" (Marx and Engels 1942:209).

Marx's logic was not only relentless, it was comprehensive. Everyone was involved, potentially if not actually. A new civilization was being built, with huge cities that agglomerated whole peoples, that subjected the country to the rule of the towns, that centralized all the means of production, concentrating property in the hands of a few, focusing governments and codes of law, clearing whole continents for cultivation, and conjuring entire populations "out of the the ground" (Marx and Engels 1942:210).

"What earlier century had even a presentiment," Marx concluded, "that such productive forces slumbered in the lap of social labour?" Who could have known that with the advent of free competition there could be such a thing as overproduction? Who could have known that there might one day be "too much civilisation, too much means of subsistence, too much industry, too much commerce" and a crisis potentially so acute as finally to cause the "whole superincumbent strata of official society" to be "sprung into the air" (Marx and Engels 1942:208–211, 217)? Who could have known that by specializing to improve their competitiveness, nations would no longer be free not to trade, and once locked into the capitalist world system, could only be driven by it into oblivion?

The analytic language that Marx used was very similar to Smith's. It was very different too. It was similar in that both of them talked of human production and labor as a total social process. It was different in that Smith saw nothing better replacing the world political economy he so graphically described. Marx saw the best as yet to come. Once the social logic of this revolutionary interlude had been played out, socialism and communism were supposed to ensue, a revolutionary vision that was to inspire millions of men and women who, like Marx, wanted to replace the capitalist world political economy with something more orderly and humane. Smith inspired generations of owners and managers who saw their task as making the system more efficient. The argument continues in both their names.

One notable difference between Smithians and Marxists today is the way Smithians talk about the economics of international politics or the politics of international economics, and Marxists talk about international political economy. Anglo-American libertarians separate politics from economics and turn the latter into the more or less quantitative study of free markets. Most European scholars, however, would be puzzled that anyone might seriously think that economics and politics can be studied apart (Caporaso 1987a:2).

The conceptual divorce of economics from politics was achieved in the nineteenth century and was due, in no small part, to the work of the English theorist William Jevons (1871). In his key text, *The Theory of Political Economy,* Jevons initiated what has been called the "marginalist" revolution—so called because of its concern with the effects of marginal changes in a commodity on production, consumption, and price. Unlike Smith or Marx, Jevons focused less on capital and labor and more on personal satisfaction and exchange. Value, he argued, was dependent "entirely upon utility," that is, upon personal benefit or satisfaction. This meant that instead of wondering, for example, as Smith did, at the wonderful way a woolen coat gets put on a day-laborer's back, Jevons wondered how it was that people managed to get them in a world where there were not enough coats to go around. This led directly to questions of supply and demand.

Jevons (1970:52, 77) believed, as Petty did, that a science of wealth making was possible and that a science of value should be expressed mathematically. Jevons had trained as a scientist and this had clearly inspired him to see "economy" not only as a separate subject but also as a "calculus." Economics was a calculus of "pleasure and pain," he believed. Its principal concern was to maximize pleasure by allowing its purchase for a minimum of pain. To Jevons, the whole theory of value and of wealth could be explained in this way. He likened it to mechanics and to the way the "theory of statics is made to rest upon the equality of indefinitely small amounts of energy" (Jevons 1970:44).

Thus it was that the classic political economy of Smith became the economics of neoclassic "marginalism." The rational choices made by Smith's self-interested citizens became "optimizing behaviour," to be quantitatively assessed. The optimizing behavior of private individuals—believed in turn to derive from the fact that "every person will choose the greater apparent good [since] human wants are more or less quickly satiated [and] prolonged labour becomes more and more painful" (Jevons 1970:88)—became the basis for a new science, one dedicated to accounting mathematically for the "efficient allocation of scarce resources among competing ends" (Caporaso 1987a:2).

Politics became residual. Students of politics were those who theorized about public policy and the relationship between the individual and the state.

The disciplinary divide thus forged between economics and politics also allowed for talk about international economics as separate from international politics, with international economics being the workings of the world market, and international politics being the workings of the world state system. There were some adventurous transdisciplinarians who talked of the politics of international economics or the economics of international politics, but they remained, until relatively recently, relatively few. Such linkages were seen, in the Anglo-American tradition at any rate, as being of peripheral concern.

The recent interest in international political economy in Anglo-American universities has largely been of the transdisciplinary kind. The collapse of the Soviet Union and the rush to embrace liberal capitalist market principles by the former East European and Soviet societies, as well as the moves by mainland Chinese in a similar direction, are supposed to have completely discredited international political economy of the Marxist sort. Marxist IPE was always anathema anyway to Anglo-American liberal capitalists, and it was a cause of considerable satisfaction to the latter when Soviet communism collapsed.

Discounting Marxist international political economy always was, and still is, a very grave mistake, however. It confuses German Marxism with Soviet or Chinese communism. Indeed, it is most ironic that Marx himself would have expected the Russian and Chinese revolutions to fail, since to get to socialism you have first, he argued, to go through capitalism. When the Russians and the Chinese jumped the historical gun, Marx would have said that this couldn't be sustained. It was capitalism in his view, not socialism, that followed on from feudalism, and that, for Marx, was a historical law.

RECURRING CONCEPTS

It is very tempting in these "postcommunist" times to write off the Marxist tradition of thought as the flawed ideology of a failed worldview. If we resist this temptation, then another question arises. Which, we might ask, is more accurate, Smith's liberalism or Marx's Marxism? Which is the more "true"? Or is "reality" best described and explained some other way in another, more neutral language, applicable to them both?

Despite an intensive search for a neutral language with which to address both kinds of classical political economy, none has yet been found that provides a clearly specified account of the international political economy that all can accept. Even the "scientific method" —so fruitful in understanding the natural universe—has been shown to be an ideologically loaded discourse when applied to IPE. This doesn't mean that such a search should be abandoned, or that we should turn our back on any attempt to be analytical. It does suggest, however, that we may always have incommensurable accounts of wealth making in the world; and that these accounts may never be reconciled because of the different values they espouse and the different views of human nature that underpin them.

This leaves us with the image of IPE as an ongoing argument between more or less coherent worldviews. The key words that recur in these worldviews, words like *state, firm, market, capital,* and *labor,* should be seen in this light. None of these terms stands alone. Each plays its part in the webs of meaning woven by each worldview.

State

Consider the concept of the state. To Smith's way of thinking, the state is a mixed blessing. State makers serve a useful purpose providing public goods like harbors and roads, courts and mass literacy, but to the most doctrinaire of such "liberals" a state-made world is a political impediment to economic activity. It only makes it harder for the world's businesspeople to provide the prosperity and peace that is the great promise of "free enterprise." In classical Marxist terms, by contrast, state makers are apologists for those who own and manage the dominant mode of production (the bourgeoisie), which in our day and age is capitalism. Rather than seeing economics and politics as separate and opposed, with economics the domain of the market and politics the domain of the state, classical Marxists see the headlong rush to accumulate capital as the defining characteristic of world affairs, and the attempt to discriminate between economics and politics as part of the bourgeois plot to mystify the process of capitalist exploitation. The state is the "executive committee" that looks after the public affairs of the governing class of bourgeois owners and managers. It "arises with, is transformed by and itself affects the accumulation of capital" (Edwards: 1985:203).

The state is a highly contingent, relatively recent, and historically novel way to organize human affairs. It was given its contemporary form as the particular solution (the Treaty of Westphalia) to a particular problem (the Thirty Years' War) in seventeenth-century Europe. It is now nominally universal, one consequence of a long and complex process of European imperialism.

States have been a "political economy" project from the beginning. The state-making practices of seventeenth-century European kings and queens, for example, required wealth. Regal power presupposed prosperity, and the royal houses of Europe saw wealth making as state making by other means. They were what would now be called mercantilists, or economic nationalists, or, more particularly, protectionists, and their ideological descendants still argue the need to maximize state strength and autonomy by using protective tariffs (duties on imports), import substitution (measures that encourage home production and local buying), and vertical integration (productive chains that minimize any potential loss to home-state entrepreneurs).

The classical mercantilist notion that the right way to augment state power is to foster production at home, buy as little as possible from abroad, and accumulate wealth in the convenient form of precious metals, still has great emotional appeal. With very few exceptions, however, state makers today are liberal marketeers as well. They believe in "rationality," "efficiency of supply and demand," and "free" and "open" competition, while black markets from Myanmar to Azerbaijan are said to testify to the power of liberal "economics" to find ways, even where these are formally denied, to meet human wants and needs.

The state presupposes other states. State makers know they live in a world of other state makers, running other, formally equal, formally autonomous territorial domains, all committed, by an elaborate kind of gentlemen's agreement, to not interfering in each other's affairs.

Modern state makers also know they live in the middle of an industrial revolution, a revolution that has magnified by a factor that can no longer be calculated the human capacity to make things and to provide services. This much-enlarged capacity has changed radically the meaning of state making, as well as many of the means by which it gets done.

Industrial capitalism has replaced the mostly mercantile form that preceded it to become the dominant ideology of an age so productive one could well be excused for seeing politics as contingent upon economics. Having entered the most materially dynamic phase in all human history, everything seems to shine in the light of that fact—the state included. Marxist theorists in particular would see the "national state" this way, that is, as "only part of the overall structure of power in a global capitalist society" (Picciotto 1991:60).

The development such productivity makes possible has clearly advantaged the state, though it doesn't always advantage particular citizens who live therein. Indeed,

> there are a number of states in the world where development means only the development of the state itself or, at most, the state sector. In fact, in a number of cases, the development of the state has been the best predictor of the underdevelopment of society. . . . Some scholars have, consequently, defined development as the process in the name of which the state mobilizes resources internally and externally and, then, eats them up itself, instead of allowing them to reach the bottom and the peripheries of the society (Nandy 1992:270).

Liberally inclined scholars, though they readily admit that markets have "developmental poles" and can cause inequalities, believe that everyone is better off the more that state makers allow free enterprise. Admittedly, free enterprise is not equal either. Knowledge and capital, "the two [factors of production] that have most easily escaped the control of the state and that can most easily slip across territorial frontiers," certainly move more freely than "labour and land" (Strange 1988:15). But open commerce is supposed to work to the mutual benefit of all, and in the liberal worldview states and their citizens cannot help but develop. In its most idealized version, the "tide of economic growth lifts all boats together" (Gilpin 1974:42).

Marxist-style scholars respond by asking what kind of social relationships the state represents (Holloway 1994:27). They see state makers protecting capitalists and defending the social disparities that are capitalism's key consequence. And they talk about the powers of the state being used to augment the wealth of the bourgeoisie (Braverman 1974:286). In some cases, like Germany or Japan, the state was built at the same time as capitalism, and has been integral to it in every way. In others, like England or the United States, "the capitalist class . . . marked off for the government a more circumscribed sphere of operations, and . . . the growth of . . . interventionism on the part of the state . . . appeared to develop as a struggle against capital" (Braverman 1974:285).

The debate goes on. Meanwhile, of course, most people cope as best they can with whatever worldview those in power happen to visit upon them.

Firm

Another feature of the basic debate about political economy is the liberalist emphasis on the "market" as the conceptual counterpart to the "state." Gilpin, for example, begins his book *The Political Economy of International Relations* by juxtaposing market and state. "The parallel existence and mutual interaction of 'state' and 'market' in the modern world," he says, "create political economy." The state, on the one hand, is a territorial entity, and state making is designed to engineer loyal citizens, well-defined frontiers, and a domestic monopoly (supposedly legitimate) of the use of force. It is the domain of political science. The market, on the other hand, is a transactional entity, and marketeering involves contracts, buyers and sellers, price signals, and supply and demand. It is the domain of economics (Gilpin 1987:8, 10–11). Gilpin, need one say, is a self-professed liberal. Eden, on the other hand, is not. She specifically dismisses Gilpin's dichotomy and posits instead, as the more "appropriate" counterpoint to the state, the "multinational enterprise" or "firm." The largest six hundred of these, Eden says, currently produce one-quarter of the world's wealth, and the "crucial problem" now, she believes, "is the tension between states and multinationals, not states and markets" (Eden 1993:26). She would locate states within the market, rather than juxtaposing them, and she would see firms as the "key nonstate actor" in both "domestic and international markets." Strange (1991a:44) also talks of the need to acknowledge the way large firms now operate globally. She says attention now has to be given to "state-to-firm" and "firm-to-firm" interactions as well as to the more familiar "state-to-state" ones. She castigates international relations analysts for "self-protective myopia" in neglecting these interactions. This, she says, has stunted the growth of IPE and kept such concerns on the disciplinary margins when they ought to be at its core (Strange 1991b:102).

While it is certainly correct to accuse "international relationists" of myopia, liberal analysts like Gilpin, for example, do give pride of place to the state-market dichotomy, and they do talk about multinational enterprises (Gilpin 1975; 1987:Ch. 6) in exactly the terms that Strange recommends. Gilpin (1987:262) makes a point of highlighting, for example, the "complex pattern of relationships among corporations, home governments, and host countries that has increasingly politicized foreign investment both at home and abroad." And he clearly notes the way "who benefits" is determined not only by firms seeking comparative advantages but also by state makers' attempts to control such firms to suit themselves.

Liberals tend to see firms as ultimately benign, responding to market opportunities to the ultimate benefit of all. Trolling the world for productive opportunities and profits, these vast commercial conglomerates are part of the nineteenth-century liberal dream of a universal end to human poverty. In this dream global firms put "to their best uses . . . like a good housekeeper, the world's resources and abilities" in such a way as to serve "not merely the survival of the economically fittest but the great cause of liberty, the cause of inventive art and the fertility of the untrammeled mind against the forces of privilege and monopoly and obsolescence." By doing so—and this is one of the most appealing aspects of this powerful vision—they are also supposed to serve the causes of "peace, . . . international concord," and "economic justice" as well (Keynes 1933:36).

Liberalists like the famous English economist John Maynard Keynes who are mercantilists too worry about the costs of global enterprise, particularly for citizens in the hands of state makers who act more out of self-interest than out of any sense of duty to the nation as a whole. Global firms seek to maximize profits. State makers seek to protect state independence and security. Signing over to global firms access rights to large amounts of a national resource, natural or human, can compromise independence and security. And though state makers retain the power to regulate the local practices of multinational enterprises, this power may not always amount to much, either because of collusion between particular state makers and firm managers, or because exercising such power may mean revenue loss or increased unemployment or loss of access to technology.

Even more so than the mercantilists, Marxists see global firms as rapacious and malevolent; as "imperialistic predators, exploiting all for the sake of the corporate few" (Gilpin 1987:231). This is not a matter of states contending with the global market, or states and firms contending with each other within that market. It is a question of the way in which industrial capitalism works, and of the way in which industrial capitalism has become a global system. To maximize the amount of capital they can make from capital (the point of the process, anyway) capitalists have historically increased the size of the production process and formed monopolies, either by beating out the competition or by coming together under the same managerial structures. In the United States, at the end of the nineteenth century, the rapid growth of capitalist monopolies of this kind led to what Braverman (1974:265) describes as the "peculiar shape of a movement for reform." Trust-busting by the U.S. Congress, instead of breaking monopolies, only hastened the process of "concentration by outright mergers." This fostered in turn a "corporate liberalism" that did little, in Marxist eyes, to inhibit the spread of U.S.-based firms or their use of what were later to be called "restrictive business practices."

Classical Marxists applaud the spread of transnational firms, since the quicker the capitalist mode of production becomes global, the quicker its contradictions will become manifest, and the quicker the whole system will collapse. Neo-Marxists, concerned with the capacity capitalists have shown for sustaining their system, and concerned as well with the way capitalists create underdevelopment as well as development in the world, are less convinced the end is nigh, and less happy with the extent to which global firms perpetuate world poverty and neoimperialist exploitation.

The debate goes on. Meanwhile people live in a world political economy built in considerable part by transnational, multinational companies that supply them with a wide range of commodities; if, that is, they are able to pay for them.

Market

Having briefly explored the firm as a counterpoint to the state, I want to return to the market and to consider in a little more detail the arguments about what "marketeering" entails.

In liberalist terms, markets are the spontaneous result of the human desire to benefit by exchange. In a marketplace buyers and sellers meet to exchange goods and services, and the prices are set by haggling. In premodernist societies markets were only a small part of life. In modernist, market economy ones, however, marketeering goes on throughout them, and the haggling is done in much more stylized ways. It is the lack of regulation that so appeals to liberals, hence their aversion to "all attempts to limit the market" (Berthoud 1992:77) and their embrace of market values as definitive of contemporary "development."

Classical liberals believe that the evolution of market societies from markets was a natural evolution and a wholly beneficial one. They believe that markets set the "best" prices and are the most supportive of productive and commercial creativity. They see marketeering as not just one way to make exchanges but as the best and only way (Berthoud 1992:70).

At the global level classical liberals see the comparative advantages particular states possess leading spontaneously to markets and marketeering. They consider this a good thing. Mercantilists have never been so convinced, of course, remaining wary of the ways in which global exchange can undermine state self-sufficiency and arguing for controls that can protect state integrity and strength. But classical liberals see such protectionism as misconstrued. They say it inhibits free competition across borders, thereby sheltering the inefficient and distorting price.

Classical Marxists take a very different view, construing the market in terms of the mode of production of the day. Thus a slave-owning society has a slave-owning market, a feudal society has a feudal market, and a capitalist society has a capitalist market. To a Marxist, the key characteristic of the capitalist market is not the "opportunity or choice" that so fascinates liberals but rather "compulsion."

> Material life and social reproduction in capitalism are universally mediated by the market, so that all individuals must in one way or another enter into market relations in order to gain access to the means of life; and the dictates of the capitalist market—its imperatives of competition, accumulation, profit maximization, and increasing labor productivity—regulate not only all economic transactions but social relations in general. As relations among human beings are mediated by the process of commodity exchange, social relations among people appear as relations among things, the "fetishism of commodities" in Marx's famous formula (Wood 1994:15).

Marxists see the global market as the consequence of capitalist imperialism, and the setting up of this market as having been highly coercive. Though there has been competition between capitalist imperialists and the states they control, this has not been as important, in the classical Marxist view, as the way in which capitalist imperialists have tried to monopolize the world market and exploit the world's workers. Here we have a revolutionary rather than an evolutionary process. It is not the revolutionary outcome of technological change either, where industrial machines need to be used nonstop to justify their installation, thus making of labor as much a commodity as that made by the machines (Polanyi 1957). Here the revolutionaries are capitalists, that is, the people who produce not for use but for profit. This is the so-called market principle. They make this profit from the workers, to whom they pay only part of the value of the work the workers do. This in Marxist parlance is the capitalist market principle.

We have on the one hand, then, the notion of the market as a self-regulating, relatively impersonal place and marketeering as the guarantee of an efficient relationship between "what people want and what is produced." The weak, the useless, and the inefficient may go to the wall but this is what keeps the system strong, and a strong system is ultimately to the benefit of all.

On the other hand we have a very different notion of the market as a "direct instrument of class power manipulated by capital in its control of labor, not to mention as a medium of a new imperialism, in which advanced capitalist economies, with the help of the state, are imposing market 'disciplines' on the Third World and on the 'new democracies,'" and degrading the environment to boot (Wood 1994:39). Here the weak, the useless, and the inefficient are crushed as a matter of routine, and a "vicious cycle of decline" (Gilpin 1987: 21) rips whole societies apart—all to the benefit of a privileged few.

The debate goes on. Thus Gilpin, a liberal, argues that it was the market that "first released" the "forces of capitalism and . . . subsequently also channeled them" (Gilpin 1987:15–16). Thus Braverman, a Marxist, argues the opposite, namely, that it was capitalism that "transformed all of society into a gigantic marketplace" (Braverman 1974:271). Wood (1994:25) brings the concepts of market and capital together, citing as decisive the advent of a particular kind of market society, the capitalist market society, where people produce things in competition with each other, rather than just exchanging things.

Meanwhile, people make do and get by as best they can, largely oblivious to these conceptually abstract concerns, but living nonetheless under conditions dictated by one or the other of them.

The island villager, for example, who lives entirely by subsistence, catching fish and growing fruit and vegetables, lives outside the global market. If she goes to the nearest town once a week to sell some of her surplus and to buy there cloth or a radio, then at that point she enters the world market. If she sees an outboard motor and decides she would like to have one for the family canoe, that means a much larger sum of money and recurrent costs like repairs and fuel. For that she may have to sell her capacity to work for a wage, as a housemaid, for example, to the wife of the expatriate doctor at the local hospital. Or her husband may have to go to work on a nearby copra plantation, where a large multinational firm buys his labor for an hourly, daily, or weekly wage. At that point he or she enters the capitalist world market, and life can change dramatically. Entering this market means not only cash in hand, it means direct exposure to the capitalist market culture, where a belief in "progress," competitive profit making, the private possession of property, entrepreneurial flair, and work itself are all highly regarded. Some or all of these values may clash with those of the culture from which the villager comes, at considerable cost to both.

Unlike the villager, the self-employed orchardist, producing apples by industrial agricultural means and competing with other orchardists to sell them to local firms who sell them worldwide, is already part of the capitalist world market. If he can't do this "efficiently," that is, if the pesticides he uses on the apples make him too ill to work, for example, then other orchardists sell what he would have done and his little manufacturing unit dies. So he bulldozes out all his orchard trees and goes to work for a wage, planting pine for a government department, and growing organic vegetables before and after work and on the weekends. He becomes, that is, a "proletarian," and his status as a free and independent proprietor is destroyed. This profound and highly personal defeat eventually kills him.

Such people are not fictional. Little stories like these are legion. Telling one or two, however, helps remind us of the human experiences that abstract concepts like "the market" try to document. The words we use when we discuss such concepts denote lived human lives. It is all too easy for detached analysis to forget this fact. Hence the need for understandings of a less reified sort. Hence the need for more-attached analysis and for nonobjectifying ways of knowing.

Labor

"Labor" has three general meanings. It is used to denote "all productive work" (Williams 1983:177). It is used in a more specialized sense to denote one of the factors of production, which also include money, land, machinery, natural resources, knowledge, and skills. And it is used to refer to the social class of those who work.

Laboring has been a basic feature of human life throughout history. Laboring for a wage is a relatively new experience, however, and the vast scale on which this now occurs is newer still. The labor power that the worker puts on the market for a wage, selling it for use like any other commodity, is a familiar concept in classical liberal political economy. Smith himself (1892:49–68) wrote about wages. Marx, however, argued that it was the "appropriation" of labor power through the wage mechanism that allowed capitalists to make their profits. This appropriation process he considered to be definitive of contemporary capitalism. "Only that worker is now 'productive,'" he said, "who produces surplus value for the capitalist, and thus promotes the self-expansion of capital" (Marx 1946:552).

What if no one wants to buy the labor power the worker offers for sale? Unemployment follows, which in a society no longer reliant upon subsistence, means no money to buy commodities for use, such as food. Given the growing reach of the capitalist market today this makes all the more significant the contemporary levels of unemployment.

In liberalist terms, this is a temporary phenomenon. If marketeering is allowed full rein, the consequent upsurge in entrepreneurial activity is bound to sweep up those unemployed. The cause of their unemployment is immaterial. Whether due to wage-greed (that is, workers pricing themselves out of the market) or innovations in labor-saving technology (robots, for example), the problem of unemployment always responds best to unfettered free enterprise.

In Marxist terms, it is quite a different matter. The unemployed are the reserve labor army, permanently on call and a sobering reminder to those in more-regular jobs of what awaits them if they don't toe the line and produce their quota of surplus value. Unemployment is currently running at about 10 percent throughout the industrialized world. In the nonindustrialized parts it is significantly worse (UNDP 1993:35). Where there is growth, it is increasingly "jobless growth," and where recessions are on the wane, they are jobless, too (UNDP 1993:36). Is there comfort to be drawn from the fact that "informal" employment is increasing at the same time? Does it help to have work of a low-wage, impermanent kind? Not in Marxist terms, where this is just one more measure of the exploitative character of a capitalist world political economy.

Capital

In classical liberal terms, "capital" refers to various "factors of production." These are the inputs to any production process. Whether "fixed," as in the form of machinery, or more movable, as in the form of "working" capital like money, inputs such as these are combined to make commodities for the market.

The image such a definition provides is that of a factory, where things make other things. There is hardly a human being in sight here.

The classical Marxist approach could not be more different. "Capital is not a thing," said Marx, "but a social relation between persons" (albeit a relation "determined by things"). Marx wrote a major work under this conceptual heading. In it he defines capital as money, though he's at some pains to emphasize from the outset that he means by this money that circulates (Marx 1946:132, 849).

Money that does not circulate, he says, is not capital. It is money as money only. For example, if I sell something, and with the money I make I buy something, the money that comes to me from the original sale goes back into the commodity I then buy and my money is gone. This is money as money. If, however, I use money to buy something with and I then sell what I've bought for money again, the money circulates. It becomes "capital" (Marx 1946:133). Selling to buy may help satisfy my wants. It won't make me more money, though. Money that circulates, on the other hand, will. Putting it out of circulation is only the prelude to bringing it back "enlarged." Out of circulation it takes the form of commodities, but the capitalist knows that "all commodities, however paltry they may look or however evil they may smell, are in faith and in truth money." They are (in what must be the most bizarre metaphor Marx ever used) "inwardly circumcised Jews" (Marx 1946:140). Capitalists are those who consciously move money around. They have no interest in what money can buy. Their motive is the "increasing appropriation of abstract wealth" (Marx 1946:138). They value only the "never-ending process of profit making"; the "urge toward absolute enrichment"; the "passionate hunt for value" (Marx 1946:138). So what, you might ask, if you don't have money to start with? Can you then be a capitalist? The answer is yes. You borrow money and you then circulate it, which makes of capitalism nothing more than the creative use of credit!

If Marx construes capital in terms of the circulation and enlargement of money, how is it that money can enlarge? What makes for the profit in this process? How is it that more money can come out of the circuit than is ever put in? Where, in other words, does the "surplus value" come from?

In its pure form circulation is an exchange of equivalents, and does not, Marx argues, create value. Surplus value can only be made from circulating money if you cheat, he says. Surplus value can be made without cheating, however, from unpaid labor. Smith was well aware of how labor makes things valuable. He considered labor to be the "real measure of the exchangeable value of all commodities." He called it the "real price of everything" and said we are rich or poor "according to the quantity of . . . labour" we command (Smith 1892:22). What Marx did, however, was go one step further to define capital as "fundamentally . . . the command of unpaid labour" (Marx 1946:580). The capitalist buys the worker's labor power, for example, paying for it only part of what it is then used to produce. The part not paid for is the surplus. This the capitalist is free to expropriate. No wonder, Marx says, as we leave the "sphere of simple circulation or exchange" we note a "change in the physiognomy" of our dramatis personae. "The one who came to the market as the owner of money, leaves it striding forward as a capitalist; the one who came to the market as the owner of labor power, brings up the rear as a worker. One of them, self-important, self-satisfied, with a keen eye to business: the other, timid, reluctant, like a man who is bringing his own skin to market, and has nothing to expect but a tanning" (Marx 1946:165).

Having talked about some of the key concepts that recur in IPE, I would like now to give a more systematic account of the attempts made historically to describe and explain how IPE works. I hope Bensusan-Butt's prospective student has not yet slunk away.

2

The Grand Narrative:
Mercantilism, Liberalism, and Marxism

❖ **Frédéric Bastiat (1909) "Petition of the Manufacturers of Candles, Wax-lights, Lamps, Candlesticks, Street Lamps, Snuffers, Extinguishers, and of the Producers of Oil, Tallow, Resin, Alcohol, and generally, of Everything connected with Lighting"**

To Messieurs the Members of the Chambers of Deputies:
Gentlemen: You are on the right road. You reject abstract theories, and have little consideration for cheapness and plenty. Your chief care is the interest of the producer. You desire to protect him from foreign competition, and reserve the *national market for national industry.*

We are about to offer you an admirable opportunity of applying your— what shall we call it? your theory? No; nothing is more deceptive than theory—your doctrine? your system? your principle? But you dislike doctrines, you abhor systems, and as for principles you deny that there are any in social economy. We shall say, then, your practice—your practice without theory and without principle.

We are suffering from the intolerable competition of a foreign rival, placed, it would seem, in a condition so far superior to ours for the production of light that he absolutely *inundates* our *national market* with it at a price fabulously reduced. The moment he shows himself our trade leaves us—all consumers apply to him; and a branch of native industry, having countless ramifications, is all at once rendered completely stagnant. This rival, who is no other than the sun, wages war to the knife against us, and we suspect that he has been raised up by *perfidious Albion* (good policy as times go); inasmuch as he displays towards that haughty island a circumspection with which he dispenses in our case.

What we pray for is, that it may please you to pass a law ordering the shutting up of all windows, sky-lights, dormer-windows, outside and inside shutters, curtains, blinds, bulls'-eyes; in a word, of all openings, holes, chinks, clefts, and fissures, by or through which the light of the sun has been in use to enter houses, to the prejudice of the meritorious manufactures with which we flatter ourselves we have accommodated our country—a country which, in gratitude, ought not to abandon us now to a strife so unequal.

We trust, Gentlemen, that you will not regard this our request as a satire, or refuse it without at least previously hearing the reasons which we have to urge in its support.

And, first, if you shut up as much as possible all access to natural light, and create a demand for artificial light, which of our French manufactures will not be encouraged by it?

If more tallow is consumed, then there must be more oxen and sheep; and, consequently, we shall behold the multiplication of meadows, meat, wool, hides, and, above all, manure, which is the basis and foundation of all agricultural wealth.

If more oil is consumed, then we shall have an extended cultivation of the poppy, of the olive, and of rape. These rich and exhausting plants will come at the right time to enable us to avail ourselves of the increased fertility which the rearing of additional cattle will impart to our lands.

Our heaths will be covered with resinous trees. Numerous swarms of bees will, on the mountains, gather perfumed treasures, now wasting their fragrance on the desert air, like the flowers from which they emanate. No branch of agriculture but will then exhibit a cheering development.

The same remark applies to navigation. Thousands of vessels will proceed to the whale fishery; and, in a short time, we shall possess a navy capable of maintaining the honour of France, and gratifying the patriotic aspirations of your petitioners, the undersigned candlemakers and others.

But what shall we say of the manufacture of *articles de Paris*? Henceforth you will behold gildings, bronzes, crystals, in candlesticks, in lamps, in lustres, in candelabra, shining forth, in spacious wardrooms, compared with which those of the present day can be regarded but as mere shops.

No poor *resinier* from his heights on the seacoast, no coalminer from the depth of his sable gallery, but will rejoice in higher wages and increased prosperity.

Only have the goodness to reflect, Gentlemen, and you will be convinced that there is, perhaps, no Frenchman, from the wealthy coalmaster to the humblest vendor of lucifer matches, whose lot will not be ameliorated by the success of this our petition.

We foresee your objections, Gentlemen, but we know that you can oppose to us none but such as you have picked up from the effete works of the partisans of Free Trade. We defy you to utter a single word against us which will not instantly rebound against yourselves and your entire policy.

You will tell us that, if we gain by the protection which we seek, the country will lose by it, because the consumer must bear the loss.

We answer:

You have ceased to have any right to invoke the interest of the consumer; for, whenever his interest is found opposed to that of the producer, you sacrifice the former. You have done so for the purpose of *encouraging labour and increasing employment*. For the same reason you should do so again.

You have yourselves obviated this objection. When you are told that the consumer is interested in the free importation of iron, coal, corn, textile fabrics—yes, you reply, but the producer is interested in their exclusion. Well, be it so; if consumers are interested in the free admission of natural light, the producers of artificial light are equally interested in its prohibition.

But, again, you may say that the producer and consumer are identical. If the manufacturer gain by protection, he will make the agriculturist also a gainer; and if agriculture prosper, it will open a vent to manufactures. Very well; if you confer upon us the monopoly of furnishing light during the day, first of all we shall purchase quantities of tallow, coals, oils, resinous substances, wax, alcohol—besides silver, iron, bronze, crystal to carry on our manufactures; and then, we, and those who furnish us with such commodities, having become rich will consume a great deal, and impart prosperity to all the other branches of our national industry.

If you urge that the light of the sun is a gratuitous gift of nature, and that to reject such gifts is to reject wealth itself under pretence of encouraging the means of acquiring it, we would caution you against giving a death-blow to your own policy. Remember that hitherto you have always repelled foreign products, *because* they approximate more nearly than home products to the character of gratuitous gifts. To comply with the exactions of other monopolists, you have only *half a motive*; and to repulse us simply because we stand on a stronger vantage-ground than others would be to adopt the equation + x + = −; in other words, it would be to heap *absurdity* upon *absurdity*.

Nature and human labour co-operate in various proportions (depending on countries and climates) in the production of commodities. The part which nature executes is always gratuitous: it is the part executed by human labour which constitutes value, and is paid for.

If a Lisbon orange sells for half the price of a Paris orange, it is because natural, and consequently gratuitous, heat does for the one what artificial, and therefore expensive, heat must do for the other.

When an orange comes to us from Portugal, we may conclude that it is furnished in part gratuitously, in part for an onerous consideration; in other words, it comes to us at *half-price* as compared with those of Paris.

Now, it is precisely the *gratuitous half* (pardon the word) which we contend should be excluded. You say, How can national labour sustain competition with foreign labour, when the former has all the work to do, and the latter only does one-half, the sun supplying the remainder? But if this *half*, being *gratuitous*, determines you to exclude competition, how should the *whole*, being *gratuitous*, induce you to admit competition? If you were consistent, you would, while excluding as hurtful to native industry what is half gratuitous, exclude *a fortiori* and with double zeal, that which is altogether gratuitous.

Once more, when products such as coal, iron, corn, or textile fabrics are sent us from abroad, and we can acquire them with less labour than if we made them ourselves, the difference is a free gift conferred upon us. The gift is more or less considerable in proportion as the difference is more or

less great. It amounts to a quarter, a half, or three-quarters of the value of
the product, when the foreigner only asks us for three-fourths, a half, or a
quarter of the price we should otherwise pay. It is as perfect and complete as
it can be, when the donor (like the sun in furnishing us with light) asks us for
nothing. The question, and we ask it formally, is this: Do you desire for our
country the benefit of gratuitous consumption, or the pretended advantages
of onerous production? Make your choice, but be logical; for as long as you
exclude, as you do, coal, iron, corn, foreign fabrics, *in proportion* as their
price approximates to *zero*, what inconsistency it would be to admit the light
of the sun, the price of which is already at *zero* during the entire day!

MERCANTILISM

As one might tell from his name, Bastiat is a Frenchman. In this
reading he accuses England ("perfidious Albion") of sending the
sun to shine on France in order to destroy the market for local manufacturers of artificial lighting. Monsieur Bastiat will have none of
it. A stronger domestic lighting industry, he says, is highly desirable. It will employ more workers and stimulate domestic production. As a consequence, laws must be passed to plunge every house
into darkness, even at high noon. The whole country, he argues, will
only benefit thereby.

Monsieur Bastiat is a mercantilist. Historically the oldest way of
thinking about the international political economy, "mercantilism"
(or "neomercantilism" as this worldview is called today, or "protectionism," which is a more descriptive label) is state making by material means. Those who propose such a worldview see in "foreign
competition" a threat to the "national market for national industry."
They see a direct relationship between state independence in finance and production, and state autonomy and power. The state
that is not in control of its money or its manufacturing and that
doesn't protect itself as a market will find itself, mercantilists argue,
weak and vulnerable in all other ways as well. The strong state will
be the one that does protect its domestic industries, while saving
hard against a rainy day.

People don't like being called doctrinaire. They like even less
being said to have an ideology. So Monsieur Bastiat, in his speech to
the Chambers of Deputies on behalf of the lighting industry, appeals directly to their members' sense of the national interest. He reminds them that the national interest is that of its producers. He
urges them not to believe abstract theories to the contrary, theories,

for example, that promise national plenty through free trade. He recommends "practice without theory and without principle." After all, someone has to stop these foreign rivals dumping cheap goods on the domestic market and driving local manufacturers out of business. The situation is clearly intolerable.

The relationship between "defense" and "opulence" (Viner 1948: 17) was first analyzed in detail by nineteenth-century Prussian scholars in their bid to highlight the importance of having a Prussian state (Viner 1948:1–2). These scholars saw in particular protectionist policies of the past a model for the present and the future. They argued, in effect, for policies that serve the same function in the international political economy as statism serves in the international state system, namely, self-help. Where my gain is seen as your loss, and vice versa; where the system as a whole is ungoverned and conflict is always imminent; in such a world, countries, they would say, should be self-sufficient and strong.

Mercantilists argue that state makers can promote their powers in one of two ways. They can try and be exclusivist, turning inward, closing down their borders and going it alone. Or they can try and be inclusivist. They can turn outward and self-aggrandize by more imperialistic means.

Exclusivity, or "classical" mercantilism, comes in different forms. At their most radical, mercantilists advocate autarky, that is, absolute autonomy and a withdrawal from the world. Those who have come the closest to this in contemporary times have been the state makers of Myanmar (Burma) and Albania. Less-radical and considerably more pervasive have been the attempts to protect the national interest with current account surpluses, that is, with attempts to export more and import less. Here the logic is to outtrade everyone else. Though this was not part of the classical mercantilist view, most mercantilists today would accept that they live in a world of other mercantilists, and that there may be good reasons for dealing with them. Their desire for state autonomy remains paramount, however, so that while it may be permissible to lend to others it is not seen as permissible to borrow from them. Thus protectionist tariffs and other controls are brought to bear, to maximize independence and minimize interdependence.

As well as these more exclusivist ways of behaving, we find a form of mercantilism that goes "out" rather than "in"; that tries to make the outside part of the inside. Autonomy and self-reliance are achieved by making others subordinate. The fight to prevail is construed in terms of the fight to control shares in "total world economic activity" (Brown 1974:27). "Trade and the flag" are moved around together.

In terms of the capitalist world market, this means not just exporting more and importing less. It means actively fighting for control of world market shares. The historic attempt by Japanese manufacturers, for example, to dominate the global color TV market might be seen in this light, since they had the full sanction and support of Japanese state makers, and indeed, their ploy was part of the overall national plan for Japanese development. To maximize global market shares to the full, you need "vertical integration," that is, control of the whole production, exchange, and distribution process from the neocolonized "paddock" to the metropolitan "patio." This was the Japanese strategy for making and importing Australian beef, for example. Everything, from the blade of grass in New South Wales to the supermarket shelf in Osaka, was owned by Japanese. This included the land, the herds, the abatoirs, the port facilities, the ships, the local transport, and the shops. Any attempt to break into the chain was met with threats of relocation. Except for the initial start-up costs and some local materials, taxes, and workers' wages after that, all the money went to Japan.

What states get by being either exclusivist or inclusivist has been much debated. Should a current account surplus be preferred as a way of protecting the domestic labor force by preventing unemployment? Is it good to promote the expansion of local manufacturing? Can such expansion be used to foster technological progress (Schmitt 1979:93–98)? Questions like these can become very pressing, particularly in times of politicoeconomic downturn. Keynes, for example, writing in 1933 in the midst of the Great Depression, saw protectionism as an imperative. Like most Englishmen of his day, he was raised to view free trade as not only rational but as part of "moral law." He came to the conclusion during the Depression, however, that international interdependence was dangerous. Let goods be "homespun," he argued. And above all, he thought at that time, let finances be "primarily national." Similar fears abound, even in nondepressed times. How often do we hear politicians and producers bemoaning the lack or loss of access to essential materials or markets abroad? How often is the banner of "responsible statecraft" raised above protectionist state policies (Schmitt 1979:109)?

❖ **David Lodge (1980) "My First Job"**

You don't have to be a Protestant to have the Protestant Ethic, I tell my students, when we come to Weber in my survey course on Sociological

Grand Theory. Look at me, I say: Jewish father, Catholic mother—and I develop an allergic rash at the mere mention of the word 'holiday', with all its connotations of reckless expenditure of time and money. Accumulate, accumulate!—that's my motto, whether it's publications, index cards, or those flimsier bits of paper that promise to pay the bearer so many pounds if he presents them to the Bank of England. Work! Strive! Excel! For the job's own sake! My students, lolling in their seats, mentally preoccupied with the problem of how to draw the dole *and* hitchhike to Greece this summer, grin tolerantly and unbelievably at me through their beards and fringes. Sometimes, to try and make them understand, I tell them the story of my first job.

Once upon a time, long, long ago, in the olden days, or, to be more precise, in the summer of 1952 (so I begin), at the age of seventeen and three-quarters, I got my first job, selling newspapers and magazines off a little trolley on Waterloo Station. It was a temporary job, to fill in a few weeks between getting my A-level results (which were excellent, I need hardly say) and going to University. There was no real economic need for me to work, and the weekly wage of £3 10s 0d (even allowing for subsequent inflation) made it scarcely worthwhile to travel up from my home in Greenwich daily. It was a matter of principle. My father, who ran his own dressmaking business employing thirty people (which he intended to hand on to me, his only child), was dubious of the point or profit of a university education, and determined that at least I should not loaf idly about the house while I waited to commence it. It was he who spotted the advert in the *Evening Standard*, phoned up the manager of the shop, and talked him into giving me the job on a temporary basis, without even consulting me. My mother looked at the advertisement. "It says, 'suitable school-leaver'," she observed.

"Well, he's left school, hasn't he?" demanded my father.

"'School-leaver' means some no-hope fifteen-year-old from a secondary modern," said my mother. "It's a euphemism." She was a well-educated woman, my mother. "Pays like a euphemism, too," she added. Years of marriage to my father had imparted a Yiddish edge to her Irish sense of humour.

"Never mind, it will give him an idea of what the real world is like," said my father. "Before he buries his head in books for another three years."

"It's true, he ought to give his eyes a rest," my mother agreed.

This conversation took place in the kitchen. I overheard it, sitting in the dining-room, going through my stamp collection (I was totting up the value of all my stamps in the Stanley Gibbons catalogue: I seemed to be worth thousands, though I had no intention of selling). I was *meant* to overhear the conversation, and to be ready to give an answer when the substance of it was formally put to me. Diplomatic leaks of this kind oiled the wheels of family life wonderfully.

My father came into the dining-room. "Oh, there you are," he said, affecting surprise, "I've found a job for you."

"What kind of job?" I enquired coyly. I had already decided to accept it.

The next Monday morning, I presented myself, promptly at 8.30 at the bookstall, a large green island in the middle of Waterloo Station. Waves of office workers arriving on suburban trains surged across the station precinct as if pursued by demons, pausing only to snatch newspapers and magazines from the counters of the shop for the next stage of their journeys by tube or bus. Inside the shop, in a cramped and stuffy little office, seated at a desk heaped with invoices and ringed with the traces of innumerable mugs of tea, was the manager, Mr Hoskyns: a harassed, irascible little man who had evidently suffered a stroke or some kind of palsy, since the right-hand side of his face was paralysed and the corner of his mouth was held up by a little gold hook and chain suspended from his spectacles. Out of the other corner of his mouth he asked me how much change I would give from a ten-shilling note to a customer who had bought three items costing ninepence, two and sixpence, and a penny-halfpence, respective. Suppressing an urge to remind him that I had just passed A-level Maths-with-Stats with flying colours, I patiently answered the question, with a speed that seemed to impress him. Then Mr Hoskyns took me outside to where two youths loitered beside three mobile news-stands. These were green-painted wooden barrows, their steeply-angled sides fitted with racks for displaying magazines and newspapers.

"Ray! Mitch! This 'ere's the new boy. Show 'im the ropes," said Mr Hoskyns, and disappeared back into his lair.

Ray was a boy of about my stature, though (I guessed) about a year younger. He was smoking a cigarette which dangled rakishly from his lower lip, and which he occasionally transferred from one side of his mouth to the other without using his hands, as if to demonstrate that in one respect at least he had an advantage over Mr Hoskyns. He kept his hands plunged into the pockets of an Army Surplus wind-breaker, and wore heavy boots protruding from frayed trousers. Mitch (I never did discover whether this was a nick-name or a contraction of a real first or second name) was very small and of indeterminate age. He had a dirty, wizened little face like a monkey's, and bit his nails continuously. He wore a collarless shirt and the jacket and trousers of two different striped suits, of the kind working-class boys often wear for Sunday best in cheap imitation of their fathers: the jacket was brown and the trousers were blue, and both garments were in a state of considerable disrepair. They looked at me in my grey flannels and the grammar school blazer which, on the advice of my mother, I had decided to "wear out" on the job, since I would have no further use for it.

"Wotcher wanner dead-end job like this for then?" was Ray's first utterance.

"I'm only doing it for a month," I said. "Just while I'm waiting to go to University."

"University? Yer mean, like Oxford and Cambridge? The Boat race and that?" (It should be remembered that going to University was a rarer phenomenon in 1952 than it is now.)

"No, London University. The London School of Economics."

"Whaffor?"

"To get a degree."

"What use is that to yer?"

I pondered a short, simple answer to this question. "You get a better job in life afterwards," I said at length. I didn't bother to explain that personally I wouldn't be looking for a job, since a thriving little business was being kept warm for me. Mitch, nibbling his fingers, stared at me intently, like a savage pigmy surprised by the appearance of a white explorer in the jungle.

Mr Hoskyns popped an angry head round the door. "I thought I said, 'Show 'im the ropes', didn't I?"

The ropes were simple enough. You loaded your trolley with newspapers and magazines, and trundled off to platforms where trains were filling up prior to their departure. There were no kiosks on the actual platforms of Waterloo Station in those days, and we were meant to serve passengers who had passed through the ticket barriers without providing themselves with reading matter. The briskest trade came from the boat trains that connected at Southampton with the transatlantic liners (remember them?) whose passengers always included a quota of Americans anxious to free their pockets of the heavy British change. Next in importance were the expresses to the holiday resorts and county towns of the south-west, especially the all-Pullman 'Bournemouth Belle', with its pink-shaded table lamps at every curtained window. The late-afternoon and early-evening commuting crowds, cramming themselves back into the same grimy carriages that had disgorged them in the morning, bought little except newspapers from us. Our brief was simply to roam the station in search of custom. When our stocks were low, we pushed our trolleys back to the shop to replenish them. Brenda, a pleasant young married woman with elaborately permed hair, who served behind the counter would give us the items we asked for and make a note of the quantities.

I did not dislike the work. Railway stations are places of considerable sociological interest. The subtle gradations of the British class-system are displayed there with unparalleled richness and range of illustration. You see every human type, and may eavesdrop on some of the most deeply emotional moments in people's lives: separations and reunions of spouses and sweethearts, soldiers off to fight in distant wars, families off to start a new life in the Dominions, honeymoon couples off to . . . whatever honeymoon couples did. I had only very hazy ideas about that, having been too busy swotting for my A-levels to spare much time for thinking about sex, much less having any, even the solitary kind. When Ray told me on my second day that I ought to have some copies of the *Wanker's Times* on my trolley, I innocently went and asked Brenda for some. The word was new to me. As for the activity to

which it referred, my father had effectively warned me off that in his Facts
of Life talk when I was fourteen. (This talk was also delivered ostensibly to
my mother while I eavesdropped in the dining-room. "I never wasted my
strength when I was a lad, you know what I mean?" my father loudly
declared. "I saved it for the right time and place." "I should think so too,"
said my mother.) Brenda turned brick red, and went off muttering to complain to Mr Hoskyns, who came bouncing out of his office, impassive on
one side of his face, angry on the other.

"What's the idea, insulting Brenda like that? You's better wash your
mouth out, my lad, or out you go on your arse." He checked himself,
evidently recognising my bewilderment was genuine. "Did Ray put you up
to it then?" He sniggered, and shook his shoulders in suppressed mirth,
making the little golden chain chink faintly. "All right. I'll speak to 'im.
But don't be so simple, another time." Across the station's expanse, lurking
beside the Speak Your Weight machine, I could see Ray and Mitch watching
this scene with broad grins on their faces, nudging and jostling each other.
"And by the way," Mr Hoskyns threw over his shoulder as he returned to his
office, "we never send out *Health and Efficiency* on the trolleys." (*Health
and Efficiency*, I usually have to explain to the children at this point, was one
of the very few publications on open sale, in those days, in which one might
examine photographs of the naked female form, tastefully disposed among
sand dunes, or clasping strategically-positioned beach-balls.)

At the end of the day we took our money to be counted by Mr Hoskyns
and entered in his ledger. On my first day I took £3 15s 6d, Mitch £5 7s 8d,
and Ray £7 0s 5d. It wasn't really surprising that I lagged behind the other
two, because they knew from experience the times and locations of the trains
that provided the best custom. By the following Friday, the busiest day of the
week, I had almost caught up with Mitch—£8 19s 6d to his £9 1s 6d—
though Ray had taken £10 15s 9d.

"What's the highest amount you've taken in one day?" I asked, as we
left the shop, pocketing our meagre wages, and prepared to join the home-
going crowds. It irked me somewhat that these secondary modern types, even
allowing for their greater experience, were able to take more cash than me. It
bothered me much more than the practical joke over *Health and Efficiency*.

"Ray took Eleven par nineteen 'n' six one Friday," said Mitch. "That's
the all-time record."

Fatal phrase! Like the smell of liquor to an alcoholic. The job was
suddenly transformed into a contest—like school, like examinations, except
that one's performance was measured in £sd instead of percentage marks. I
set myself to beat Ray's record the following Friday. I still remember the
shocked, unbelieving expressions on Ray's and Mitch's faces as Mr Hoskyns
called out my total.

"Twelve pounds eggs-*actly*! Well done, lad! That's the best ever, I do
believe."

The following day, Saturday, I noticed that Ray was assiduously working the long lines of holidaymakers queuing for the special trains to the seaside resorts, milking their custom before they ever got to the platforms where Mitch and I plied our trade. When Mr Hoskyns announced the tallies at the end of the day, Ray had taken £12 7s 8d—a new record, and particularly remarkable in being achieved on a Saturday.

Suddenly, we were locked in fierce competition. Economically, it was quite absurd, for we were paid no commission on sales—though Mr Hoskyns certainly was, and manifested understandable pleasure as our daily and weekly takings escalated. At the sound of our trolleys returning in the late afternoon, he would come out of his cubbyhole to greet us with a lopsided smile, his gold chain glinting in the pale sunlight that slanted through the grimy glass of the station roof. The old record of £11 19s 6d soon seemed a negligible sum—something any one of us could achieve effortlessly on a wet Monday or Tuesday. On the third Friday of my employment, we grossed over fifty pounds between us. Ray's face was white and strained as Mr Hoskyns called out the totals, and Mitch gnawed his fingernails like a starving cannibal reduced to self-consumption. Mitch had taken £14 10s 3d, Ray £18 4s 9d and myself £19 1s 3d.

The following week was my last on the job. Aware of this fact, Ray and Mitch competed fiercely to exceed my takings, while I responded eagerly to the challenge. We ran, literally ran, with our trolleys from platform to platform, as one train departed and another began to fill up. We picked out rich-looking Americans in the boat-train crowd and hung about in their vicinity with our most expensive magazines, *Vogue* and *Harper's Bazaar* that cost a whole half-crown each, prominently displayed. We developed an eye for the kind of young man on the "Bournemouth Belle" who would try to impress his girlfriend with a lavish expenditure of money on magazines that clearly neither of them would be reading. We shuffled our stocks and rearranged them several times a day to appeal to the clientele of the moment. We abbreviated our lunch-hour, and took our tea-breaks on the move. In takings, Ray and I were neck and neck, day by day: sometimes he was the winner by a few shillings, sometimes myself. But the real needle match between us was on the Friday, which was to be my last day of work, since I had earned some overtime which entitled me to have the last Saturday off. Both Ray and I realised that this Friday would see the record smashed yet again, and perhaps the magic figure of £20 in a single day—the four-minute mile of our world—achieved by one or other of us.

Recklessly we raced across the station with our trolleys, that day, to claim the most favourable pitch, beside the first-class compartments of departing expresses; jealously we eyed each other's dwindling stocks. Like Arab street-traders we accosted astonished passengers and pestered them to buy our wares, forcing our way into intimate circles of tearfully embracing relatives, or tapping urgently on the windows of carriages whose occupants had already settled themselves for a quiet snooze. At one point I saw Ray actually running beside a moving train to complete the sale of a copy of *Homes and Gardens.*

At the end of the day, Mitch had taken £15 8s 6d, Ray £20 1s 9d and myself £21 2s 6d. Ray turned away, sick and white, and ground the cigarette he had been smoking under his heel. Mitch swore softly and drew blood from his mutilated finger ends. I felt suddenly sorry for them both. The future stretched out for me as rosy as the table lamps of the "Bournemouth Belle". Within a few years, I had reason to hope, it would be me who would be taking his seat for luncheon on the plump Pullman cushions; and although I didn't actually guess that before many more had passed I would be catching the boat-train for the *Queen Mary* and a Fellowship in the United States, I had a hunch that such extended horizons would one day be mine. While for Ray and Mitch the future held only the prospect of pushing the trolleys from platform to platform, until perhaps they graduated to serving behind the counters of the shop—or, more likely—became porters or cleaners. I regretted, now, that I had won the competition for takings, and denied them the small satisfaction of beating me in that respect at least. But worst was still to come.

Mr Hoskyns was paying me off: three one pound notes and a ten shilling note. "You've done well, son," he said. "Sales from the trolleys have turned up a treat since you came 'ere. You've shown these two idle little sods what 'ard work really means. And mark my words," he continued, turning to Ray and Mitch, "I expect you two to keep up the good work after 'e's gorn. If you don't turn in this sort of sum *every* Friday, from now on, I'll want to know the reason why—you understand?"

The next day I overheard my parents talking in the kitchen. "He seems very moody," said my mother, "Do you think he's fallen in love?" My father snorted derisively. "In love? He's probably just constipated." "He seemed very quiet when he came home from work yesterday," said my mother. "You'd almost think he was sorry to leave." "He's probably wondering whether it's a good idea to go to University after all," said my father. "Well, he can come straight into the business now, if he wants to."

I burst into the kitchen. "I'll tell you why I'm moody!" I cried.

"You shouldn't listen to other people's private conversations," said my mother.

"It's because I've seen how capitalism exploits the workers! How it sets one man against another, cons them into competing with each other, and takes all the profit. I'll have nothing more to do with it!"

My father sank on to a kitchen chair with a groan, and covered his face with his hands. "I knew it, I knew it would happen one day. My only son, who I have been slaving for all these years, has had a brainstorm. What have I done to deserve that this should happen to me?"

So that was how I became a sociologist. My first job was also my last. (I don't call *this* a job—reading books and talking about them to a captive audience; I would pay to do it if they weren't paying me.) I didn't, as you see, go into business; I went into academic life, where the Protestant ethic does less harm to one's fellow men. But the faces of Ray and Mitch still haunt me, as I last saw them, with the realisation slowly sinking in that they were committed to maintaining that punishing tempo of work, that extraordinary volume of sales, indefinitely, and to no personal advantage, or else be subjected to constant complaint and abuse. All because of me.

After my lecture on Weber, I usually go back to Marx and Engels.

LIBERALISM

Max Weber, the German sociologist, attributed the extraordinary power of capitalism to what he called the Protestant Ethic. Driven by a desire to know they were one of the Elect, who got to Heaven when they died, the Calvinists in the Geneva of the Middle Ages chose to celebrate sobriety and industry. They worked hard, in other words, to prove to themselves that they were worthy of the spiritual honor of a divine outcome to their lives. This made them, without them even realizing it, highly competitive. Competitiveness has been a hallmark ever since of an efficient political economy. Lodge shows clearly, in the reading above, how powerful this feeling can be, and how it can overtake even someone in his first job, selling newspapers.

The boys Lodge describes at Waterloo Station were acting like mercantilists. Their behavior was highly competitive, as if one boy's gain was another boy's loss. Was this their only choice, however? Why didn't they collude, for example, dividing the work among them and sharing the wages they subsequently made? That would have been the rational way to behave. Their energies could then have been used, not against each other, but in outselling other newspaper kiosks that employed other groups of boys.

It fell to Adam Smith to show the limits of what is a mercantilist way of thinking. Mercantilists are highly defensive about winning and losing. Smith argued for the opposite. He saw opulence as the outcome of open competition, where everyone gains and no one loses. Wealth doesn't come from jealously guarding your own little patch, he said. It comes from free enterprise, and the freer the better. Thus, "every town and country," he said, " . . . in proportion as they have opened their ports to all nations, instead of being ruined by this free trade . . . have been enriched by it" (Smith: 1892:380).

A country, Smith argued, can easily import "to a greater value than it exports for half a century" (Smith: 1892:380). It doesn't matter, he said, if the "gold and silver which comes into it during . . .

this time may be all immediately sent out of it. . . . [E]ven the debts, too, which it contracts in the principal nations with whom it deals may be gradually increasing" to no ill effect if its "real wealth," the "exchangeable value of the annual produce of its lands and labor . . . during the same period, have been increasing in a much greater proportion" (Smith 1892:380–381). That's the rub. A country doesn't need to be protective if it's productive. Make enough and autonomy doesn't matter.

Smith's philosophy of free enterprise is the classically liberal one. It corresponds to the politicostrategic philosophy of self-help through cooperative interdependence. While the "bottom line" may still entail territorial defense, it's what goes on above this line that matters most. Indeed, a world in which all state makers actively embrace a nondefensive, outward-looking, open-borders approach to trade and investment is one, Smithians believe, that will never get to the bottom line.

Imagine a world, Smith seems to suggest, where self-interested men and women meet in markets to do what suits them best. In pursuing their self-interest, they carry the whole society to new heights. Prosperity and harmony are the inevitable result. "Unanimity without conformity" (Friedman 1962:23) is the fortunate consequence. Inhibit people's freedom to buy and sell, however, and this law will be prevented from working to its best effect. "It is a rather daunting thought," says Cole (1991:6–7), "that whenever an economist talks uncritically about supply and demand in a market, there is, behind those apparently uncontroversial terms, the assumption of a whole philosophy of possessive individualism and liberal politics."

The notion that there are "natural laws" that govern "individual" behavior was highly characteristic of the eighteenth century European era when Smith thought and wrote. At this time of so-called "Enlightenment" scholars began asking "what we might do on earth now, rather than what we might do to regain a glorious past, or how to reach heaven in the future" (Cole 1991:6–7). Not only did this more secular attitude make the natural universe seem more accessible, it also opened the human world to applied reason.

One such application was Smith's idea of liberal marketeering. What went on in the village square once a week, perhaps, seemed to have been made into a whole way of thinking. Profit and loss, supply and demand began to seem timeless and universal. They seemed to make possible a new human "science" of unprecedented precision, namely, economics.

The words *seem* and *seemingly* are very important here, since the "economic man" that liberal thinkers devised is a part-person, not a whole one. By assuming that he is much given to unambiguous, self-serving decisions, it does become possible to summarize his behavior, and that of all those like him, in terms of a kind of market mechanics. And this can be quite useful as a first approximation. It is only a first approximation, however, since market mechanics allows of "no leaving, no forgetting, no blunders, no impulsive decisions (made on unquestioned and possibly unintended recommendations from half-known exemplars), no adventurous or experimental decision (made to see what would happen), no developing or fading tastes, no flow of surprises and unintended and unnoticed consequences, [and] no accumulation of regrets at opportunities rejected or unperceived" (Bensusan-Butt 1980).

The assumption that what happens now on earth should be what economic man decides to do now on earth, was used to justify the entrepreneurial activity of eighteenth- and nineteenth-century European businessmen. So successful were these activities that manufacturers and traders eventually turned to the landed aristocrats who still dominated Europe and said, in effect: "Please note! We don't perform in some inferior sideshow, supplying luxuries and novelties, alleviating the occasional famine, stocking your homes and supplying your armies. We are the main players in a new game. We are the makers of national prosperity. We deserve political freedom and public acclaim."

Not all liberals accept the classical idea that markets work best when unfettered. Not all liberals believe that state makers should be excluded from markets as much as possible. Experience has shown many of them that markets can be "inefficient" and can fail. Harmony has to be helped to happen, if, for example, unequal starting conditions are not to be made by marketeers into even more unequal outcomes. Many liberals have, as a consequence, come to advocate a role for state makers as referees and facilitators. These "reformist" liberals—people like Keynes, for example, in his non-mercantilist mode—consider statist intervention to be necessary to smooth out the market's bust and boom cycles. The state provides public goods like contract adjudication procedures. It protects other public goods, like the environment, which might otherwise be damaged beyond repair before marketeers decide to make a profit from the repair process.

Reformist liberals like Gilpin believe that the world market as a whole needs an interventionist ring holder. They would look to one hegemonic country to police global free trade agreements and to act as "lender of last resort." They would invite the intellectuals of such a country to take a lead in defining ways to defend global public goods (Gilpin 1987:307).

Contemporary neoclassical liberals like Hayek ("neoliberals," as they are currently called) have never given up the idea that governments distort markets, and that markets that are fully free are the only ones to be preferred (Hayek 1988). They want what Ashley (1983:463) calls "economism." They want deregulated economies, despite the negative effects deregulation has on employment levels or national morale. These shortcomings pale, they say, beside the benefits that entrepreneurs can provide, benefits like jobs, profits, and general prosperity.

What should a state maker do? Intervene in ways that reformist liberals recommend and classical liberals deplore? Bring the state "back in"? Or get out of the market, regardless of the short-term results, and hope to Adam Smith that what follows makes enough money for enough people to police the resultant crime and revolution? No wonder the debate within the liberal ranks often seems so fierce. Lodge on his windy station platform could sense some of the awful cost of constant competition. At least, we can say, those three boys had a job. Those thrown out of work by entrepreneurs who relocate factories or who replace human labor with more machines tell a different story. Like Lodge in his lectures, it is no surprise when they turn to Marx.

❖ **Stephen Hymer (1971) "Robinson Crusoe and the Secret of Primitive Accumulation"**

> *Every living being is a sort of imperialist,*
> *seeking to transform as much as possible of*
> *the environment into itself and its seed.*—Bertrand Russell

Note on Primitive Accumulation

The word *primitive* is here used in the sense of "belonging to the first age, period, or stage," i.e. of being "original rather than derivative," and not in the sense of "simple, rude, or rough." Marx's original term was "Ursprüngliche Akkumulation," and as Paul Sweezy suggests, it would have been better translated as "original" or "primary" accumulation. But it is too late to change current usage, and the word *primitive* should be interpreted in a technical sense, as in mathematics, where a *primitive* line or figure is a line or figure "from which some construction or reckoning begins." In economics primitive accumulation refers to the period from which capitalist accumulation springs. It was not simple, though it was rude and rough.[1]

The solitary and isolated figure of Robinson Crusoe is often taken as a starting point by economists, especially in their analysis of international trade. He is pictured as a rugged individual—diligent, intelligent, and above all frugal—who masters nature through reason. But the actual story of Robinson Crusoe, as told by Defoe, is also one of conquest, slavery, robbery, murder, and force. That this side of the story should be ignored is not at all surprising, "for in the tender annals of political economy the idyllic reigns from time immemorial." The contrast between the economist's Robinson Crusoe and the genuine one mirrors the contrast between the mythical description of international trade found in economics textbooks and the actual facts of what happens in the international economy.

The paradigm of non-Marxist international trade theory is the model of a hunter and fisherman who trade to their mutual benefit under conditions of equality, reciprocity, and freedom. But international trade (or, for that matter, interregional trade) is often based on a division between superior and subordinate rather than a division between equals; and it is anything but peaceful. It is trade between the centre and hinterland, the colonizers and the colonized, the masters and the servants. Like the relation of capital to labour, it is based on a division between higher and lower functions: one party does the thinking, planning, organizing; the other does the work. Because it is unequal in structure and reward it has to be established and maintained by force, whether it be the structural violence of poverty, the symbolic violence of socialisation, or the physical violence of war and pacification.

In this essay I would like to go over the details of Crusoe's story—how, starting as a slave trader, he uses the surplus of others to acquire a fortune—in order to illustrate Marx's analysis of the capitalist economy, especially the period of primitive accumulation which was its starting point.

For capitalist accumulation to work, two different kinds of people must meet in the market (and later in the production process); on the one hand, owners of money eager to increase their capital by buying other people's labour power; on the other hand, free labourers unencumbered by pre-capitalist obligations or personal property. Once capitalism is on its legs, it maintains this separation and reproduces it on a continuously expanding scale. But a prior stage is needed to clear the way for the capitalist system and get it started—a period of primitive accumulation.

In the last part of Volume 1 of *Capital*, Marx sketched the historical process by which means of production were concentrated in the hands of the capitalist, leaving the worker no alternative but to work for him. He showed how a wage labour force was created through the expropriation of the agricultural population and he traced the genesis of the industrial capitalist to, among other things, the looting of Africa, Asia, and America "in the rosy dawn of the era of capitalist production." In the story of Robinson Crusoe, Defoe describes how a seventeenth-century Englishman amassed capital and organised a labour force to work for him in Brazil and in the Caribbean. Of course what Crusoe established was not a market economy such as emerged in England but a plantation and settler economy such as was used by capitalism in the non-European world. It might therefore be called the story of primitive underdevelopment.

Defoe (1659–1731) was particularly well placed to observe and understand the essence of the rising bourgeoisie and the secrets of its origins. The son of a London butcher, he was engaged in the business of a hosiery factor and a commission merchant until he went bankrupt. During his life he wrote many essays and pamphlets on economics, discussing among other things, banks, road management, friendly and insurance societies, idiot asylums, bankruptcy, academies, military colleges, women's education, social welfare programs, and national workshops. He was one of the first writers to rely on the growing market of the middle class to earn his living.[2]

(1) Merchants' Capital

Robinson Crusoe's story can be told in terms of a series of cycles, some running simultaneously, through which he accumulates capital. In the early days these take the form M-C-M, i.e. he starts off with money, exchanges it for commodities, and ends up with more money. In the later phases when he is outside the money economy, they take the form C-L-C, as he uses his stock of commodities to gain control over other people's labour and to produce more commodities, ending up with a small empire.

Robinson Crusoe was born in 1632. The son of a merchant, he could have chosen to follow the middle station of life and raise his fortune "by application and industry, with a life of ease and pleasure." Instead he chose to go to sea—partly for adventure, partly because of greed.

In his first voyage he starts off with £40 in "toys and trifles," goes to the Guinea coast (as mess-mate, and companion of the captain whom he befriended in London), and comes back with five pounds nine ounces of gold worth £300. This is the first circuit of his capital. He leaves £200 of this sum in England with the captain's widow (the captain died soon after their return) and, using the remaining £100 as fresh capital, sets off on a second voyage as a Guinea trader in order to make more capital. Instead he meets with disaster. The ship is captured by Moors and he becomes a slave in North Africa. He escapes slavery in a boat taken from his master, accompanied by a fellow slave Xury, a black man, to whom he promises, "Xury, if you will be faithful to me, I'll make you a great man." Together they sail a thousand miles along the coast of Africa, until they are met and rescued by a Portuguese captain.

Fortunately for Robinson, there is honour among capitalists. The captain, who is on his way to Brazil, feels it would be unfair to take everything from Robinson and bring him to Brazil penniless. "I have saved your life on no other terms than I would be glad to be saved myself. . . . When I carry you to Brazil, so great a way from your own country, if I should take from you what you have, you will be starved there, and then I only take away that life I have given."

Robinson of course does not tell the captain that he still has £200 in England. Instead, he sells the captain his boat (i.e. the boat he took when he escaped) and everything in it, *including Xury*. An African is an African, and only under certain conditions does he become a slave. Robinson has some pangs of guilt about selling "the poor boy's liberty who had assisted me so faithfully in procuring my own." However, the captain offers to set Xury free in ten years if he turns Christian. "Upon this, and Xury saying he was willing to go to him, I let the captain have him" (for sixty pieces of eight). Commodities are things and cannot go to market by themselves. They have to be taken. If they are unwilling, they can be forced.

Robinson arrives in Brazil where he purchases "as much land that was uncured as my money would reach, and formed a plan for my plantation and settlement, and such a one as might be suitable to the stock which I proposed to myself to receive from England." He soon finds "more than before, I had done wrong in parting with my boy Xury," for he needed help and found there was "no work to be done, but by the labour of my hands."

He sends a letter to the widow in England through his Portuguese captain friend instructing that half of his Pds200 be sent to him in the form of merchandise. The captain takes the letter to Lisbon where he gives it to some London merchants who relay it to London. The widow gives the money to a London merchant who, "vesting this hundred pounds in English goods, such as the captain had writ for, sent them directly to him at Lisbon, and he brought them all safe to me to Brazil; among which, without my direction (for I was too young in my business to think of them), he had taken care to have all sorts of tools, ironwork, and utensils necessary for my plantation, and which were of great use to me."

The cargo arrives, bringing great fortune to Robinson. The Portuguese captain had used the £5 the widow had given him for a present to purchase and bring to Robinson, "a servant under bond for six years service, and would not accept of any consideration, except a little tobacco which I would have him accept, being of my own produce." Moreover, he is able to sell the English goods in Brazil "to a very great advantage" and the first thing he does is to buy a Negro slave and a second indentured servant.

This series of transactions presupposes an elaborate social network of capitalist intercommunications. The mythical Robinson is pictured as a self-sufficient individual, but much of the actual story, even after he is shipwrecked, shows him as a dependent man belonging to a larger whole and always relying on help and co-operation from others. The social nature of production turns out to be the real message of his story as we shall see again and again. There is no real paradox in this. To capitalism belong both the production of the most highly developed social relations in history and the production of the solitary individual.

Robinson now integrates himself into the community as a successful
planter and accumulates steadily. But he cannot be content and soon leaves
"the happy view I had of being a rich and thriving man in my new
plantation, only to pursue a rash and immoderate desire of rising faster than
the nature of the thing admitted."

The plantations in Brazil were short of labour, for "few Negroes were
brought, and those excessive dear" since the slave trade at that time was not
far developed and was controlled by royal monopolies of the kings of Spain
and Portugal. Robinson had told some friends about his two voyages to the
Guinea Coast and the ease of purchasing there "for trifles not only gold dust
but Negroes in great numbers" (NB. that the trifles listed are beads, toys,
knives, scissors, hatchets, bits of glass, and the like—all but the first two
are by no means trifles, as Robinson would soon find out). These friends
approached him in secrecy with a plan for outfitting a ship to get slaves
from the Guinea Coast who would then be smuggled into Brazil privately
and distributed among their own plantations. They asked Robinson to go as
"supercargo in the ship to manage the trading part and offered [him] an equal
share of the Negroes without providing any part of the stock."

Robinson accepts, and it is on this voyage that his famous shipwreck
occurs. Years later, in the depths of isolation, he had cause to regret this
decision which he views in terms of his original sin of "not being satisfied
with the station wherein God and nature had placed [him] . . . "

"What business had I to leave a settled fortune, a well-stocked
plantation, improving and increasing, to turn supercargo to Guinea, to fetch
Negroes, when patience and time would have so increased our stock at home
that we could have bought them from those whose business it was to fetch
them? And though it had cost us something more, yet the difference of that
price was by no means worth saving at so great a hazard."

In fact he comes out ahead for by the end of the story Robinson has
succeeded in accumulating much faster than if he had remained content, for
he adds a new fortune from his island economy to the growth of his plantation. True, he must suffer a long period of isolation, but in many ways his
solitary sojourn represents the alienation suffered by all under capitalism—
those who work and receive little as well as those like Robinson who
accumulate and always must Go on, Go on.

(2) Island Economy: The Pre-Trade Situation

The key factors in Robinson Crusoe's survival and prosperity on his island
in the sun are not his ingenuity and resourcefulness but the pleasant climate
and the large store of embodied labour he starts out with. In thirteen trips to
his wrecked ship he was able to furnish himself with many things, taking a
vast array of materials and tools he never made but were still his to enjoy.
These he uses to gain command over nature and over other men. Of chief
importance in his initial stock of means of production is a plentiful supply

of guns and ammunition, which give him decisive advantage in setting the terms of trade when his island economy is finally opened up to trade.

Robinson himself is fully aware of the importance of his heritage (see table 1). "What should I have done without a gun, without ammunition, without any tools to make anything or work with, without clothes, bedding, a tent, or any manner of coverings?" he asks. And "by making the most rational judgment of things every man may be in time master of every mechanic art. I had never handled a tool in my life, and yet in time, by labour, application, and contrivance, I wanted nothing but I could have made it, *especially if I had had the tools*" (emphasis added). A European is a European and it is only under certain conditions that he becomes a master. It was not their personal attributes that gave Robinson and other European adventurers their strength vis-à-vis non-Europeans but the equipment they brought with them, the power of knowledge made into objects. This material base was the result of a complicated social division of labour of which they were the beneficiaries not the creators.

Table 1   Items Taken by Robinson Crusoe from the Shipwreck

Defence:	ammunition, arms powder, 2 barrels musket bullets, 5–7 muskets, large bag full of small shot
Food:	biscuits, rum, bread, rice, cheese, goat flesh, corn, liquor, flour, cordials, sweetmeats, poultry feed, wheat and rice seed
Clothing:	men's clothes, handkerchiefs, coloured neckties, 2 pairs of shoes
Furniture and miscellaneous:	hammock, bedding, pens, ink, paper, 3 or 4 compasses, some mathematical instruments, dials, perspectives, charts, books on navigation, 3 Bibles
Tools:	carpenter's chest, 203 bags full of nails and spikes, a great screwjack, 1 or 2 dozen hatchets, grindstone, 2 saws, axe, hammer, 2 or 3 iron crows, 2 or 3 razors, 1 large scissors, fire shovel and tongs, 2 brass kettles, copper pots, gridiron
Raw materials:	rigging, sails for canvas, small ropes, ropes and wire, ironwork, timber, boards, planks, 203 hundredweight of iron, 1 hundredweight of sheet lead
Animals:	dog, 2 cats
Things he misses badly:	ink, spade, shovel, needles, pins, thread, smoking pipe

---

His island is a rich one, again thanks in part to the activities of other people. He surveys it with little understanding since most of the plants were unfamiliar to him. He makes no independent discovery but finds certain familiar items—goats, turtles, fruits, lemons, oranges, tobacco, grapes—

many of which I imagine could not have got there except if transplanted by previous visitors from other islands. His own discovery of agriculture is accidental. Among the things he rescued from the ship was a little bag which had once been filled with corn. Robinson seeing nothing in the bag but husks and dust, and needing it for some other purpose, shook the husks out on the ground. A month or so later, not even remembering he had thrown them there, he was "perfectly astonished" to find barley growing.

Conditioned by capitalist tradition, Crusoe tried to keep account of his activities and "while my ink lasted, I kept things very exact; but after that was gone, I could not, for I could not make any ink by any means I could devise." He draws up a cost-benefit analysis of his position, stating in it "very impartially like debtor and creditor, the comforts I enjoyed, against the miseries I suffered." He finds his day divided into three. It took him only about three hours going out with his gun, to get his food. Another portion of his day was spent in ordering, curing, preserving, and cooking. A third portion was spent on capital formation, planting barley and rice, curing raisins, building furniture and a canoe, and so forth.

This passion for accounting might seem to confirm the economists' picture of Robinson as the rational man par excellence, allocating his time efficiently among various activities in order to maximize utility. But then comes this astonishing observation, "But my time or labour was little worth, and so it was as well employed one way as another"! Contrary to the usual models of economic theory, Robinson Crusoe, producing only for use and not for exchange, finds that there is no scarcity and that labour has no value. The driving force of capitalism, the passion for accumulation vanished when he was alone. "All I could make use of was all that was valuable. . . . The most covetous, griping miser in the world would have been cured of the vice of covetousness, if he had been in my case."

Robinson's own explanation of this phenomenon is mainly in terms of demand. Because he is alone, his wants are limited and satiated before he exhausts his available labour time:

> I was removed from all the wickedness of the world here. I had nei-
> ther the lust of the flesh, the lust of the eye or the pride of life. I had
> nothing to covet; for I had all that I was now capable of enjoying. I
> was lord of the whole manor; or if I pleased, I might call myself king,
> or emperor over the whole country which I had possession of. There
> were no rivals. I had no competitor . . .

This is true as far as it goes, but it is one-sided. Robinson's greed went away because there were no people to organise and master. Marx's propo-sition was that surplus labour was the sole measure and source of capitalist wealth. Without someone else's labour to control, the capitalist's value system vanished: no boundless thirst for surplus labour arose from the nature of production itself; the goals of efficiency, maximization, and accumulation faded into a wider system of values.

Later when Robinson's island becomes populated, the passion to organize and accumulate returns. It is only when he has no labour but his own to control that labour is not scarce and he ceases to measure things in terms of labour time. As Robinson's reference to the miser shows, it is not merely a question of the demand for consumption goods. The miser accumulates not for consumption but for accumulation, just as the purposeful man in the capitalist era, as Keynes noted, "does not love his cat, but his cat's kittens; not, in truth, the kittens, but only the kittens' kittens, and so on forward forever to the end of cat-dom. For him jam is not jam unless it is a case of jam tomorrow and never jam today."[3] Money and capital are social relations representing social power over others. Regardless of what goes on in the minds of misers and capitalists when they look at their stock, it is power over people that they are accounting and accumulating, as they would soon find out if they, like Robinson, were left alone.

Robinson is partially aware of this when he meditates on the uselessness of gold on his island:

I smiled to myself at the sight of this money. "O drug!" said I aloud, "what are thou good for? Thou art not worth to me, no not the taking off of the ground, one of those knives is worth all this heap; I have no manner of use for thee; e'en remain where thou art, and go to the bottom as a creature whose life is not worth saving." However, upon second thoughts, I took it away . . .

He thus negates the Mercantilist system which made a fetish out of gold, but does not fully pierce the veil of money to uncover the underlying basis of surplus labour—does not in his theories, that is; in his daily practice he is fully aware of the real basis of the economy. This shows up when he discusses the concept of Greed. In Robinson's eyes, his original sin is the crime of wanting to rise above his station instead of following the calling chosen for him by his father. Isolation and estrangement are his punishment, and he feels that his story should teach content to those "who cannot enjoy comfortably what God has given them." He feels guilty for violating the feudal institutions of status, patriarchy, and God. He does not consider that when he accumulates, he violates those whom he exploits—Xury, the Africans he sold into slavery, his indentured servants, and soon Friday and others. From the ideological point of view, Robinson is a transitional man looking backward and upward instead of forward and downward. This is why he learns nothing (morally speaking) from his loneliness. The miser is not in fact cured, the vice of covetousness easily returns.

Since the relationship of trade, accumulation, and exploitation is so crucial to understanding economics, we might dwell on it a little longer. The argument can be traced back to Aristotle, who felt that a self-sufficient community would not be driven by scarcity and accumulation, since natural wants were limited and could easily be satisfied with plenty of time left over for leisure. Such a community would practice the art of householding which has use value as its end. But Aristotle, an eyewitness to the growth of the market at its very first appearance, noted that there was another art of wealth getting—commercial trade—which had no limit, since its end was the accumulation of exchange value for its own sake. Aristotle was more interested in the effects of the rise of commerce than in its base and did not make the connection between exchange value and surplus labour. But it was there for all to see. The emergence of the market in ancient Athens was a by-product of its imperial expansion, the looting of territories liberated from the Persians, the collection of tribute and taxes from other Greek states for protection, and the forced diversion of the area's trade to Athens' port.[4]

Keynes, though analytically imprecise, glimpsed the same point in his article on "National Self-Sufficiency" (*Yale Review*, 1934) where he instinctively saw that some withdrawal from international trade was necessary to make the life made possible by science pleasant and worth-while. He wanted to minimise rather than maximise economic entanglements among nations so that we can be "our own masters" and "make out favourite experiments toward the ideal social republic of the future." He was all for a free exchange of ideas, knowledge, science, hospitality, and travel, "but let goods be home-spun whenever it is reasonably and commercially possible, and, above all let finance be primarily national." He knew that it was not invidious consumption that was the problem, but the desire to extend oneself by penetrating foreign markets with exports and investment, which in the end comes down to an attempt to transform as much as possible of the world into oneself and one's seed, i.e., imperialism.

To return to Robinson Crusoe. It is important to note that his isolation was accompanied not so much by loneliness as by fear. The first thing he did when he arrived on his beautiful Caribbean paradise was to build himself a fortress. It was only when he was completely "fenced and fortified" from all the world that he "slept secure in the night." His precautions during the first eleven years when he is completely alone are astonishing. Yet during these years he is in no danger from wild animals or any living thing. His chief problem comes from birds who steal his seeds. He deals with them with dispatch, shooting a few and then "I took them up and served them as we serve notorious thieves in England, viz., hanged them in chains for a terror to others." And, as we shall see in the next section, when signs of other human beings come to him, he does not run out with joy, ready to risk everything to hear a human voice after so many years in solitary confinement. Instead his fears and anxieties rise to a frenzied pitch, and he fences and fortifies himself more and more, withdrawing further and further into isolation.

Perhaps this is what one should expect from a man isolated for so long a period. But at times it seems to me that Defoe, in describing Robinson

Crusoe, was not only talking about a man who by accident becomes isolated, but is presenting an allegory about the life of all men in capitalist society—solitary, poor, uncertain, afraid. The isolation is more intense in Robinson's mind than in his actual situation. For what comes out clearly, in encounter after encounter, is that whenever Robinson has to face another person he reacts with fear and suspicion. His isolation, in short, is no more nor less than the alienation of possessive individualism, repeated a million times in capitalist society, and in our days symbolized by the private civil-defense shelter protected from neighbours by a machine gun.

(3) Opening Up of Trade: Forming an Imperial Strategy

The opening up of his economy to the outside world does not come to Robinson Crusoe in the form of abstract prices generated in anonymous markets but in the form of real people with whom he must come to terms. After fifteen years on the island, he comes upon the print of a naked man's foot on the shore. His first reaction is fear. He was "terrified to the last degree, looking behind me at every two or three steps, mistaking every bush and tree, and fancying every stump at a distance to be a man."

He goes to his retreat. "Never frightened hare fled to cover, or fox to earth, with more terror of mind, than I." From then on he lived "in the constant snare of the fear of man . . . a life of anxiety, fear and care."

He thinks of destroying his cattle enclosure, cornfield, and dwelling, "that they might not find such a grain there . . . and still be prompted to look further, in order to find out the persons inhabiting." He builds a second wall of fortifications, armed with seven muskets planted like a cannon and fitted "into frames that held them like a carriage, so that I could fire all the seven guns in two minutes' time. This wall I was many a weary month a-finishing and yet never thought myself safe till it was done." He pierces all the ground outside his wall with stakes or sticks so that in five or six years' time he had "a wood before my dwelling growing so monstrous thick and strong that it was indeed perfectly impassable; and no men of what kind soever would ever imagine that there was anything beyond it."

Three years after he sees the footprint, he comes across bones and other remains of cannibalism. (We leave aside the historical question of whether or not cannibalism was practised by the Caribbeans. It is enough that Robinson thought so. European readiness to believe other people were cannibals, regardless of fact, plays the same role in determining trade patterns as the inter-European solidarity exhibited, for example, between the Portuguese captain and Robinson.) He withdrew further and "kept close within my circle for almost two years."

Gradually fear wears off, and he begins to come out more. But he proceeds cautiously. He does not fire his gun, for fear it would be heard, and he is always armed with a gun, two pistols, and a cutlass. At times he even thinks of attack, and builds a place from which he can "destroy some of these monsters in their cruel bloody entertainment and, if possible, save the victim they should bring hither to destroy." But then he thinks, "These people had done me no injury . . . and therefore it could not be just for me to fall upon them." He chastises the Spaniards for their barbarities in America "where they destroyed millions of these people . . . a mere butchery, a bloody and unnatural piece of cruelty, unjustifiable either to God or man; as for which the very name of a Spaniard is reckoned to be frightful and terrible to all people of humanity or of Christian compassion." He decides it is "not my business to meddle with them unless they first attacked me."

During the next few years he keeps himself "more retired than ever," seldom going from his cell. Fear "put an end to all invention and to all the contrivances I had laid for my future accommodations." He was afraid to drive a nail, or chop a stick of wood, or fire a gun, or light a fire for fear it would be heard or seen. He wants "nothing so much as a safe retreat," and finds it in a hidden grotto. "I fancied myself now like one of the ancient giants which were said to live in caves and holes in the rocks, where none could come at them." Yet even in this deep isolation, it is only people that he feared. With some parrots, cats, kids, and tame seafowl as pets, "I began to be very well contented with the life I led, if it might but have been secured from the dread of the savages."

In his twenty-third year he finally sights some of the Caribbeans who periodically visit the island. He first retreats to his fortifications; but, no longer "able to bear sitting in ignorance," he sets himself up in a safe place from which to observe "nine naked savages sitting round a small fire." Thoughts of "contriving how to circumvent and fall upon them the very next time" come once more to his mind and soon he is dreaming "often of killing the savages." His loneliness intensifies when one night he hears a shot fired from a distressed ship and next day finds a shipwreck. He longs for contact with Europeans. "O that there had been one or two, nay, or but one soul saved out of this ship, to have escaped to me, that I might have one companion, one fellow creature to have spoken to me and to have conversed with!"

His thoughts move from defense to offense. His moral misgivings about Spanish colonization recede into the background, and he begins to form an imperial strategy. The plan comes to him in a dream in which a captured savage escapes, runs to him, and becomes his servant. Awaking, "I make this conclusion, that my only way to go about an attempt for an escape was, if possible, to get a savage into my possession: and if possible it should be one of the prisoners." He has some fears about whether he can do this and some moral qualms about whether he should; but though "the thoughts of shedding human blood for my deliverance were terrible to me," he at length resolved "to get one of these savages into my hands, cost what it would."

About a year and a half later a group of about twenty or thirty Caribbeans come ashore. Luck is with him. One prisoner escapes, followed by
only two men. "It came now very warmly upon my thoughts and indeed
irresistibly, that now was my time to get me a servant, and perhaps a
companion or assistant." Robinson knocks down one of the pursuers and
shoots a second. The rescued prisoner, cautious and afraid, approaches. "He
came nearer and nearer, kneeling down every ten or twelve steps. . . . At
length he came close to me, and then he kneeled down again, kissed the
ground, and laid his head upon the ground, and taking me by the foot, set my
foot upon his head; this, it seems, was in token of swearing to be my slave
forever." Robinson has his servant. An economy is born.

(4) Colonization

Friday, tired from his ordeal, sleeps. Robinson evaluates his prize. The
relationship they are about to enter into is an unequal and violent one.
("Violence," writes R. D. Laing in *The Politics of Experience*, "attempts to
constrain the other's freedom, to force him to act in the way we desire, but
with ultimate lack of concern, with indifference to the other's own existence
or destiny.") It requires an ideological superstructure to sustain it and make it
tolerable. Friday is an independent person with his own mind and will. But
Robinson's rule depends upon the extent to which his head controls Friday's
hand. To help himself in his daily struggle with Friday, Robinson begins to
think of Friday not as a person but as a sort of pet, a mindless body that is
obedient and beautiful. ("The use made of slaves and of tame animals is not
very different; for both with their bodies minister to the needs of life."
Aristotle, *The Republic*.) The following is a verbatim quote of his description
of Friday, except for the substitution of "she" for "he", "her" for "him". This
is not done to suggest homosexuality but to emphasize how rulers conceive
of the ruled only as bodies to minister to their needs. (To quote Aristotle
again, "the male is by nature superior, and the female inferior; and the one
rules, and the other is ruled.")

> She was a comely, handsome woman, perfectly well made, with
> straight strong limbs, not too large, tall and well-shaped, and as I
> reckon, about twenty-six years of age. She had a very good counte-
> nance, not a fierce and surly aspect, but seemed to have something
> very manly in her face and yet she had all the sweetness and softness
> of a European in her countenance too, especially when she smiled.
> Her hair was long and black, not curled like wool; her forehead very
> high and large; and a great vivacity and sparkling sharpness in her
> eyes. The colour of her skin was not quite black, but very tawny: and
> yet not of an ugly yellow, nauseous tawny, as the Brazilians and Vir-
> ginians, and other natives of America are; but of a bright kind of a

dun olive colour that had in it something very agreeable, though not very easy to describe. Her face was round and plump; her nose small, not flat like the Negroes', a very good mouth, thin lips, and her fine teeth well set, and white as ivory.

Robinson has a gun, but he cannot rule by force alone if he wants Friday to be productive. He must socialize his servant to accept his subordinate position. Robinson is at a great advantage for he has saved the man's life, but a careful program is still necessary, going through several stages of development, before the servant internalizes the authoritarian relationship and is able to act "independently" in a "dependent" fashion. The parallels between Robinson's education of Friday, and the actual procedures of colonization used in the last two hundred years are striking.

Step 1: The first thing Robinson does is set the stage for discourse by giving himself and Friday names that are humiliating to Friday and symbolic of his indebtedness. "First I made him know his name should be Friday, which was the day I saved his life; I called him so for the memory of the time; I likewise taught him to say Master, and then let him know that was to be my name."

Step 2: Robinson further establishes relative status by covering Friday's nakedness with a pair of linen drawers (taken from the shipwreck) and a jerkin of goat's skin and a cap of hareskin he had made himself. He "was mighty well pleased to see himself almost as clothed as his master."

Step 3: Robinson gives Friday a place to sleep between the two fortifications, i.e., a middle position, partly protected but outside the master's preserves. He sets up a burglar alarm so that "Friday could in no way come at me in the inside of my innermost wall without making so much notice in getting over that it must needs waken me," and takes other precautions such as taking all weapons into his side every night. Yet as Robinson says, these precautions were not really needed, "for never man had a more faithful, loving, sincere servant than Friday was to me; without passions, sullenness, or designs, perfectly obliged and engaged; his very affections were tied to me like those of a child to a father; and I dare say he would have sacrificed his life for the saving of mine upon any occasion whatsoever." The allocation of space helps remind Friday of his position and keep him subordinate.

Step 4: Friday is then given the skills necessary for his station and his duties, i.e., the ability to understand orders and satisfy Robinson's needs. "I . . . made it my business to teach him everything that was proper to make him useful, handy, and helpful; but especially to make him speak and understand me when I spoke."

Step 5: Next comes a crucial moment in which Robinson, through a cruel show of force, terrifies poor Friday into complete submission. Robinson takes Friday out and shoots a kid with his gun. (He is no longer afraid of being heard.)

The poor creature, who had at a distance indeed seen me kill the savage, his enemy, but did not know or could imagine how it was done,
was sensibly surprised. . . . He did not see the kid I had shot at or per-
ceive I had killed it, but ripped up his waist-coat to feel if he was not
wounded, and as I found presently, thought I was resolved to kill him,
for he came and kneeled down to me, and, embracing my knees, said
a great many things I did not understand; but I could easily see the
meaning was to pray me not to kill him.

In this ritual death and rebirth, Friday learns the full extent of
Robinson's power over him. Robinson then kills various animals, and teaches
Friday "to run and fetch them" like a dog. But he takes care that Friday
never sees him load the gun, so that he remains ignorant of the fact that you
have to put in ammunition.

Step 6: The first stage of initiation is completed, Robinson can move on
to establishing the social division of labour on a more subtle base. He
teaches Friday to cook and bake, and "in a little time Friday was able to do
all the work for me, as well as I could do it for myself." Then Robinson
marks out a piece of land "in which Friday not only worked very willingly
and very hard, but did it cheerfully." Robinson explains that it was for corn
to make more bread since there were now two of them. Friday, by himself,
discovers the laws of property and capitalist distribution of income in fully
mystified form. "He appeared very sensible of that past, and let me know
that he thought I had much more labour upon me on his account than I had
for myself, and that he would work the harder for me, if I would tell him
what to do."

Step 7: Graduation: Robinson now instructs Friday in the knowledge of
the true God. This takes three years, during which Friday raises such difficult
questions that Robinson for a time withdraws, realizing that one cannot win
by logical argument alone, and only divine revelation can convince people of
Christianity. Finally, success. "The savage was now a good Christian." The
two become more intimate, Robinson tells Friday his story and at long last
"let him into the mystery, for such it was to him, of gunpowder and bullet
and taught him how to shoot." Robinson gives Friday a knife and a hatchet
and shows him the boat he was planning to use to escape.

Step 8: Eternal Policeman: Even after granting independence, Robinson
cannot trust Friday. The master can never rest secure. One day, while watching the mainland from the top of a hill on the island, Robinson observes

an extraordinary sense of pleasure appeared on Friday's face . . . and
a strange eagerness, as if he had a mind to be in his own country
again; and this observation of mine put a great many thoughts into
me, which made me at first not so easy about my new man Friday as
I was before; and I made no doubt but that if Friday could get back to

his own nation again, he would not only forget all his religion, but all his obligation to me; and would be forward enough to give his countrymen an account of me, and come back, perhaps with a hundred or two of them, and make a feast upon me, at which he might be as merry as he used to be with those of his enemies, when they were taken in war.

Robinson continuously pumps Friday to see if he could uncover any cracks; then he feels guilty over his suspicion. Imperialism knows no peace.

(5) Partnership and Expanded Reproduction

For roughly ten years, between the time he first saw the print of a foot in the sand until he met Friday, Robinson Crusoe led a life of fear, anxiety, and care during which time his productive activities were reduced to a minimum and he scarcely dared to venture outside the narrow confines of his strongholds. When Friday comes he becomes expansive again, teaching, building, accumulating. Though no mention is made of accounting, one can deduce that labour again became valuable, for Robinson is once more purposeful, and interested in allocation and efficiency, as he orders, causes, gives Friday to do one thing or another, instructs him, shows him, gives him direction, makes things familiar to him, makes him understand, teaches him, lets him see, calls him, heartens him, beckons him to run and fetch, sets him to work, makes him build something, etc. etc. Through his social relation with Friday, he becomes an economic man. Friday becomes labour and he becomes capital—innovating, organizing, and building an empire.

About three years after Friday arrives, Robinson's twenty-seventh year on the island, an opportunity for enlargement comes. Twenty-one savages and three prisoners come ashore. Robinson divides the arms with Friday and they set out to attack. On the way, Robinson again has doubts as to whether it was right "to go and dip my hands in blood, to attack people who had neither done or intended me any wrong." "Friday," he observes, "might justify it, because he was a declared enemy, and in a state of war with those very particular people; and it was lawful for him to attack them," but, as he could not say the same for himself, he resolves unilaterally for both of them not to act unless "something offered that was more a call to me than yet I knew of."

The call comes when he discovers one of the victims is a white man and he becomes "enraged to the highest degree." As it turns out, the prisoner is a Spaniard; given what Robinson had previously said about Spanish colonial policy, one might have thought he would have some doubts about what was lawful. But he does not, and along with Friday, attacks—killing seventeen and routing four. (Friday does most of the killing, in part because he "took his aim so much better" than Robinson, in part because Robinson was directing and Friday doing.) The Spaniard is rescued and they find another victim in a boat who turns out to be Friday's father, his life luckily saved because his fellow captive was white.

Now they were four. Robinson has an empire which he rules firmly and justly with a certain degree of permissiveness and tolerance.

> My island was now peopled, and I thought myself very rich in subjects; and it was a merry reflection, which I frequently made, how like a king I looked. First of all, the whole country was my own property, so that I had an undoubted right of dominion. Secondly, my people were perfectly subjected. I was absolute lord and lawgiver; they all owed their lives to me, and were ready to lay down their lives, if there had been occasion of it for me. It was remarkable, too, we had but three subjects, and they were of three different religions. My man Friday was a Protestant, his father was a pagan and a cannibal, and the Spaniard was a Papist. However I allowed liberty of conscience throughout my dominions.

The period of primitive accumulation is over. Robinson now has property. It is not based on his previous labour, but on his fortunate possession of arms. Though his capital comes into the world dripping blood from every pore, his ownership is undisputed. Friday was not a lazy rascal spending his subsistence on more riotous living, yet in the end he still has nothing but himself, while the wealth of Robinson Crusoe increases constantly although he has long ceased to work.

With time, more people arrive on his island. Robinson shrewdly uses his monopoly of the means of production to make them submit to his rule. As the empire grows, its problems become more complex. But Robinson is ever resourceful in using terror, religion, frontier law, and the principle of delegated authority to consolidate his position and produce a self-producing order.

Robinson learns that there are fourteen more Spaniards and Portuguese staying with the Caribbeans, "who lived there at peace indeed with the savages." They had arms but no powder and no hope of escape, for they had "neither vessel, or tools to build one, or provisions of any kind." Robinson of course has the missing ingredients for their rescue, but how can he be sure he will be paid back? "I feared mostly their treachery and ill usage of me, if I put my life in their hands, for that gratitude was no inherent virtue in the nature of man; nor did men always square their dealings by the obligations they had received so much as they did by the advantage they expected."

Robinson cannot depend on the law to guard his property. Instead he uses religion. Europeans do not require so elaborate a socialization procedure as Friday because they have come by education, tradition, and habit to look upon private property as a self-evident law of nature. The Spaniard and Friday's father are to go to where the other Europeans are staying. They would then sign a contract, "that they should be absolutely under my leading, as their commander and captain; and that they should swear upon the Holy Sacraments and the Gospel to be true to me and to go to such Christian country as that I should agree to, and no other; and to be directed wholly and absolutely by my orders." Robinson converts their debt to him into an obligation towards God. Thus men are ruled by the products of their mind.

The trip is postponed for a year, while Robinson's capital stock is expanded so that there will be enough food for the new recruits. The work process is now more complicated because of the increase in numbers. A vertical structure separating operations, co-ordination, and strategy is established on the basis of nationality—a sort of multinational corporation in miniature. "I marked out several trees which I thought fit for our work, and I set Friday and his father to cutting them down; and then I caused the Spaniard, to whom I had imparted my thought on that affair, to oversee and direct their work."

When the harvest is in, the Spaniard and Friday's father are sent out to negotiate. While they are away, an English ship arrives at the island. Robinson is filled with indescribable joy at seeing a ship "manned by [his] own countrymen, and consequently friends." Yet at the same time, "some secret doubts hung about [him]," for perhaps they were thieves and murderers. This we have seen is a typical reaction of Robinson Crusoe to other people; it is a prudent attribute in a society of possessive individuals where all are the enemy of each. *Caveat Emptor.*

Some of the crew come ashore with three prisoners. When the prisoners are left unguarded, Robinson approaches them: "I am a man, an Englishman, and disposed to assist you, you see; I have one servant only; we have arms and ammunition; tell us freely, can we serve you?" The three prisoners turn out to be the captain of the ship, his mate, and one passenger. The others are mutineers, of whom the captain says, "There were two desperate villains among them that it was scarce safe to show any mercy to"; but if they were secured, he believed "all the rest would return to their duty."

The charges being laid, a quick decision and verdict is reached. Robinson sides with authority. The captain offers a generous contract to Robinson: "Both he and the ship, if recovered, should be wholly directed and commanded by me in everything; and if the ship was not recovered, he would live and die with me in what part of the world soever I would send him; and the other two men the same." Robinson asks for much less: recognition of his undisputed authority while they are on the island, free passage to England for himself and Friday if the ship is recovered.

The men who brought the captain ashore are attacked. The two villains are summarily executed in the first round, the rest are made prisoners or allowed to join the captain and Robinson. More men are sent to shore from the ship, and are soon captured. One is made prisoner, the others are told Robinson is governor of the island and that he would engage for their pardon if they helped capture the ship. The ship is seized with only one life lost, that of the new captain. Robinson, still posing as governor, interviews the five prisoners and hearing the "full account of their villainous behaviour to the captain, and how they had run away with the ship and were preparing to commit further robberies," offers them the choice of being left on the island or being taken to England in chains to be hanged. They choose the island and Robinson is so much the richer. Law makes criminals and criminals make settlers. In a repeat of his lesson to the birds, Robinson orders the captain "to cause the new captain who was killed to be hanged at the yardarm, that these men might see him."

On the 19th December, 1686, twenty-eight years and two months after his arrival, Robinson goes on board the ship, taking with him his great goatskin cap, his umbrella, one of his parrots, and the money he had taken off the ship. He also takes Friday but does not wait for the return of Friday's father and the Spaniards. Instead he leaves a letter for them with the prisoners being left behind, after making them "promise to treat them in common with themselves."

He returns to civilization and discovers capital's power for self-sustaining growth. His trustees

> had given in the account of the produce of my part of the plantation to the procurator fiscal, who had appropriated it, in case I never came to claim it, one third to the kind, and two thirds to the monastery of St. Augustine, to be expended for the benefit of the poor and for the conversion of Indians to the Catholic faith; but that if I appeared, or anyone for me, to claim the inheritance, it should be restored: only that the improvements, or annual production, being distributed to charitable uses, could not be restored.

He was thus a rich man, "master all of a sudden of about £5,000 sterling in money, and had an estate, as I might well call it, in Brazil, of about a thousand pounds a year, as sure as an estate of lands in England."

He also had his island to which he returns in 1694. He learns how the Spaniards had trouble with the villains when they first returned but eventually subjected them, of their battles with the Caribbeans, "of the improvements they made upon the island itself and of how five of them made an attempt upon the mainland, and brought away eleven men and five women prisoners, by which, at my coming, I found about twenty young children on the island." Robinson brings them supplies, a carpenter, and a smith and later sent seven women "such as I found proper for service or for wives to such as would take them."

Before he leaves the island, he reorganizes it on a sound basis. Dividing it into parts, he reserves to himself the property of the whole, and gives others such parts respectively as they agreed upon. As to the Englishmen, he promised to send them some women from England, "and the fellows proved very honest and diligent after they were mastered and had their properties set apart for them." With property and the family firmly established, the ground is clear for steady growth.

(6) Moral

We may stop at this point and consider the very high rate of return earned by Robinson on his original capital of £40. He cannot be said to have worked very hard for his money, but he was certainly a great organiser and entrepreneur, showing extraordinary capacity to take advantage of situations and manage other people. He suffered the pains of solitude and the vices of greed, distrust, and ruthlessness, but he ends up with "wealth all round me" and Friday—"ever proving a most faithful servant upon all occasions."

The allegory of Robinson Crusoe gives us better economic history and better economic theory than many of the tales told by modern economics about the national and international division of labour. Economics tends to stay in the market place and worry about prices. It has more to say about how Robinson's sugar relates to his clothing than how he relates to Friday. To understand how capital produces and is produced, we must leave the noisy sphere of the market where everything takes place on the surface and enter into the hidden recesses of the factory and corporation, where there is usually no admittance except on business.

Defoe's capitalist is transported to a desert island outside the market system, and his relations to other people are direct and visible. Their secret of capital is revealed, namely, that it is based on other people's labour and is obtained through force and illusion. The birth certificate of Robinson's capital is not as bloody as that of many other fortunes, but its coercive nature is clear.

The international economy of Robinson's time, like that of today, is not composed of equal patterns but is ordered along class lines. Robinson occupies one of the upper-middle levels of the pyramid. (The highest levels are in the capitals of Europe.) Captains, merchants, and planters are his peer group. With them he exchanges on the basis of fraternal collaboration. (Arab captains excepted.) They teach him, rescue him, do business for him, and keep him from falling beneath his class. He in turn generally regards them as honest and plain-dealing men, sides with them against their rebellious subordinates, and is easy with them in his bargaining. Towards whites of lower rank he is more demanding. If they disobey, he is severe; but if they are loyal, he is willing to share some booty and delegate some authority. Africans and Caribbeans are sold, killed, trained, or used as wives by his men, as the case may be. About the white indentured servants, artisans, etc., little is said by Defoe in his story.

The contradictions between Robinson and other members of the hierarchy give the story its dynamics. He is forever wrestling with the problem of subordinating lower levels and trying to rise above his own. The fact that he does not see it this way but prefers to make up stories about himself makes no difference. He denies the conflict between himself and Friday by accepting Friday's mask of willing obedience. And he conceives of his greed as a crime against God instead of against man. But his daily life shows that his social relations are antagonistic and that he knows it.

In the last analysis, however, the story is only partly dialectical. We hear only of how Robinson perceives the contradictions and how he resolves them. In this work of fiction he is always able to fuse two into one. In actual life one divides into two, and the system develops beyond the capitalist's fantasy of proper law and order. Economic science also needs the story of Friday's grandchildren.

MARXISM

Marx did not believe in the harmony of the market. He emphasized the contradictions of capitalism instead, contradictions that exist, as Hymer points out, from the very beginning. Every society, Marx says, is riven by class conflict. As the mode of production of the day is destroyed by such conflict, another arises, like a phoenix, to take its place. This is riven in turn by the conflicts it engenders, and so history goes.

The mode of production of Marx's time was industrial capitalism. It remains so today. The class conflict within capitalism, Marx said, is between those who own the means of production and those who work for these owners for wages. It is labor power that provides, in Marx's view, the ultimate source of value. As a recent analyst put it,

> in every society the material environment is changed through production into things that individuals want to use. The type of technology will . . . determine the technical division of labor, but . . . the drive to increase labor productivity and, therefore, improve the profitability of a particular enterprise creates a tendency for the profitability of capital . . . to fall. This . . . leads to increased pressure by capitalists on the labor force to increase profitability,

a process of escalating exploitation that only exacerbates class conflict and that "cannot be resolved by the action of the state. . . . Rather, the state reflects the imbalance of class forces and acts in favour of the interests of the dominant class" (Cole 1991:11).

Ultimately, Marx believed, capitalism would come to an end. Whether it was brought down by angry workers or the laws of capitalist dynamics, capitalism could not last. Nor should it, since in Marx's view the best was yet to come. With capitalism out of the way, the immense productive power of the species that capitalism itself had helped liberate could then be used to create communities that were fair, efficient, and democratic. The state, without a class rationale, would "wither away." All that would be left of it would be "mere administration."

To a mercantilist, capitalism is most readily understood in terms of consumption. It means the consolidation of capital in the form of land, and the accumulation of capital in the form of finance. To a liberal, capitalism is most readily understood in terms of exchange. It denotes the use of capital to make more capital. It denotes the pursuit of profit in the context of a self-regulating market. To a Marxist, however, capitalism is best understood in terms of its prodigious productivity. Its productivity is made possible by paid wage laborers whose work is exploited, as was that of the slaves and serfs of previous modes of production, to provide capitalists with privileges they don't themselves work to earn. From the sixteenth century on it is this way of producing things that has come to predominate. This doesn't make the capitalist world market the definitive way to produce commodities. It is, however, the main way it is done at the moment.

How such a system arose is much debated. Some cite as decisive the influx of precious metals into Europe that followed the European discovery of the New World. Some cite as the key cause the accumulation of wealth through trade with the Indies. Others cite the technological improvements made possible by progress in the natural sciences. Others again cite population growth, or a revolution in religious convictions (such as the spread of Protestantism). Hymer, in his analysis of Robinson Crusoe, emphasizes Marx's concept of cycles of capital accumulation. Like Crusoe's, the story of early capitalism is a story, Hymer says, of "primitive accumulation." It is a story of "conquest, slavery, robbery, murder, and force"; of cheap labor, colonial possessions, and the surplus they provide.

This list begs as many questions as it answers, however. Similar causes to those existing at the beginnings of the capitalist world system can be shown to have existed elsewhere at other times, and yet capitalism was not their result. On the other hand we find, where capitalism does not even exist, people articulating a capitalist worldview. It is said, for example, that "the America of the eighteenth century was economically primitive, but it is in the maxims of Franklin that the spirit of bourgeois capitalism . . . finds . . . its . . . most lucid expression" (Tawney 1930).

In historical terms, capitalism and state making are clearly cognate. You can make a state, in the liberal or mercantilist sense, without relying on capitalists; and you can be a capitalist without having to help, or be helped by, makers of states. To a Marxist, however, the one is in effect the other. In Marxist terms, you would expect state makers and capitalists to arrive on the historical stage together, since state making, after all, is just one dimension of the capitalist mode of production. It is where the owners of capital order their public affairs.

While more than one attempt has been made to impose a single public order on the capitalist world system, none has yet prevailed, unless you think the global bourgeoisie are already cohesive enough to amount to a global ruling class. Capitalism has also not yet collapsed. Capitalists continue to find ways to survive, plowing profits back into "welfare state" provisions that buy off dissent, seeking new markets for their commodities and exploiting cheap sources of supply to make this possible. The imperialism of the nineteenth century has given way to the neoimperialism of the twentieth, while control of territory and all that it contains has given way to the kind of collusion between global capitalists and local "comprador elites" that makes such territorial intervention unnecessary.

Classical Marxists applaud the march of capital, assuming that the sooner the world has been revolutionized in this way, the sooner the class conflict it creates will destroy it, and the sooner socialism will ensue. They cheer the bourgeoisie along, while scanning the social horizon for hopeful signs of revolutionary zeal on the part of the world working class.

Reformist Marxists (otherwise known as neo-Marxists) are keenly aware of the staying power of the capitalist system. They see Marx's laws of capitalist dynamics, like the law of the falling rate of profit, failing to take effect. Particularly in his later works Marx came to believe that the action of these laws would cause capitalism to collapse of its own accord. So far it hasn't, and reformist Marxists have had to explain why.

So far, also, the revolutionary potential of capitalism has taken much longer to realize than Marx, particularly in his earlier analyses, seemed to assume. They have had to worry, not only that the revolution seems to be much delayed, but also about the ways in which it might have become stuck, skewed, or put in reverse. Reformist Marxist theorists, for example, write about the frozen class relationships that seem to have stopped the growth of a revolutionary working class in its tracks. World systems theorists (Wallerstein 1979) and the so-called dependency theorists (Cardoso 1972) talk in Marxist terms about the lopsided structures that have characterized capitalism since it started in the sixteenth century. What with centers dominating peripheries, and with semiperipheries in between, revolution has not had much of a chance. Development theorists talk about the "development of underdevelopment" (Frank 1978) and how a united world working class has been fragmented by nationalism, not united by their common hatred of the bourgeosie. Like Godot, the "lonely hour of the last instance" hasn't come.

With exploitation, poverty, and suffering still endemic, what is to be done? Reformist Marxists are surrounded by the casualties of capitalism. They stand in the middle of a long, violent war that cripples and kills for profit alone. Who can intervene? Reformist Marxists don't find it easy to turn to state makers for help, since, by their own lights, state makers are there to protect the interests of the capitalists, not those of the poor working class. So reformist Marxists tend to turn instead to the margins of the capitalist system and more particularly, to the "social movements" they find there. These movements articulate the concerns of a wide range of people who are integral to the system but who have little voice in it. These people are manifestly there, but they have been made invisible—at least in the eyes of those who determine the terms of public debate. These movements speak out on behalf of the millions of women, blacks, indigenous peoples, greens, and others for whom capitalism does not deliver the goods.

Although these movements can do considerably less to protect the exploited from capitalist greed than state makers can, they have not, on the whole, been bought off either. At least from the higher moral ground that social movements usually stand on some pressure can be put on state makers, and while this pressure may have little practical effect, where else is there to turn until capitalism collapses or is overthrown?

NOTES

1. Stephen Hymer is professor of Economics at the New School for Social Research. He writes, "I would like to thank Heidi Cochran, Harry Magdoff, and Frank Rossevelt for their help. I have not seen the Buñuel movie of Robinson Crusoe but have been influenced by a second-hand account of it."

2. For studies of Defoe dealing with economic aspects see: E. M. Novak, *Economics and the Fiction of Daniel Defoe*, University of California Press, 1962. H. M. Robertson, *Aspects of the Rise of Economic Individualism*, Cambridge University Press. Ian Watt, *The Rise of the Novel*, Chatto and Windus, 1957; Peregrin Books, 1963. Dorothy Van Ghent, *The English Novel*, Harper Torchbook, 1961, chapter on Moll Flanders. Brian Fitzgerald, *Daniel Defoe*, Secker Warburg, 1954. Pierre Macherey, *Pour une Theorie de la Production Litteraire*,

François Maspero, 1966. John Richetti, *Popular Fiction Between Defoe and Richardson.*

3. J. M. Keynes, "Economic Possibilities for our Grandchildren," in *Essays in Persuasion*, W. W. Norton & Co., Inc., 1963, p. 370.

4. See Karl Polyani, "Aristotle Discovers the Economy," in K. Polyani et al., *Trade and Markets in the Early Empires*, New York: Free Press, 1957; and A. French, *The Growth of the Athenian Economy*, London: Routledge and Kegan Paul, 1964.

3

Contending Narratives:
A Postmodern IPE?

❖ Cynthia Enloe (1990) "Women in Banana Republics"

It is always worth asking, "Where are the women?" Answering the question reveals the dependence of most political and economic systems not just on women, but on certain kinds of relations between women and men. A great deal has been written about countries derisively labelled "banana republics." They are described as countries whose land and soul are in the clutches of a foreign company, supported by the might of its own government. A banana republic's sovereignty has been so thoroughly compromised that it is the butt of jokes, not respect. It has a government, but it is staffed by people who line their own pockets by doing the bidding of the overseas corporation and its political allies. Because it is impossible for such compromised rulers to win the support of their own citizens, many of whom are exploited on the corporation's plantations, the government depends on guns and jails, not ballots and national pride.

The quintessential banana republics were those Central American countries which came to be dominated by the United Fruit Company's monoculture, the US marines and their hand-picked dictators. Their regimes have been backed by American presidents, mocked by Woody Allen, and overthrown by nationalist guerrillas.

Yet these political systems, and the international relationships which underpin them, have been discussed as if women scarcely existed. The principal actors on all sides have been portrayed by conventional commentators as men, and as if their being male was insignificant. Thus the ways in which their shared masculinity allowed agribusiness entrepreneurs to form alliances with men in their own diplomatic corps and with men in Nicaraguan or Honduran society have been left unexamined. Enjoying Cuban cigars together after dinner while wives and mistresses powder their noses has been the stuff of smug cartoons but not of political curiosity. Similarly, a banana republic's militarized ethos has been taken for granted, without an investigation of how militarism feeds on masculinist values to sustain it. Marines, diplomats, corporate managers and military dictators may mostly be male, but they tend to need the feminine "other" to maintain their self-assurance.

One of the conditions that has pushed women off the banana republic stage has been the masculinization of the banana plantation.

Banana-company executives imagined that most of the jobs on their large plantations could be done only by men. Banana plantations were carved out of wooded acres. Clearing the brush required workers who could use a machete, live in rude barracks, and who, once the plantation's trees were bearing fruit, could chop down the heavy bunches and carry them to central loading areas and from there to the docks, to be loaded by the ton onto refrigerator ships. This was men's work.

Not all plantation work has been masculinized. Generally, crops that call for the use of machetes—tools that can also be used as weapons—are produced with large inputs of male labour: bananas, sugar, palm oil. Producers of crops that require a lot of weeding, tapping and picking hire large numbers of women, sometimes comprising a majority of workers: tea, coffee, rubber.

Nor is the gendered labour formula on any plantation fixed. Plantation managers who once relied heavily on male workers may decide to bring in more women if the men become too costly; if their union becomes too threatening; if the international market for the crop declines necessitating cost-cutting measures such as hiring more part-time workers; if a new technology allows some physically demanding tasks to be done by workers with less strength. Today both sugar and rubber are being produced by plantation companies using more women workers than they did a generation ago. What has remained constant, however, is the presumption of international corporations that their position in the world market depends on manipulations of masculinity and femininity. Gender is injected into every Brooke Bond, or Lipton tea leaf, every Unilever or Lonrho palm-oil nut, every bucket of Dunlop or Michelin latex, every stalk of Tate & Lyle sugar cane.

Like all plantation managers, banana company executives considered race as well as gender when employing what they thought would be the most skilled and compliant workforce. Thus although the majority of banana workers were men, race was used to divide them. On United Brands' plantations in Costa Rica and Panama, for instance, managers recruited Amerindian men from the Guaymi and Kuna communities, as well as West Indian Black men and hispanicized Latino men. They placed them in different, unequally paid jobs, Latino men at the top (below white male managers), Amerindian men at the bottom. Amerindian men were assigned to menial jobs such as chopping grass and overgrown bush, thus ensuring that Latino men's negative stereotypes of Amerindians—*cholos*, unskilled, uncultured natives—would be perpetuated. The stereotypes were valuable to the company because they forestalled potential alliances between Latino, Black and Amerindian men over common grievances.

> *Manager:* It's easier to work with *cholos*. They're not as smart and don't speak good Spanish. They can't argue back at you even when they're right. . . . Hell, you can make a *cholo* do anything.

Latino foreman: My workers are [not] *cholos.* . . . It's different here.
Sure I can grab them [Latino and Black male workers] and make them
work faster; but the consequences will catch up with me tomorrow.
We're not *cholos* here . . . you understand?

To say, therefore, that a banana plantation is masculinized is not to say
that masculinity, even when combined with social class, is sufficient to forge
political unity. On the other hand, the presumption that a banana plantation is
a man's world does affect the politics of any movement attempting to
improve workers' conditions, or to transform the power relationships that
comprise a "banana republic".

A banana plantation's politics are deeply affected not just by the
fact that the majority of its workers—and virtually all of its managers and
owners—are men, but by the *meaning* that has been attached to that masculinization. Even male banana workers employed by a foreign company that,
in alliance with local elites, had turned their country into a proverbial banana
republic, could feel some pride. For they were unquestionably performing
men's work. They knew how to wield a machete; they knew how to lift great
weights; they worked outside in close co-ordination with trains and ships.
Whether a smallholder or a plantation employee, a banana man was a *man*.

> Tourist, white man, wipin his face,
> Met me in Golden Grove market place,
> He looked at m'ol'clothes brown wid stain,
> An soaked tight through wid de Portlan rain,
> He cas his eye, turned up his nose,
> He says, "You're a beggar man, I suppose?"
> He says, "Boy get some occupation,
> Be of some value to your nation."
>
> I said, "By God and dis big right han
> You mus recognise a banana man . . .
> Don't judge a man by his patchy clothes,
> I'm a strong man, a proud man, an I'm free
> Free as dese mountains, free as dis sea,
> I know myself, an I know my ways,
> An will say wid pride to de end o my days
>
> Praise God an m'big right han
> I will live an die a banana man."

In the 1920s when banana workers began to organize and to conduct
strikes that even the US government and local elites had to pay attention to,

their demands reached beyond working conditions to political structures. These workers' protests took on strong nationalist overtones: the local regime and foreign troops were as much the target of their protests as the plantation companies. But so long as banana plantation work was imagined to be men's work, and so long as the banana workers' unions were organized as if they were men's organizations, the nationalist cause would be masculinized. A banana republic might fall, but patriarchy remained in place.

Women Weed, Women Clean

The banana plantation has never been as exclusively male as popular imagery suggests. It takes women's paid and unpaid labour to bring the golden fruit to the world's breakfast tables.

A banana plantation is closest to a male enclave at the beginning, when the principal task is bulldozing and clearing the land for planting. But even at this stage women are depended upon by the companies—and their male employees—to play their roles. As in the male-dominated mining industry from Chile to South Africa and Indonesia, companies can recruit men to live away from home only if someone back home takes care of their families and maintains their land. The "feminization of agriculture"—that is, leaving small-scale farming to women, typically without giving them training, equipment or extra finance—has always been part and parcel of the mas-culinization of mining and banana plantations. The male labour force has to make private arrangements with wives, mothers or sisters to assure them of a place to return to when their contracts expire, when they get fed up with supervisors' contemptuous treatment or when they are laid off because world prices have plummeted. Behind every all-male banana plantation stand scores of women performing unpaid domestic and productive labour. Company executives, union spokesmen and export-driven government officials have all preferred not to take this into account when working out their bargaining positions. International agencies such as the International Monetary Fund scarcely give a thought to women as wives and subsistence farmers when they press indebted governments to open up more land to plantation com-panies in order to correct their trade imbalances and pay off foreign bankers.

Once the banana trees have been planted, women are likely to become residents and workers on the plantations. Plantation managers, like their diplomatic and military counterparts, have found marriage both a political asset and a liability. On the one hand, having young male workers without wives and children has advantages: the men are in their physical prime, they are likely to view life as an adventure and be willing to tolerate harsh working and living conditions. On the other hand, young unattached men are more volatile and are willing to take risks if angered precisely because they will not jeopardize anyone's security aside from their own. This makes the married male worker seem more stable to a calculating plantation manager. He may demand more from the company in the form of rudimentary amenities for his wife and children, but he is more likely to toe the company line for their sake.

Women are most likely to be employed by the banana companies if the plantation cannot recruit men from a low-status ethnic group, like Amerindians in Central America, to do the least prestigious and lowest-paid jobs. In all sorts of agribusiness, women tend to be given the most tedious, least "skilled" jobs, those that are most seasonal, the least likely to offer year-round employment and those company benefits awarded to full-time employees. Weeding and cleaning are the quintessential "women's" jobs in agriculture, both in socialist and capitalist countries.

Bananas today are washed, weighed and packed in factories on the plantations before being transported to the docks for shipment overseas. Inside these packing houses one finds the women on the modern banana plantation. They remove the bunches of fruit from the thick stems, an operation that has to be done carefully (one might say skilfully) so that the bananas are not damaged. They wash the bananas in a chemical solution, a hazardous job. They select the rejects, which can amount to up to half the bananas picked in the fields. Companies often dump rejected bananas in nearby streams, causing pollution which kills local fish. Women weigh the fruit and finally attach the company's tell-tale sticker on each bunch. They are paid piece-rates and foremen expect them to work at high speed. In between harvests they may have little work to do and not receive any pay. At harvest time they are expected to be available for long stretches, sometimes around the clock, to meet the company's tight shipping schedule.

Tess is a Filipino woman who works for TADECO, a subsidiary of United Brands, Philippines. She works on a plantation on the country's southern island, Mindanao. A decade-long war has been fought in the area between government troops and indigenous Muslim groups protesting against the leasing of large tracts of land either to multinational pineapple and banana companies or to wealthy Filipino landowners, who then work out lucrative contracts with those corporations. Tess herself is a Christian Filipina. She, like thousands of other women and men, migrated, with government encouragement, to Mindanao from other islands in search of work once the bottom fell out of the once-dominant sugar industry. She works with other young women in the plantation's packing plant, preparing bananas to be shipped to Japan by Japanese and American import companies. She is paid approximately $1 a day. With an additional living allowance, Tess can make about $45 a month; she sends a third of this home to her family in the Visayas.

Tess uses a chemical solution to wash the company's bananas. There is a large, reddish splotch on her leg where some of the chemical spilled accidentally. At the end of a day spent standing for hours at a time, Tess goes "home" to a bunkhouse she shares with 100 other women, twenty-four to a room, sleeping in eight sets of three-tiered bunks.

Many women working on banana plantations are young and single, and, in the Philippines, often have secondary-school or even college educations. They may be the daughters of male employees, or they may be recruited from outside. They are subjected to sexual harassment in the packing plants and can be fired if found to be pregnant. The life of a banana washer is dull and isolated: "We have no choice than to stay here. First, the company is quite far from the highway and if we . . . spend our fare what else would be left for our food?"

Large banana companies—Geest in Britain, United Brands, Del Monte and Dole in the United States and Japan's Sumitomo—also require workers at the other end of the food chain, in the countries where they market their bananas. The docks, the trucks and the ripening plants reveal how company managers shape the sexual division of labour. Stevedores in every country are thought of as doing a classic "man's" job, though again ethnic politics may determine which men will unload the bananas from the company's ships. Today in Japan, where immigrant labour is being increasingly relied upon to do the low-status, low-paid jobs, Filipino men do the heavy work of transferring bananas from ships to trucks. The job has become so closely associated with the fruit that to be a longshoreman in Japan is to be a "banana". Women are hired in all the consumer countries to weigh and sort at the ripening plant before the fruit heads for the supermarket. Food processing is as feminized—as dependent on ideas about femininity—as nursing, secretarial work and sewing.

Women are hired by the banana companies to do low-paid, often seasonal jobs that offer little chance of training and promotion; some involve the hazards of chemical pollution and sexual harassment. But many women still seek these jobs because they seem better than the alternatives: dependence on fathers or husbands (if they are employed), life on the dole (if work is not available), work in the entertainment industry around a military base, subsistence farming with few resources, emigration.

Many women are heads of households and take exploitative jobs in order to support their children; other women see their employment as part of being dutiful daughters, sending part of their meagre earnings back to parents, who may be losing farm land to agribusinesses. Neither women nor men working on any plantation—banana, tea, rubber, sugar, pineapple, palm oil, coffee— are simply "workers." They are wives, husbands, daughters, sons, mothers, fathers, lovers; and each role has its own politics. The politics of being a daughter, a mother or a wife allows First World and Third World governments to rely on international plantation companies, which in turn are able to recruit and control women workers and win the consumer loyalty of women buyers. "Daughter," "mother," and "wife" are ideas on which the international political system today depends.

A POSTMODERN IPE?

Where are the women in IPE? They are there, as Enloe demonstrates. The system depends on them. And yet analyses of IPE are
mostly made as if women did not exist. The conventional study of
IPE mostly details the doings of men and their maleness and how
this maleness is maintained. These are important features of IPE
and topics of considerable analytic interest. So, however, is the fact
of gender bias itself, and the ways gendering is done in IPE so as to
privilege diverse patriarchal and fraternal practices.

Gender bias and the production of patriarchy are apparent in
each of the analytic languages discussed above. It is bias and hierarchy of a particular sort, however. While most people are born bi-
ologically sexed in either a male or female form, gender roles are
social constructs, and most people behave as their cultures have
taught them to. There are considerable variations between what
cultures expect of their women and men, and as a cosequence I
should write "people who are 'women'" instead of "women" as
such, and "people who are 'men'" instead of "men" as such. In the
interests of uncluttered prose I shall take this formulation as read
wherever "men" or "women" appear. I do want to emphasize,
however, that the conventional ideologies of IPE were all formulated in England, Scotland, and continental Europe and as a consequence they all show a clear preference for English and Scottish
and European models of gender difference.

As to mercantilism, for example, the state whose autonomy is so
highly prized is a gendered construct, spoken for and thought about
in ways typical of European stereotypes. Orthodox mercantilism assumes that state makers are competitive and violent, for example,
and that there can be no relationships between such state makers
other than those of constant vigilance and eternal suspicion. Orthodox mercantilists actively deny the potential for global community,
and it is this kind of argument that distorts our understanding of
how the world works and how it could work (Tickner 1992:79–80;
Hartsock 1983; Peterson and Runyan 1993; Sylvester 1994; Beckman
and D'Amico 1994). The result is patriarchal mercantilism and not
matriarchal mercantilism. Matriarchal mercantilism may well be a
contradiction in terms. Even if it isn't, most feminists would see matriarchal mercantilism as being more affirmative than that of the
patriarchal sort, if only because it would be more likely to produce
living beings than opulence or commodities.

As to liberalism, the self-maximizing, rationalistic, economic
man at the heart of what was originally a Scottish and English

worldview can only be seen as a culturally specific and highly gendered construct. In his orthodox form this opportunistic individual is notably male. Based by classical liberals like Adam Smith, not necessarily on themselves but certainly on cultural stereotypes with which they were familiar, he is a highly reduced version of a human being. He is competitive and calculating. And he is only interested in material self-gratification.

It is the height of cultural arrogance to see such traits as existing "prior to and apart from community" (Tickner 1992:73), as orthodox liberals do. It is to promote an ideology that is emphatically not shared by many men and most women. It is a limited and limiting belief, and while it can, and has, worked market wonders, it has done so very unevenly and at considerable cost.

This cost has notably been borne by the female half of the species. Though its status as a statistic is somewhat unclear, a conclusion attributed in 1981 to a UN report by the Committee on the Status of Women maintains that "while women represent half the global population and one-third of all working hours, they receive only one-tenth of world income and own less than 1 percent of world property" (Tickner 1992:75). Even as a ballpark figure this indicates something of the size of the gender injustice liberal marketeering involves. It is females more than males who have been impoverished in the process of world development—an effect most notable in the poorer, agricultural parts of the world where firms, seeking low-wage, unskilled workers, find an abundant supply of female labor. It is also male makers of states in debt who choose to submit to the rigors of classical liberalism as the price for international balance-of-payments relief and who then visit these rigors disproportionately on women, since it is the women, of course, who are expected to provide most of the services that the men in government decide to cut.

This dismal picture is well documented by more than one UN agency. By the end of the United Nations Decade for the Advancement of Women (1975–1985), for example, it was apparent that "with few exceptions . . . women's relative access to economic resources, income, and employment ha[d] worsened, their burdens of work ha[d] increased, and their relative and even absolute health, nutritional, and educational status ha[d] declined" (Sen and Grown 1987:16). The 1989 World Survey on the Role of Women in Development confirmed this conclusion. Reviewing the world political economy at that time, it said, "poverty among women has increased, even in the richest countries [while] for the majority of developing countries, economic progress for women has virtually stopped" (UN 1989:5–6). In global terms, that is, poor women are getting poorer, more women are getting poor, and women are getting poorer compared to men (Pettman 1991:123).

As to Marxism, it is apparent that by emphasizing class and the class-making consequences of modes of production, both classical Marxists and neo-Marxists are able to ignore the significance of gender and the gender-specific nature of human reproduction.

Consider how classes change as modes of production do. Then consider how the general pattern of gendering practices remains the same regardless. While slave owners have given way to feudal lords, who have given way in turn to capitalist rentiers and entrepreneurs, men have remained dominant regardless. While slaves have been replaced by serfs, who have been replaced in turn by free wage laborers, women have remained subordinate throughout. One would expect, in Marxist terms, women who become free wage-workers to bear the same relationship to owners of capital as men do. However, they don't. There are two classes of proletarian, a female class and a male class, and of the two the male is the more privileged. One would expect in Marxist terms a gender-neutral bourgeoisie. However, it isn't. This would suggest that the social construct *gender* is more basic than the Marxist social category *class*, and that the feminist concept of patriarchy is more basic than the Marxist concept of capitalism. It also shows how male capitalists receive most of the undeclared gender dividend. The patriarchal consequence is imperial. Not for nothing does Mies (1988) call women the world's "last colony."

Consider how gendering practices are used to consign women to the home, to perform there, on account of their gender status alone, the family labor necessary to reproduce the species. Not for nothing do analysts on the margins of IPE see the trend toward a global division of labor between waged male and unwaged female workers as intrinsic to the capitalist mode of production. Indeed, without the systematic devaluation of housework, the systematic attempt to define women universally as housewives (Mies 1986:116), and the systematic subsidy that the women who mostly do such housework provide, it is not unfair to argue that capitalism could not have succeeded. Again, because of their focus on class, Marxists fail to appreciate the radical significance of the social construction of gender or the radical inequality that gendering entails. Again, it has fallen to feminists to point out the revolutionary potential of a model of international political economy predicated on the "production of life rather than the production of things and wealth" (Tickner 1992:96).

Women's movements argue from a wide variety of perspectives. I don't mean to suggest by choosing a reading from Enloe alone, or by talking about a feminist critique of the orthodox analytical languages, that there is only one such critique. Quite the contrary, feminist critiques proceed from highly diverse standpoints and cover the full gamut of ideological views.

The same applies to any other social movement. Critiques of IPE in environmental terms, for example, range from light to deep green; from radical ecology to liberal attempts to find market solutions to problems of overpopulation, pollution, and resource depletion; from recycling and organic gardening to the overthrow of the world capitalist system.

Petty's dream of finding one quantitative solution to the problems posed by IPE was distinctively modern. The rejection of Petty's dream in favor of a plurality of perspectives is distinctively postmodern. Singular truths stultify, postmodernists say, and in critiquing all attempts to arrive at such limited and limiting outcomes, they help give voice to those who have been silenced by modernist thinking. What we hear from those who have been stifled are voices in the plural, however, not one voice that speaks for each social movement.

What are we to make of this Babel? We not only have the orthodox analytical languages to contend with. We also have them in their extremist and reformist forms. And we now have critiques by women, greens, indigenous peoples, and religious groups, too. It is a veritable riot of analysis and argument. What should we do to come to terms with such a range of ideas and opinions?

First of all, we should accept that IPE will ultimately defy definitive explanation. It is such a complex array of repeated human practices that we will never exhaust its capacity for surprise.

Second, we should recognize that complex though the subject is, IPE is not chaotic. IPE events do not occur completely at random, otherwise we could say nothing at all about the subject, except perhaps this one thing. There are patterns to IPE. They are not precise or very clear but they do exist. What is more, different analytic languages have been devised to describe and explain these patterns. These languages differ because they differ in the assumptions they make about human nature and the value premises each adopts. They all claim to represent IPE in its essentials. They each have large numbers of adherents. None, however, has ever received universal acclaim.

Third, we should appreciate that, if we want a comprehensive knowledge of IPE, we will have to understand all of the different ways in which it is described and explained and not just one or two of them. Unlike the blind men and the elephant, we are going to have to fumble our way around the whole beast. If we want to know its shape and size, we won't be able to stay in one place, proclaiming in effect that elephants are anacondas because we happen to be clutching the trunk. No one would believe us, anyway, particularly when they are saying that elephants are wrinkly trees, or ropes with tassles at the end.

This means that we are also on occasion going to contradict ourselves. Like Walt Whitman, however, we are going to have to work at being large enough to contain contradictions. We are going to have to work at an understanding of IPE as an ongoing argument about and among radically divergent analytic languages.

Arriving at such an understanding does not mean we should run these languages in parallel like disengaged soliloquies. Nor does it mean staging a raucous kind of cat fight between them. It means understanding how orthodoxies become like the air we breathe and the water we drink. It means actively trying to account for them all and for diverse unorthodoxies, too, relinquishing thereby any one-dimensional account of IPE. It means, in short, becoming more eclectic.

There is, after all, no "correct" or permanently preferable approach to IPE. Moreover, "how" we talk about IPE determines in turn "what" we make of it in substantive terms. The ways in which we describe and explain IPE help constitute in turn the very world we are describing and explaining.

Nowhere is this more apparent than in the policy choices that present themselves in response to specific issues.

Consider, for example, the issue of a crippling, state-specific debt. Mercantilists would not have gotten into debt in the first place. If their protectionism was of the in-turned kind, they would have protected their finances by not borrowing from foreign banks. If it was of the out-turned kind, they would have built up trade surpluses, which they might then have lent to others. They would not, however, have compromised their sovereignty by putting themselves in such a mendicant position.

Liberals, by contrast, see debt crises as primarily an economic issue (albeit one with political consequences). They look for macroeconomic shocks or market imperfections. Extremist liberals opt for solutions that involve less government intervention and more openness to the world market. Reformist liberals sanction more government intervention than this. They might recommend debt-servicing agreements, perhaps, to promote market revival.

Marxists see debt crises as the predictable work of capitalist profit-predators. Extremist Marxists see revolt on the part of the exploited as the inevitable outcome. The owners of debt they see as living on borrowed time. Reformist Marxists, who have watched capitalists mount the rescue of their system more than once and who are less optimistic about Marx's laws of history finally prevailing, advocate default.

Gender-sensitive analysts highlight the extent to which the debt burden falls more heavily upon women than on men. They prescribe policies that deal, in various ways, more fairly with that fact.

Deep greens want small-scale, ecologically aware communities that disaggregate the state, and its debt burden with it, while light greens argue for market strategies that expand production and trade, make interest repayments, but not at the expense of the environment.

And so on.

Unlike academics, policymakers do have to make a choice. They can't stop at analysis. Surely it is better to choose from a full range of ideological options, however, than to privilege one analytic language only. The alternative is to dismiss in advance all contending points of view, along with any potential contributions other points of view might make. And given the paucity of creative policies in the world, that would seem to be rash at best and ideologically arrogant at worst.

Consider, for example, a regional famine. There is, first, the problem of talking about any famine in objectivizing terms. After all, the commitment to the practices that caused the famine in the first place are hardly likely to collapse under the "accumulated weight" of "exquisite papers prepared for . . . seminars in political economy" (Robert Martin, cited in Staniland 1985:192). Famine is appalling by any measure of human suffering. Talking about famine in an abstract way can seem, as a consequence, extraordinarily inappropriate. We do talk about famine in this way, however, in the hope that the knowledge we get will help us to choose the best policies and to alleviate the most suffering.

Abstraction by policymakers requires ideological choices, however. Should potential helpers join a UN agency or a nongovernmental aid organization, for example, or would they save more lives bombing the headquarters of selected international corporations? Should they lobby for more international aid? Or should they just sit and wait for capitalism to self-destruct in the hope that a less famine-prone system can then be put in its place?

As a victim, is it best to try and overthrow the local government and install a regime more dedicated to food self-sufficiency? Should international travel corporations be invited to make a comparative advantage out of the famine itself? They could make a tourist spectacle out of the starving people and pay a percentage of their profits to provide some sort of famine relief (thereby reducing comparative advantage, but helping alleviate the famine nonetheless)? Should the famine be encouraged in the hope that the advantage of being famine-stricken will help bring the whole global system down so that something more humane can then be put in its place? Should immediate efforts go toward empowering women, who, given the primary role they play in food provision, are best placed to do the most good?

It is not hard to recognize here different and highly divergent points of view. Extremist liberals look as ever for marketeering solutions, though to them a truly liberal IPE would not have famines in it in the first place. Famines occur because of market distortions.

Reformist liberals argue for state intervention, such as more effective global social welfare policies—perhaps a kind of world dole. Extremist Marxists see the end of capitalism as nigh and gleefully await its demise. Reformist Marxists argue for intervention meanwhile and the delinking of famine-stricken countries from the global political economy. Feminists paint the problem in terms of patriarchy. Greens do so in terms of environmental degradation. And so on.

The arguments ramify, and the longer they continue the more obvious it becomes that choices are being made on the basis of different analytic languages about how the world works and how it should work.

These languages are impossible to reconcile because the particular interests they promote and protect represent different assumptions about human nature and human values. Despite claims that "state automony" or "free marketeering" or "anti-imperialism" or "female liberation" will provide the key interpretive principle, in IPE in practice such overarching claims have never been accepted as universally applicable. Which is why "claims to have 'the' theory are invariably false, certainly arrogant, and possibly dangerous" (Staniland 1985:204). The arguments continue, both between and within the realms of discourse defined here, and so they should. Without these arguments all change would be at an end, and we really would then be stuck with this as the best of all possible worlds.

To show how integral analytical languages are to our understanding of IPE and how differently they interpret its practices or processes, it is worth considering, as well as the couple of issues discussed above, a few contemporary industries (Galloway 1991). What these industries are doesn't particularly matter. Nor do I want to discuss them at any great length. What I do want to do is lay each industry out as an argument, so that we can see and hear various analytic voices at work as clearly as possible.

The industrial civilization of our day relies on myriad machines. These machines magnify enormously people's muscle power and mental capacities. Of the machines used in industrialized countries none are more important than those of transport and communications. Indeed, it has become something of a cliché in analyses of IPE to acknowledge the significance of global changes in these technologies; which is understandable when we recall, for example, how our species has gone from moving around on foot or with the help of animals, to landing craft on the moon, within one generation. Many of the people in the world still do move around on foot or with the help of animals, though most have other options now, and it is this change that is revolutionary (Owen 1987:1).

In terms of transportation, the liberal conception of comparative advantage would make no sense at all without the capacity to move people and freight in large quantities from one country to another. While autarkic mercantilists do not need international transport, the more imperialistically minded mercantilists certainly do. It would be impossible, for example, to sustain vertically integrated productive chains without ships and planes, trucks and trains. Marxists have long appreciated the way in which capitalist expansiveness has been contingent upon advances in transport technology. How, after all, can industries draw "raw material . . . from the remotest zones" without transport, and how can capitalists get their products "consumed not only at home, but in every quarter of the globe" if there is no way to get them there (Marx and Engels 1942:209)?

While world transportation has grown at an extraordinary rate, it has also grown very unevenly. We live as a consequence on a planet "partly mobile and affluent and partly immobile and impoverished" (Owen 1987:6; Button and Rothengatter 1993).

In terms of communications, too, technological advances have been very fast and their effects have been very uneven. In the case of communications, the added factor of rapid growth in human powers of computation has made for what is now called an "information revolution." While information has become a factor of production in its own right, this does not mean that manufacturing is becoming less important. It means, rather, that intellectual labor and intellectual capital have become more important in relation to physical labor and material capital (Wriston 1992:6).

In mercantilist terms, the information revolution makes state autonomy virtually impossible to maintain and raises profound fears.

In liberalist terms, it makes possible a world market of exemplary purity; one that has already created, it is claimed, a "new . . . monetary standard," an "information standard" no less, that like a "giant vote-counting machine" provides a "running tally on what the world thinks of a government's diplomatic, fiscal, and monetary policies" (Wriston 1992:9). No wonder analysts talk of the world's electromagnetic spectrum as being a more valuable natural resource than oil (Frederick 1993:121).

In Marxist terms, though the selling of mental labor for a wage may have become relatively more important than the selling of manual labor, the ruling-class appropriation of surplus value goes on regardless. It doesn't matter from their perspective whether the labor is knowledge-intensive or not.

Marxists also note that the transnational flow of information is increasingly dominated by a "handful of huge conglomerates" that now control "most of the world's important newspapers, magazines, books, radio and television outlets, cinema, recording industries, and videocassettes" (Frederick 1993:124). So concentrated has this oligopoly become that one analyst sees the whole electronic highway as the potential province now of just "seven American [business] men" (Harris 1995:81).

None of which would matter except that concentration of ownership means that what goes along the electronic highway can be, and is, homogenized and controlled to maximize profit and to foster the culture of capitalism itself. Thus the traffic flow along the electronic highway can be, and is, directed largely one way, with the global North telling the global South what to think, how to feel, and when to laugh. Cultural "dependency" and cultural imperialism are ongoing consequences, with new disparities opening up daily between the "info-rich" and the "info-poor" (Frederick 1993:146).

Social movements like the Association for Progressive Communications, which was founded in 1990, labor mightily in the global public interest to provide a freer flow of information, alternative news services, and other ways of talking about all of these issues. One does wonder, however, about those who are still effectively silent because they are not plugged in. What would they say if they had the chance? Would they see "plugging in" as beneficial, anyway? One also wonders whether there is not behind the association's enthusiasm for global civil society, alternative news sources, and freer information flows, the same Enlightenment agenda that has fostered liberalism for more than two hundred years. And while liberalism has been a very creative ideology, it is not the only one, and it has not been an unmixed blessing.

The new cybernations forming in the cyberspace that computers and communication technologies have created are in a sense Enlightenment rationalism's new frontier. It is not certain, however, that we should be embracing wholeheartedly such an abstracted, objectifying medium. Even liberals have started pointing out that people are not "thinking machines," since they absorb "at least as much information from sight, smell and emotion as they do from abstract symbols" (*Economist*, March 5, 1994:11). While we push on with rationalist experiments like the Internet, we are reminded by other social movements of a less technology-centered kind that our nonrational selves are equally intrinsic. At the cutting edge of the communications revolution we find the same feeling that led me to write this book.

One of the industries made possible by contemporary transportation and communications is tourism. This industry is arguably now the largest in the world. While there are many kinds of tourism and many different kinds of tourist (Murphy 1985:6), it can be said of all of them that tourism is "as much ideology as physical movement. It is a package of ideas about industrial, bureaucratic life . . . it is about power" (Enloe 1990:28, 40).

The size of the contemporary tourism industry, plus the sense that much more may be going on here than mass attempts to get a suntan, would suggest we take it very seriously indeed. It is curious, therefore, that we do not. Perhaps it seems too frivolous still. If so, one would then expect scholars to have the same attitude to the political economy of the world's entertainment empires, and yet, the corporate control of Hollywood and the cultural imperialism that Hollywood film and television industries make possible are familiar enough topics to analysts of IPE; likewise, discussions of who controls the satellite television broadcasting "footprints" in Asia. The neglect of an industry as large as and as significant as tourism appears in this light to be doubly strange. Perhaps, in the end, why tourism is "not discussed as seriously . . . as oil," for example, tells us more about the "ideological construction of 'seriousness' than about the political economy of tourism itself" (Enloe 1990:40).

The size and significance of tourism of all kinds can make state makers highly ambivalent about opening their borders to tourists. Seasonal hordes of foreign visitors can be seen as having undesirable politicoeconomic and politicocultural effects. They build up "dependence," it is said, while trivializing local ways of life. Mercantilistic state makers may, as a consequence, impose restrictions on tourists to slow the undesired effects of large transcultural flows on local peoples. Frances Bugotu of the Solomon Islands, for example, later to head the South Pacific Commission, waged a long-running campaign to prevent the extension of the airstrip at Honiara, the nation's capital, to stop jumbo jets from landing there and bringing in larger numbers of tourists. State makers can also decide to bow to the inevitable, however, while trying to control the industry in such a way as to maximize state autonomy. They may, for example, prohibit foreign charter airlines from providing internal flights, for example, thus protecting national carriers and maximizing revenues, much as Kenya once did.

Liberal state makers, on the other hand, argue for open borders and for every commercial effort to meet the demand for tourism. They provide all the necessary permissions to allow the freest tourist trade possible. They see tourism as one way to exploit a country's comparative advantage, and particularly so for materially poor states with little else to export. They want to turn "underdevelopment" to advantage. They consider it an asset to be "unspoiled," "exotic" even, and they actively promote local scenery and cultural "color" as commodities for foreign consumption. The developmental consequences can, indeed, be problematic, but that does not stop the "It's Better in the Bahamas" and the "Enjoy Paradise, Enjoy Puerto Rico" campaigns. Richter, for example, tells of being asked to provide a report on tourist "development" for the state makers of Belize. "A cursory reading on the country led me," she says,

> to conclude that . . . it needed a sewage system for its capital city before it needed to develop tourism. . . . Later I discovered that another tourism consultant . . . had told them the same thing in an earlier . . . report. It was shelved. Eventually a tourism consultant will help Belize develop tourism. It is less certain when someone will help Belize develop Belize (Richter 1989:19).

Liberal state makers, and particularly the more reformist liberal state makers, are unimpressed by such a conclusion. Indeed, they see building sewage systems as contingent upon the income the tourist industry provides. And they argue that it is the tourist industry itself that provides the incentive to build such sewers.

In Marxist parlance, tourism is one more capitalist ploy. Every alienated worker is a potential tourist. He or she seeks to escape from workplaces robbed of meaning by the wage relationship and emptied of purpose by labor for exchange rather than use. Tourism, in this regard, is more a matter of a flight from the capitalist world economy, than a going toward a holiday abroad (Richter 1989:208).

For the capitalist, whether in collusion with the state maker or one and the same person, tourism is the chance to exploit a need to profitable effect; to accumulate more capital, that is, by satisfying people's desires for out-of-country experiences. Monopolies will be preferred. For example, by integrating diverse firms—travel agencies, tour operators, transportation companies, hotels—into transnational production chains, profits can be maximized. Into these carefully constructed funnels it is then possible to pour millions of people, to parade them past natural objects, historical monuments, collections of artifacts, and diverse caricatures of local cultures, while providing food and fun to highly profitable effect. Indeed, it is possible to build "entire infrastructure[s]" in this way with "foreign goods, controlled by foreigners, and used by foreigners," while repatriating all the profits abroad (Richter 1989:181).

This, in Marxist terms, is neoimperialism. No one's territory has been taken away. It has been merely rented, and facilities have been installed on it for either large-scale, charter travel for the masses, or small-scale, capital-intensive travel for the wealthy. Tourist masses blotting whole landscapes by the sheer weight of their numbers may prompt the odd mercantilistic reaction but those in the best position to implement such controls are usually those most integral to the system, in which case they are likely to favor neoimperialism rather than neomercantilism. The tourists with the greatest wealth intrude in other ways. The facilities for them may be more discreet, but they will also be more expensive, more dependent on outside management, more conspicuous about the levels of consumption they make possible, and more resented by the locally deprived. Mercantilism may rear its head here too, though again, what state makers are going to convert back into housing for the poor, perhaps, luxurious "plant" and equipment they may want to enjoy themselves? What state makers are going to build (though it takes the same investment) modest hotels for use throughout the country by both national and international visitors, rather than a capital city status symbol to the nation and themselves?

Notable throughout the tourist industry as a whole is the role played by women. Not only are most of the service jobs involved in tourist care done by females (for example, chambermaiding), but females also play an important part in the international trade in one particular global commodity, namely, sex. Sex tourism is big businesss. The sexuality of Asian women, for example, commodified and sold worldwide, is a case in point. The trade in Asian sexuality "feeds off and into representations of colonial and third world women as passive/exotic. . . . Media images, tourist brochures and airline advertising like the Singapore 'girl' associate the Asian woman with male adventure and female availability. . . . They join the . . . scenery as 'unspoiled' and natural resources, there for the taking" (Pettman 1991:13). The exploitation of women, children, and men too in this way is one particularly sorry form of masculinist imperialism. It is also an integral part of the story of world development; of indebted countries, desperate for foreign currency; and of "structural adjustment," as contrived and executed by men. The critique of this trade illustrates well the socially created and culturally differentiated nature of the demand, highlights the diverse networks of production, shows how the industry could not function on its current scale without global transportation and communication (men flying into Bangkok, for example), depicts in graphic detail the use of individuals as commodities, and outlines the limits of mercantilist, liberal, and Marxist analyses (since the sex trade doesn't threaten national power, doesn't promote greater individual liberty—but can certainly constrain or eliminate it—and isn't adequately comprehended in class terms).

A pornographic trade of a very different sort is exemplified by John Jane's classic, first published in 1898, *All the World's Fighting Ships*. It seems there is no living in a capitalist state system without the "merchants of death" and in a liberal world political economy without their glossy, colorful brochures and advertising material, each one a graphic example of industrial capitalism at its most obscene (amnonc 1995:1). Jane's book on ships was the first in what is now a wide range of specialized periodicals that not only sell information about world armaments but also about the kind of commercial opportunities the manufacture of and the trade in armaments provide. Jane's is exemplary in this regard: it currently publishes, for example, an International Defense Directory that lists not only 36,000 senior defense personnel but also 16,400 defense companies and organizations and the manufacturers of 3,500 types of defense-related products from over 180 countries. In the defense business, "accurate information" not only means the difference between life and death. It also means whether to trade and invest or not.

Two notes run through the catalog account of the publishing services that Jane's provides—that of the need for military hardware and intelligence, and that of the unparalleled commercial opportunities that meeting such needs can provide. These two notes are in perfect counterpoint. There is the bass of the one crying, "Beware, beware." There is the descant of the other promising more-lethal capacities for your lira, more mangled multitudes for your lempira, or whatever else your currency might be.

In mercantilist terms, the armaments trade is anathema. Self-sufficiency in weapons production and supply is basic to sovereign autonomy. How is it possible, for example, to be "independent" if the fighter planes in one's national air force need spare parts from somewhere else?

As industrial production chains have become more international and as finished goods have come to incorporate components from more and more dispersed manufacturing sites, mercantilist concerns have been shared more widely. State making has historically entailed war making, and war is seen in mercantilist terms as always immanent. Worst case scenarios abound, keeping the pressure on to be armed and ready. In mercantilist terms, "weapons, being the source of power (analogous to specie [i.e., gold or silver])," should not be traded "except for strictly political reasons" (Krause 1992:14). Hence the mercantilists measure state "power" in terms of industrial self-sufficiency and not just in terms of armed forces.

Not every state maker has the means to make the arms needed for war, however; hence the arms trade. In extremist liberal terms, of course, armaments are commodities, just like any other, and laissez-faire production and trade, even armaments production and trade, benefits all. Trade means growth, growth means prosperity, and prosperity means peace. In liberal parlance, therefore, arms dealing actually makes for peace. Unlike mercantilists, liberals see no need to place restrictions on arms making and arms trading. To liberals, state makers who subsidize domestic armaments industries to reinforce their autonomy undermine the benefits that comparative advantage and the global division of labor bring. Where state makers subsidize such industries to make for themselves a comparative advantage, however, as the former Czechoslovakia did in explosives technology, then extremist liberals would say that they should be allowed to sell their explosives worldwide on the open market. The market nexus of supply and demand will set the price, and the prosperity that results will reduce any necessity to use such explosives for anything other than peaceful purposes. Indeed, how such explosives get used raises political questions, extremist liberals say, that are essentially separate from those of market economics, and impinge upon that market only at peril to the prosperity and peace it provides. The lethal irony, for example, in the historical fact that in 1899 "British soldiers were shot down by British guns that British armaments firms had sold to the Boers"; that in 1914 "German soldiers were killed by German guns manned by the armies of King Albert and Czar Nicholas II"; and that examples like these are legion should not obscure the more fundamental fact, as extremist liberals see it, that trading enough guns is a route to wealth, and wealth in turn precludes war.

Reformist liberals don't believe marketeers can be relied upon to provide such public goods as law and order. They are more likely as a consequence to argue for state intervention to prevent marketeers from trading themselves to death. Reformist liberals are aware, in other words, that markets left alone do not provide for national security. Adam Smith himself acknowledged that among the possible "market failures" was the failure to secure a country's defense.

The concern for national security is antiliberal in the classical sense, and there is a deep ambivalence through all liberal thinking about whether to privilege the market or the state. Smith, though a classical liberal, was also a mercantilist. He was concerned to secure the wealth of nations, after all, not the wealth of the individuals who are brought together in the world market. And though the logical consequence of classical liberal thinking is a world of individuals, not states, few liberals are prepared to be less nationalistic just to be intellectually consistent.

Reformist liberals argue for a referee at the global level as well. In a self-help world state makers retain the right to bear arms. A world of armed sovereign states makes necessary (reformist liberals argue) a hegemonic state capable of intervening to prevent individual members of the system of states from using their arms to threaten the system as a whole, and the global market that that system makes possible.

In Marxist terms the focus falls on who owns and manages the factories and supply chains, and who works for them. The robust character of capitalism is clearly manifest in the way major armaments manufacturers survive the defeat of governments in war and go on to rearm whoever prevails in the subsequent peace. Here we get a good glimpse of a map behind the usual map of the world on the wall. Do Japanese state makers sustain Mitsubishi, for example, or does Mitsubishi sustain Japanese state makers?

Extremist Marxists await the revolutionary overthrow of the whole capitalist system. The exploitation characteristic of such a system is the necessary precursor to its collapse, they say. So they are not likely to want to intervene to control armaments flows to poor countries, for example, for use in repressing local populations, since the system must "ripen" before it will fall, and armaments industries are part of the ripening process. Since the masses will need weapons when they ultimately revolt, armaments industries are necessary to provide the proletariat with arms when the revolution finally comes.

Reformist Marxists, concerned about capitalism's continued survival, and concerned, too, about the way capitalists who make arms continue to work not only for their own survival but for the ongoing worldwide exploitation of working people, seek controls on arms. In a state-made world, state makers are the ones best placed to effect these controls. Where state makers serve the interests of capitalists, however, this becomes irrelevant. Thus military officers from "developing" countries are trained in "developed" ones to respect not only the rules of strategic global practice but those of capitalist marketeering as well. Under such circumstances reformist Marxists can turn only to the social movements of "the people" themselves, and to the court of world opinion.

Feminist movements have explored in some detail the links between males, masculinity, and war. The "boys" will have their "toys," whether because of a surfeit of testosterone or some more culturally induced cause, and the armaments industry is there to provide the brightest and shiniest possible. State making is closely allied, both historically and systemically, with war making, and war making, for whatever reason, has always been a highly gendered activity, with males doing the fighting and females relegated to support roles while providing some of the rationale.

Like the gender construction of human society, the global arms industry is highly hierarchic. The United States and the former Soviet Union provided two-thirds of all global arms over the whole post–World War II period. Though still highly hierarchic, the world's armaments industry is diffusing, however. "In 1945," for example, "only 4 countries outside the developed world produced military equipment (Argentina, Brazil, India, and South Africa)." Today "about 40 do so" (Roberts 1995:7).

The diffusion process is not a typically liberalist one. Arms are not typical commodities, and they have not followed the way in which international divisions of labor are typically made (Krause 1992:92, 125, 213–214). The politicoeconomic story of diffusion, at least in the capitalist world, has been a mix of hard-sell capitalism and the mercantilist desire of state makers in countries without advanced metallurgical or chemical industries to be able to make sufficient quantities of modern weapons regardless. The combination of push by armaments entrepreneurs and pull from state makers wanting to be self-sufficient has made for a web of coproduction, offset, and licensing arrangements (Williams 1986). These have made for many more sites of weapons manufacture. These forces have also, however, tied countries into vertically integrated chains that constitute a global version of the military-industrial complex.

Vertical integration of the kind apparent in the armaments industry is also apparent in the agricultural industry. The large transnational agribusinesses build chains of production and supply that reach unbroken "from field to table." The tables the transnational chains supply are not local ones, though. They are at a considerable distance, and they are mostly in the "developed" countries of the global North (George 1986:158).

The transnational food industry uses local land and labor, but the food produced is "almost always for export" to those who can pay most. "Like mining," George (1986:159) observes, these are "truly 'extractive industries,'" and like mining, not only their human but also their environmental costs can be considerable. Whether in terms of the consequences of land clearance (Amazonia), or the effect of chemical fertilizers on water supplies (Taiwan), or the effect of synthetic industrial pesticides on those who work in the industry and consume its products (everywhere), the costs of industrial agriculture are high and rising.

Most state makers place a priority on food self-sufficiency. The mercantilist strategy would be to ensure complete self-supply and agricultural autonomy. In extremist liberal terms, however, the opposite applies. It is the mass manufacture of food and its sale on markets for profit, these liberals say, that is the only way to feed people and to solve the world's hunger problems. Free market industrial food manufacture may well be harmful to the environment, as well as to small, family-level farms and people who don't fit corporate plans for the "rationalization" of production, but it is plans like these, liberals argue, that a hungry world requires.

It is the harm such rationalization represents and the capacity it has to undermine the market that reformist liberals find worrying in turn. Being multinational, agribusinesses can maximize their profits by manipulating worldwide the mix of the factors of production they use. Profit for agribusiness can very easily mean unemployment for "rationalized" workers, for example, or environmental decay. Knowing that they've been rationalized for the good of the market can be scant comfort to those who find they're unable to sell their labor. Finding your forests razed for wood chips in the name of market efficiency can be equally distressing.

To a Marxist, most immediately apparent is the way, in "less developed" countries, the export of primary products is used to "structurally adjust," that is, to qualify countries for debt relief loans from organizations like the IMF and the World Bank. They note the use of arable land to produce luxury food products for the global North (McMichael and Myhre 1991:100). And they note the way rural proletarians provide surplus value using capital-intensive, highly mechanized, industrial farming techniques. They see this as exploitation, not adjustment.

To an extremist Marxist, the global pattern is reminiscent of nineteenth-century Europe. "All the varied horrors we look back upon with mingled disgust and incredulity," George (1986:23) argues,

> have their equivalents, and worse, in the Asian, African and Latin American countries where one in ten people live in absolute poverty and where, just as the "propertied classes" of yesteryear opposed every reform and predicted imminent . . . disaster if

eight-year-olds could no longer work in the mills, so today those groups that profit from the poverty that keeps people hungry want to keep the status quo between the rich and poor worlds.

A social picture like this, in Marxist terms, is a potentially revolutionary one.

To a reformist Marxist, the tragedy is the ongoing lack of revolutionary change and the ongoing cost in human life and suffering. The tragedy is how avoidable world hunger happens to be. Scarcity and famine are entirely preventable, they say. With what we know and with the resources at our command we could easily feed all earth's people and more. "Hunger is not [in this repect] a scourge . . . [it's a] scandal" (George 1986:23).

To various feminist social movements the scourge is sex-specific as well, and so is the scandal. The industrialization of agriculture and the marketeering to which liberals claim the world owes its living have not provided equally for women as opposed to men. Liberal feminists argue as a consequence for equality of opportunity. Socialist feminists argue for equality of treatment. Radical feminists argue for an inversion of the status quo; for better-fed women, that is, and worse-fed men.

One final example of how ideologies contest the definition of a major global industry can be found not in food but in pharmaceuticals and drugs.

Pharmaceuticals are mostly made in the industrialized world for the industrialized world, and more particularly, in those countries where the industry was first built, namely, the United States, the United Kingdom, Japan, Belgium, Germany, France, Italy, the Netherlands, Sweden, Switzerland, and most recently, China. The largest markets carry more than twenty thousand individual medicines (Ballance 1992:3–4).

Mercantilist self-sufficiency in basic pharmaceutical supplies is possible in principle for any state. In practice, however, a fully fledged industry making the main drugs of mass relevance from raw materials requires a level of manufacturing sophistication well beyond that of most poorer countries. These must trade. They must go to the world marketplace, which is where the extremist liberals say they should have been from the start. Reformist liberals, by contrast, aware of the disparities in health care that marketeering results in, aware as well of how closely good health and human capital are allied, advocate greater state care. Extremist Marxists see such disparities as a structural feature of capitalism and as part of its revolutionary potential. Reformist Marxists, meanwhile, worry about ways to protect the pharmaceutically exploited. They are the most likely to be advocating prevention as an alternative to cure, and treatment regimes other than allopathic ones.

The manufacture of and the trade in illicit drugs make up a large industry of their own. How large is impossible to say. For heroin, worth ounce for ounce ten times as much as gold, for cocaine, worth in the United States up to $40,000 a kilo wholesale, and for marijuana, it is certainly not inconsiderable. In the case of cocaine, for example, a figure of a thousand metric tons has been put upon Latin American production alone, with worldwide seizures making up only a fraction of that figure (*Economist*, December 24–January 6, 1995:20).

Commodities valued so highly are bound to attract the opportunistic intervention of entrepreneurs, and so they have, producing and trading freely despite statist regulators and the U.S. "war on drugs." This war is a metaphorical one with "no frontiers and no fronts. . . . The 'enemy' is not in uniform, and he does not fight in formations. The nature of the threat is indirect and underground" (Levitsky 1992:160). In extremist liberal terms, regulation is uncalled for, since people should be free to consume what they want and can pay for. There should be no licit/illicit distinction at all. People who choose illegal drugs should have the right to do so, though the nature of what constitutes free choice in this regard is much debated, and clearly has a lot to do with the culture in which the individual lives. Smith's hidden hand rolls reefers, in liberal parlance, and harmony, prosperity, and peace quite naturally prevail.

Reformist liberals wonder about the viability of a market that has such detrimental effects, even for cultures where illegal drugs play a more accepted part. They see the need for state intervention to mitigate those effects.

In extremist Marxist terms, drug trafficking is a capitalist plot, doomed to fail. Like religion, illegal drugs are opiates for the masses— literally so. Those who own and manage the means of drug production and distribution are certainly capitalists, though how their business might contribute to capitalism's collapse is not clear. Perhaps it saps the entrepreneurial spirit of the bourgeoisie or the will to work of the proletariat. Short of revolution we find exploitation aplenty, however, whether it be of peasant growers or criminalized consumers.

Reformist Marxists, who seek to protect the exploited, recommend reformist liberal intervention by the state. State makers, in Marxist terms in thrall to the bourgeoisie, are problematic people to turn to, however. Marxist reformers talk about civil society instead and the social movements that seek change by grassroots means. The drug trade relies, as they see it, on the uneven development of the world political economy. The problem of "hard drugs" is most apparent, they claim, in "precisely those urban centres in North America and Europe that have suffered the greatest job losses as a result of . . . 'the demise of manufacturing industry'" (Taylor 1994:494). On a global scale, it is "precisely those countries which have been disadvantaged in the new international global political economy, in part because they have not developed an indigenous industrial or financial commercial class," that now have to rely on the sale of "whatever agricultural product they can produce, with minimal technology," namely, drugs (Taylor 1994:495). Coca bushes can be harvested only a year and a half after they are first planted, and they can be harvested three or four times a year for up to twenty years. They provide, in other words, an early and a steady crop return (President's Commission 1986:29). This blanket conclusion does not explain why those countries in the global South who are manifestly "disadvantaged" and yet have not turned to the drug-growing and trading option, should have chosen differently. Nor does it explain the "de-developing" regions in the global North that are not notable drug users either. But there is enough of a correlation here to give us pause. Nor is the state much of a help in the cases where the correlation is clear; which leaves people having to somehow help themselves.

I hope by now it is reasonably clear that how we talk about an issue really does determine what we make of it in substantive terms. Try holding a drinking glass upright against a wall and drawing a line around it. You get a rectangle. Turn the glass on its end and you get a circle. It's the same object, the same subject, the same reality, but you have two different shapes. It really does depend on how you look at it. No one way is more "correct" than the other, though this doesn't stop the rectangular people arguing with the circular people about the relative merits and demerits of their respective points of view, and of the analytic languages they choose to use. Because their premises are different, however, their arguments never end. They could only be reconciled by a cosmic perspective that could see all sides at once, or rather, by someone who could see a drinking glass as a sphere, since only a sphere has the same shape from any angle.

There are all kinds of interconnections between these particular industries, just as there are many more industries that could have been discussed. There are connections between recreational spending on illegal drugs and tourism, for example. There are tensions between recreational spending on things like tourism and illicit drugs, and spending on necessities like food or pharmeceuticals or the products of other industries, such as oil. There are connections between money laundering and computing. It was not my point to pursue these connections here, rather I wanted to demonstrate the radical influence perspective has upon what we understand to be of significance in IPE and to note the limits any perspective places upon what we see and do. Knowing about limits is the first step toward transcending them. That goes, as Enloe knows, for the rationalist-objective approach to IPE as a whole. But why reflect any further? Let's return to someone who knows what I mean, and what is more, can make the point in experiential terms.

4

From "International Political Economy" to "World Political Economy"

❖ Anthony Sampson (1973) "The Barbecue"

It was in Brussels, at the annual ITT [International Telephone and Telegraph] barbecue of managers from all over the world, that I first felt the full impact. It was just after the ITT scandal had broken in Washington and Chile, after the giant corporation had been accused of bribing the Nixon government to drop an anti-trust suit, and of trying to undermine the elections in Chile. I was already interested in multinational corporations, and I had become specially curious about this conglomerate, with its astonishing jumble of world interests, from telephones to cosmetics, from hire-cars to hams, with an apparently unstoppable power to operate beyond the reach of governments. I had been talking to people both inside and outside the company, and to my surprise I had been invited, as a solitary journalist, to attend this self-contained company function.

It was a strange setting, which seemed outside time or place. It was at the "Executive Mansion", a big bourgeois house in a suburb of Brussels, which ITT maintains as a company club and a centre for entertainment. A marquee had been put up in the garden, draped with blue and white ITT bunting, and Belgian waiters were cooking steaks and sweet corn on the charcoal grills, while the polyglot managers queued up docilely with their plates. The American contingent, sixty of them, had flown over two days before, for their monthly inspection of the European accounts: they had the dazed, sleep-walking look of people still confused by jet-lag, and some of them (I confirmed) still kept their watches on New York time, in case they had to ring up the head office.

It was not immediately easy to tell the Europeans from the Americans, except perhaps from the shoes and trousers; for the Europeans, too—whether Swedish, Greek or even French—had a hail-fellow style and spoke fluent American, joking and reminiscing about old times in Copenhagen and Rio. I soon had a sense of being enveloped by the company, by its rites, customs and arcane organogram, of being swept right away from Brussels, or Europe, or anywhere.

After a good deal of back-slapping, shoulder-punching and story-telling, the executives sat down to their meal on trestle-tables in the marquee. There was no special seating plan; the atmosphere was determinedly democratic

99

and unsnobbish. But in the middle a bald hearty man was pointed out to me, the young president of ITT Europe, Mike Bergerac; and next to him looking small by comparison was an owlish figure in a neat dark suit. This, I recognised, was the master-mind behind the whole corporation—Harold Sydney Geneen.

After the meal, there were speeches. An Italian manager told a long funny story in comic Italian-American about marriage and sex. There were references to how famous ITT had become in the past weeks, and how they no longer needed to read company reports to learn news of their company; they could read it in the newspapers. Then Mike Bergerac made another humorous speech, in praise of Geneen, speaking in a Californian drawl, with an easy-going, open-air casualness which made it hard to believe that he had ever been French. The climax of his joke came when he revealed that Geneen had recently been to London, where he had been observed—improbably enough—enjoying watching a game of cricket at Lords. Bergerac then suddenly brandished a cricket-bag, out of which he produced a cricket bat, stumps and pads (they had been flown over at the last moment, I was told by my neighbour, by ITT's advertising men in London). He held them up, one by one, while the executives rocked with laughter and Geneen too laughed with an impish grin which lit up his face.

Then Geneen stood up. He continued the joke, swinging the bat with remarks about batting for business, bowling fast balls and needing strong pads. But the picture of Geneen as the cricketer never really seemed convincing; and he quickly went on to talk about ITT, with more jokes about the terrific publicity, and how this was a "non-sandwich evening" (most of the evenings when the Americans come over are spent in late-night conferences, with only time for a sandwich).

As soon as he spoke, for all the informality, it was clear that he domi-nated the whole gathering, like a headmaster at the end of term pretending to be one of the boys, but fooling none of them. He talked about record profits, continuing expansion, successful delegation and multinational co-operation. His eyes gleamed as he went on about ITT's brilliant performance. He ended by saying, "I want you to know that I'm having a lot of fun, and I want you to have fun, too."

There was a surge of applause. It seemed clear that he really was having fun; though I was less sure that the rest were. Yet listening to the jokes and the speeches, one would not think that this company had just been through a barrage of public criticism, examination and censure. I asked the head of public relations, Ned Gerrity, what effect he thought the scandal had had on ITT's business. He said it had really established the company's corporate identity: "The bookings for Sheraton hotels have been a record."

After the speeches, the managers walked around the garden and the house, drinking and chatting about turnover and inventories. They were hearty in a rather tense way, like a reunion of alumni who are not quite sure

how well they know each other. The tension was heightened by the presence
of the bosses—the senior vice-presidents who had flown over from New
York, who wandered round warily. There was Tim Dunleavy, a big jolly
Irishman with tousled hair, who had the cosy look of a teddy-bear, but whose
jollity was said to be only a smokescreen for a steel-trap mind. There was
Jim Lester, inscrutable with his narrow eyes and circumflex mouth, like a
sad mandarin; his implacable exterior, I was told, concealed an implacable
interior. There was Ned Gerrity, regarded as the eyes and ears of his master,
Geneen; a leathery man with pebble glasses, loping round the lawn with his
cigar rolling round his mouth.

The gathering was as emphatically masculine as a regiment or a football
club; there was not even a waitress. The whole *esprit* was one of challenge
and ordeal, with a whiff of grapeshot in the air: the appearance of a girl
would have shattered the spell.

Later in the evening I was taken to meet Geneen, who was standing
talking in the now almost-empty marquee. It was a surprising encounter. I
was introduced as an English writer, and he told me immediately how much
he liked England, where he had been born, and how he loved coming back to
London. Then he went on to explain how he had admired the British Empire,
and was sorry it had been given up so hastily. Why didn't the British government support the White Rhodesians? Didn't they realise that four-fifths of
the British people were behind Ian Smith? He went on to talk about America's difficulties with the rest of the world—how her oil supplies were in
danger, and how eventually she might need to move into the Arab countries
to protect them. As he warmed to his tirade, his whole frame came to life; he
began gesturing, pointing, and laughing, his fingers darting around touching
his nose, his ear, his chin, as if weaving some private spell; his greeny-brown
eyes twinkled, and he grinned and laughed like a gargoyle. He seemed no
longer a dark-suited owlish accountant, but more like an imp or a genie:
almost like Rumpelstiltskin, magically turning thread into gold. I noticed that
a clutch of vice-presidents were standing round listening, watching him
carefully: they laughed when he laughed, and nodded when he nodded.

Businessmen, he explained, are the only people who know how to create
jobs, and make work for people; he was responsible for 400,000 employees,
all over the world, and it was his duty to lobby governments on their behalf,
as effectively as he could. What do governments know about providing jobs?
Why does the American government waste time with anti-trust questions,
when it should be supporting the big corporations which are battling with the
Japanese, and contributing to the balance of payments? As for these liberal
newspapermen who attack big business, what do *they* know about making
jobs? I interrupted him to say: "Perhaps *I'm* a liberal newspaperman!" He
looked at me in disbelief and roared with laughter, with the others in chorus.

He argued for three-quarters of an hour in the marquee, treating me
patiently, with amused tolerance, as a wayward sceptic who would soon see

the true light of reason: he even sent a message afterwards, saying how much he'd enjoyed the talk. We parted amicably, with mutual incomprehension. But in this marquee, like a nomad's encampment, I had begun for a moment to get the feel of being inside this amazing corporation, to glimpse it through the eyes of the master and followers. From their camp they looked out onto a world benighted with prejudice and unreason; where governments were merely obstructing the long march of production and profit; where nations were like backward native tribes, to be placated, converted, and overcome.

That barbecue evening aroused my curiosity, more than it satisfied it. It seemed like a caricature, exaggerating all the characteristics of these new organisms, the multinational corporations, and raising in an extreme form the question: who, if anyone, can control them? Here was a giant company which had just undergone this extreme public battering, apparently emerging all the prouder and more unified from the ordeal, as if it were a pirate ship that had slipped through a naval engagement. Its duality looked baffling; on one side it presented itself as a highly responsible world organisation, constantly mindful of its 200,000 shareholders, its 400,000 employees, its seventy host nations, and held together with an accounting system of the strictest control: in the words of its advertisements "serving people and nations everywhere." Yet on the other side, in the marquee I had the powerful impression that here was a company that was accountable to no nation, anywhere; and held together and inspired by one man, against whom no-one cared to argue. A man, moreover, who in spite of his famous accounting skills and discipline, yet had the unmistakable style of a buccaneer—who could stir up others with purpose and excitement, luring them away from their families and homes into a world of hectic travel, late-night meetings, constant pressure and outrageous demands.

How did such a company come about, and how had it so inexorably increased its scope? How can one man dominate a corporation and hold together an industrial empire making thousands of products across half the world? How can governments ever control such an organism which is, like a jellyfish, both everywhere and nowhere? And how does the multi-national corporation, of which ITT is a convenient caricature, fit in with modern notions of politics and diplomacy? How does it, or should it, relate to the nation-state, to the Common Market or to the models of world trade? . . .

"He's Captain Ahab, really," said one Geneen-watcher, and I could see what he meant—the monomania and obsession, the magnetic ascendancy he cast over his crew in the hunt for the whale. But as I continued my own travels, I came to think that Geneen and his corporation resembled not so much the crew of the *Pequod*, as the white whale itself; a leviathan secretly encircling the world, usually detectable only by the turbulence of the water, but suddenly showing one side of its huge strange shape, or spouting dark water, first in one corner of the globe, then a few days later at the opposite end; becoming a legend for ubiquity, immortality, and supernatural strength.

The emerging world business civilization has its roots deep in European culture, but its branches and flowers are now found everywhere in the world. Driven by a passionate commitment to liberal capitalism, men like the managers of Sampson's ITT are a new kind of citizen. They carry a national passport—or two or three—but their real passport is their contract of employment with the company for which they work. They belong not so much to an international political economy but a world political economy. They are cosmopolitan members of a global market that they build as they go.

This market is growing fast. What are its most significant features? Sampson suggests a few—multinational corporations, for example, changing patterns of employment, changing balances of productive power. These are all important features, but they are not the only ones. Moreover, each feature can be read from a different analytic perspective using different analytic languages. Features are as features are said to be.

GROWTH IN PRODUCTION

To liberals the most important development in modern times has been the way markets have merged to define virtually every society in the world. Marketeering mores have become part and parcel of virtually every human culture. Rather than haggle together once a week in the village square, for example, we have countless chances, as buyers and sellers, to meet together to effect the exchange of goods and services. Markets are now ubiquitous, and the rules and understandings they require are ubiquitous, too. Like the state, their predominance today is a strange and wondrous thing. In historical terms, it is unique.

The market is now available virtually everywhere. In some places this is so all day and every day. In an intensely marketized country like Japan, for example, street vending machines have been installed every hundred meters or so. They operate nonstop, peddling not only a wide range of foods and drinks, but compact discs, camera film, postcards and stamps, magazines and comics, dry cell batteries, used underwear and phone cards. By 1993 there were 5.5 million such machines, one for every twenty-two people in the country, and this, one should add, is just the curb-side fringe of a vast commercial web woven through the entire fabric of Japanese society.

In a marketized world marketeering, in the sense of market-specific behavioral practices, also becomes ubiquitous. Cultural values change to account, for example, for commodity display (advertising), stimulated desires (the "cult of the new"), status defined in terms of possessions ("you can't take it with you but you can have it now"), a cultivated neglect of environmental degradation (unquestioning acceptance of inbuilt obsolescence, for example), masculinized competitiveness (sales campaigns), and an extraordinary emphasis upon the getting and relinquishing of the main medium of exchange (namely, money).

To Marxists the point of the market is that it is a capitalist market. Williams (1983:50–52) says that calling someone a "capitalist" goes back to the eighteenth century, which is also about the time that "capital" began to be used as a specialized term to denote not just capital stock, like land, machinery, materials, or workers' skill levels, but capital as money invested to earn interest. *Capitalism,* as a word describing a "particular economic system," didn't appear until early in the nineteenth century, however, and it wasn't until later in the century that it began to be used, most notably by Marx himself, to denote privatized ownership of the means of production, in association with free wage labor.

Not all analysts see capital or even the market itself as the most basic feature of the growth process. Some, for example, see the advent of industry and the Industrial Revolution as the distinguishing feature of the world political economy. It is the Industrial Revolution, they argue, that is primarily responsible for the extraordinary productivity of contemporary human beings (Landes 1969). "Since the Industrial Revolution," says Gilpin (1987:98), "the major cause of economic growth has been a series of technological innovations that have provided new opportunities for investment and economic expansion."

Gilpin's use of the adjective *economic* to denote a discrete realm of human endeavor is the clue here. Gilpin, as noted earlier, is a reformist liberal. As such he is more inclined to think in terms of wealth making as separate from, say, politics. He thinks of technological change as having a life of its own. Other liberals, by contrast, particularly the more classically oriented ones, see industrialization making a difference only where free play is given to entrepreneurs. Marxists see industrialization as the means peculiar to the contemporary mode of production, with all that that entails. Being capitalist industrialization is what makes all the difference. To feminists, it is most notably patriarchist industrialization. To environmentalists, it is Pandora's box; and so on

The growth of the international political economy has entailed growth in both breadth and depth. The system itself has gotten bigger, and the interactions in every part of it have become more intense. It is a phenomenon so profound that the concept of an international political economy, while still a meaningful one, has to be considered now in the context of another that is becoming equally if not more important, namely, that of a global political economy.

Global Firms

The global political economy is dominated not only by state makers, but also by the heads of transnational firms or corporations—men like Geneen of ITT, described so graphically by Sampson. "During the early 1990's," according to one UN report, "at least 37,000 parent firms controlled over 206,000 foreign affiliates" (UNCTAD 1994:4). In 1992 the largest one hundred of these firms (excluding the banking and finance ones) controlled about $3.4 trillion in global assets, over one-third of which were held outside the countries where these firms were based (UNCTAD 1994:5).

Headquartered almost exclusively in the capitals of the countries of the European Union, as well as the United States, Japan, Australia, Canada, Finland, New Zealand, Norway, Sweden, and Switzerland, the top two among the top one hundred global firms, in terms of assets located abroad, are currently oil companies. Preeminence in the sense of assets abroad reflects the nature of the oil industry, and in particular, how geographically dispersed and capital-intensive it is. If companies are ranked in terms of quality service, however, visionary management, market responsiveness, financial soundness, or the example they set to others, then in the Asian region at any rate, where a survey of 4,500 professionals was conducted to determine the relative ranking of multinationals, the market leader is the beverage firm Coca-Cola, closely followed by Motorola and McDonald's (Leger 1994:38–39).

All the top firms are notably transnational, either standing alone in foreign domains or meshing with local concerns (UNCTAD 1994:136). This meshing process is one of the most notable features of the world political economy. "Globalization is ultimately the product of decisions taken by firms," according to UNCTAD (1994:158), a conclusion borne out by the finding that five hundred global firms among them do four-fifths of all the production in the world, and only fifteen firms control between them the world trade in "all basic commodities, from food to minerals" (Gurtov 1994:29).

Taken as a group it is the computer and electronic firms that hold the most assets abroad. These are followed closely by mining and petroleum, chemical and pharmaceutical, car-making, and food and beverage firms. Taken as a whole this makes global firms "major organizers of economic activity and an important source of capital, technology, managerial and organization know-how for both developed and developing economies" (UNCTAD 1994:163)—much as Sampson says.

This is not to mention the role of global firms as the employers, directly and indirectly, of 150 million workers in high-technology secondary, that is, industrial, and tertiary, that is, service, industries (UNCTAD 1994:164). While this may be only 6 percent of the world's paid labor force, it is the leading edge of this force. Marxists in particular talk about the "incorporation of labor from many countries into an integrated worldwide corporate productive structure" (Hymer 1979:75).

Firms are in the world market to outproduce and outsell each other, but technological change can also make what a particular firm offers obsolete. This provides firms with a pressing reason for constant research and innovation. This assumes the financial means to do so, which is why global firms have grown in parallel with the global capital market (Hymer 1979:82). The demand for credit on the part of global firms gets met from the world's supply of stored value, and the "savings of many nations" get mobilized for this purpose (Hymer 1979:82).

Marxists in particular point to the symbiotic nature of this relationship, and the common sense of cause it creates between owners and managers of firms and capital. It is Marxists, too, who draw attention to what global firms do to labor. "Increased cooperation" between the workers of the world can only appear to the capitalist as "increased competition" (Hymer 1979:85), since to maximize their profits, global firms must, among many other things, buy labor power as cheaply as possible. "It costs $25 an hour," for example, "to employ a production worker in Germany (including non-wage costs such as social-security contributions) and $16 an hour in America; but only $5 in South Korea, $2.40 in Mexico, $1.40 in Poland and 50 cents or less in China, India and Indonesia" (Woodall 1994:14). Depending on how labor-intensive the production process happens to be, the cost of making finished goods may include only a small amount of what is paid to labor. If firms are trying to make money in highly competitive markets, however, every cost advantage can matter, even seemingly small ones.

Laborers do come to the capitalists, but on the whole, capitalists take their production processes to the workers. Contemporary production technologies make this much more feasible. Capitalists also prevail upon state makers to use state borders to impede migration flows. This keeps the global labor force fragmented and therefore easier to control and easier to exploit. With the help of state makers, capitalists can also maintain, "by force or by education, the general structural conditions which cause laborers to come to work each day and to accept the authority of the capitalist and his right to higher income, either as managerial compensation or as interest and dividends" (Hymer 1979:86).

Global Production

Sampson describes ITT as an "industrial empire making thousands of products across half the world." It is productiveness of this sort, and on such a scale, that has changed the international political economy into a world one.

At the end of the last century and in the first years of this one global production chains were mostly to be found in the primary sector (agriculture). They have been moving ever since into the secondary (industrial) and tertiary (service) ones. "As a result," UNCTAD (1994: 146) believes, "a substantial share of global output [four-fifths, by Gurtov's reckoning] is being reorganized under the common governance of TNC's. . . . Trade and technology transfers . . . are being taken out of the market and internalized within TNC networks." This means that, "from being a collection of independent national economies linked primarily through markets, the world economy is becoming, for the first time, an international production system, integrated increasingly through numerous parts of the value-added chain of production" (UNCTAD 1994:146).

What are we to make of this process? The quotation above is couched in liberal language. The notion of "national economies" and of a "world economy" as discrete entities only makes sense in liberal terms. To the more extreme liberal, producers are not required to develop a "social outlook commensurate with the social production they create," since the system is supposed to deliver such an outcome automatically. Reformist liberals are more pessimistic, however, retaining a place for state makers somewhere "above . . . the market so that the waste of externalities can be reduced and the conflicts between capitals and between capital and labor can be ameliorated" (Hymer 1979:77).

Mercantilists reject outright the way in which liberal reformists still expect the state to operate "with its hands tied." Global firms, they say, should serve the "national interest" or be regulated accordingly (Hymer 1979:78).

Marxists decry the "costs [under capitalism] of constant rivalry, the inability [of the system] to meet social needs, and the frustration of human development." They decry, too, the authoritarian way in which firms, and particularly global firms, keep the worker largely ignorant of the "cooperative process of which he is part," and the way in which they alienate the worker from "his work, his instruments and machines, and his product" (Hymer 1979:77).

The globalization of production is most readily apparent to Marxists. Liberals and mercantilists talk about entrepreneurs connecting up national economies, creating flows of goods and money. Theirs is a world economy of international exchange. Marxists, however, talk of global firms like ITT commanding integrated production chains that maximize value surpluses by myriads of transnational means. Theirs is a world political economy of production. It is one where "international" is unequivocally "global" and where "production" is "productivity" on a truly global scale (Robert 1992:175).

Global Divisions of Labor

Global firms have been instrumental not only in integrating production chains but in bringing about radical changes in the international division of labor.

The classical international division of labor involved the exchange of industrial goods for primary commodities. It involved industrialized countries exporting finished goods to nonindustrialized ones, and importing primary commodities (raw materials) in return. This pattern has changed. Global firms now put manufacturing and assembly plants in relatively remote locations because of the tax-and-labor-cost advantages and the chance to avoid strict environmental protection laws. They keep the knowledge-intensive parts of the production chain in more technologically advanced places, but the unskilled and semiskilled labor-intensive parts they put where workers are cheaper. Instead of the poorer countries on the world's productive peripheries exporting only raw materials, we then get them making and trading finished goods as well (Fröbel et al. 1978).

This is the new international division of labor. It involves the exchange of industrial goods for primary commodities and cheap labor, and while the analysis above suggests that global firms brought this about, it has also been argued that state makers in a number of poorer countries helped bring it about, too. In the 1930s and during World War II a number of these countries built labor-intensive import substitution industries in their bid to save foreign exchange and become more "developed." Exports from these industries had a significant impact on parallel industries in developed states. Global firms began to invest in the more successful of the peripheral manufacturing concerns, and a new international division of labor was created (Dolan 1991:4).

This is not all the new international divison of labor involves, however. Capitalist firms in the world's productive cores have continued to promote industrial research. This has enabled them to change from more "material-intensive" products and processes to lesser ones. "Fifty to 100 pounds of fiberglass cable," for example, "transmit as many telephone messages as does one ton of copper wire [and] requires no more than five percent of the energy needed to produce [it]. . . . Thus it is quite unlikely that raw material prices will ever rise substantially as compared to the prices of manufactured goods (or high-knowledge services such as information, education or health care) except in the event of a major prolonged war" (Drucker 1989: 290–291).

This has put considerable pressure on those peripheral countries that provide obsolescing mineral and energy resources. Resources have value because of the industrial technologies that turn them into commodities. The technologies that make these resources worth using are changing, however. Core countries are staying well ahead, and any prospect of a commodities squeeze being put on them as resources deplete has so far not materialized.

In more-extremist liberal terms, the change in the international division of labor is to be welcomed. Since the international economy is a self-equilibrating one, the end result of money flows and the world trade in managerial expertise, raw materials, and machinery is an international division of labor nobody planned but everyone benefits from (Caporaso 1987b:4). Labor, in these terms, is only part of what makes for any finished product. International divisions of labor result from entrepreneurial decisions about how to combine all the factors of production to optimal effect. It is no more than Smith's pin-making process on a world scale. The result is much magnified production capacities, but there is no more to it than that.

In more-extremist Marxist terms, the significance of the changing international division of labor is notably greater, simply because the role that Marxists see labor power performing in the production process is much greater. At the same time as global firms began to move their factories to cheap labor countries, for example, automated robot workers also began to eliminate opportunities for blue collar employment in those where labor was more expensive. This trend became so marked that analysts began to wonder whether or not in a few years countries like the United States and Japan would be employing "no larger a proportion of the labor force in manufacturing" than they currently employ in farming that is, "at most, ten

percent" (Drucker 1988:291–292). If this trend were to become a definitive feature of the world political economy, then we would see the
"uncoupling of manufacturing production from manufacturing
employment" (Drucker 1988:291)—a revolutionary change indeed.
Without other ways of reemploying those put out of work, this change
could even be revolutionary in the extremist Marxist sense. It is no
accident, therefore, that extremist liberals take such an interest in controlling crime, since this is one of the most direct consequences of
high, chronic unemployment. It is no accident that reformist liberals
want to bring the state back in. Or that mercantilist cries to "keep the
jobs at home" and "buy local, or else" continue to have such appeal.

Fordism and Post-Fordism

The most characteristic way to manufacture large numbers of cheap,
standardized commodities is that pioneered by Henry Ford. Using
"large factories with dedicated machinery that produced large runs,"
with "well-paid workers" in large, homogeneous, strictly supervised
groups, performing "single tasks in a long line," and with large stocks
of components kept ready to feed onto an assembly line kept in constant operation, Ford was able to produce prodigious quantities of
reliable, affordable cars (Dolan 1991:18). The speed with which his
methods were copied is the best measure of their success.

"Fordism," as this method has been called, involved not only production lines. It also involved a "rough compromise" among capitalists, workers, and state makers whereby each recognized the need to
tie wage increases to increases in productivity. Such a compromise
was common after World War II in most of the richer countries. It lasted as long as profits rose enough to satisfy capitalists, levels of consumption remained satisfactory to workers, and the welfare nets set
by state makers remained wide enough to catch most of those who fell
out of the system (Dolan 1991:1–2).

Post-Fordism, by contrast, denotes a production process of "flexible specialization," competitive "differentiation," and quality control
(Dolan 1991:18). The decomposition of production into three stages—
design/engineering, manufacturing, and assembly—and the advent
of improved transport and communications have been discussed
already in the context of firms, global production, and the global division of labor. As noted, the possibilities for profit such highly adapt-
able production provides have made it highly attractive to capitalist
investors worldwide.

Post-Fordism also refers to the way overproduction (or undercon-
sumption) in the developed countries has prompted capitalists to

invest elsewhere in a bid to halt the decline in their rates of profit. The chance factories will relocate has helped create considerable fear among the work force in richer countries. Job losses always seem imminent now. These fears have been translated, with the help of those capitalists who feel threatened too, into calls on state makers to implement mercantilist measures to protect those Fordist industries at most risk, and to foster at the same time the development of more technologically advanced research and service concerns. State makers have responded by calling for a return to more-extremist liberal marketeering methods. They have begun deregulating, thus shifting as much responsibility as they can for the social costs of what is happening to the marketeers themselves. Reformist liberals look for state-based ways to save marketeers from themselves. The more extremist Marxists see the whole process as typical of a mode of production in a frenzy before it falls over. Neo-Marxists remain concerned that yet again capitalism has bought a reprieve by highly exploitative means.

THE UNEVENNESS OF THE GROWTH IN PRODUCTION

The IPE is becoming bigger and more integrated. It is evident that this is an uneven process, however, and that this unevenness has several different dimensions.

Ideologies

"In our view," said U.S. Vice-President Al Gore at the United Nations Social Summit in Copenhagen in March 1995, "only the market system unlocks a higher fraction of the human potential than any other form of economic organization, and has the demonstrated potential to create broadly distributed new wealth."

Cuba's President Fidel Castro said, "In a world where the rich are becoming richer and the poor are growing poorer there can be no social development. Where there is no human feeling there can be no human rights."

Gabon's President Omar Bongo said, "You take advantage of Africa and when your belly is full you tell Africa not to be awkward" (Black 1995:4).

As the world political economy has grown, so too have the range of views about how to describe and explain it. These views are highly disparate. In this sense they represent a highly uneven understanding of a major dimension of world affairs. From the protectionist defense of state autonomy; the Gore-style defense of free marketeering; the

Marxist emphasis on understanding capitalism; or the critiques from the ideological margins by environmentalist, feminist, or indigenous people's movements; the analysis of the productivity of the world political economy is nothing if not diverse. It is also heartfelt. As many found in Copenhagen, the tension between these different views can be high, and the disputes about their policy implications can be bitter indeed.

For the forty years of the Cold War this disparity took the form of a grand ideological dichotomy, that between the liberal capitalist West and the command socialist East. The growth of the world political economy took place in two separate zones, each one expressive of its own philosophy and each one explicitly committed to outdoing the other. In the event it was the command socialists who were outdone. The Soviet experiment with highly centralized, statecentric developmental planning collapsed. Chinese state makers began to "marketeer." Liberal capitalism became hegemonic, though as the debates at Copenhagen showed, it remains radically contested still.

Temporality

The growth in the productivity of the international political economy has been very uneven over time. Though this growth has been "truly remarkable," representing a "prolonged and massive increase in aggregate wealth per capita . . . over several centuries" (Gilpin 1987: 100), it has also varied considerably. The rate of change has been far from constant. Price levels have risen and fallen, and growth has gone from boom to bust and back again to boom.

These cycles have been of considerable interest to business theorists. Some discern a systematic pattern of upward and downward swings that is anything from three to fifty years long. Some describe alternating periods of rapid and slow growth but find nothing systematic about that fact at all. Others see such variations as mere epiphenomena, preferring to find in the march of humankind a single historical line.

Whatever one makes of their causes and consequences, recessions and outright depressions have recurred throughout the period of overall growth, both large and small. There have also been periods of indifferent and very strong growth, also large and small. In general periods of downturn the inclination is to opt for mercantilist policies in the attempt to protect national populations from global malaise. In times of upturn the inclination is to opt for more-liberal policies in the attempt to cash in on the general mood of entrepreneurial optimism.

"In summary," Gilpin (1987:105) says, the world political economy has experienced a "traumatic experience" approximately every fifty years or so. Since the last such experience was the advent of recession in 1973 (the end of a twenty-year boom), we can, by this logic, expect the next big slowdown in the 2020s (a return version, perhaps, of the Great Depression of the 1930s). Gilpin also notes that these "erratic . . . shifts have been global phenomena. Originating in the core economies, their effects have been transmitted . . . to the extremities of the planet, shattering individual economies and setting one . . . against another as each nation has tried to protect itself." These times of "expansion and contraction," he says, "have also been associated with profound shifts in the structure of the international . . . system."

In liberal terms, the most popular explanation of these economic cycles is that of technological change. New productive inventions inspire new investments that lead to new spurts in growth. Once these spurts peter out, growth slows. This is not a problem, however, if the efficient are unimpeded, since marketeers can create new equilibriums if free to do so. Hence the importance that all liberals attach to free enterprise.

In Marxist terms, a more likely explanation of the changes in growth speed over time is the combined effect, under capitalism, of the oversupply of commodities, the overconcentration of capital in fewer and fewer hands, and falling rates of profit. Because of these trends capitalism is seen as internally contradictory and prone to recurrent crises. Neo-Marxists like Lenin argue that the effects of these trends also force capitalists to seek markets, investment opportunities, and cheap supplies of the factors of production wherever they can find them. Capitalists do this not only to maximize their profits but to forestall the inevitable collapse of the capitalist system as a whole. They do it to buy off the downtrodden workers with goods and better wages. They stagger in the process from self-serving rescue mission to self-serving rescue mission, and the global experience of their doing so is bust and boom.

Geography

The growth in the productivity of the global political economy has also been uneven in geographic terms. There have been systemic growth poles for the last four hundred years, and a "major objective of states," Gilpin (1987:99) says, throughout this entire time has been to constitute one of them. The Portuguese, the Spanish, and the Dutch dominated the preindustrial international political economy by turns. A revolution in "steam power, iron metallurgy, and textiles" (Gilpin 1987:98) brought Britain to the fore, and the diffusion of Britain's Industrial Revolution created new high-growth areas—in North

America, Germany, and Japan. Despite two disastrous wars, the first in Europe and the second in Europe, Asia, and the Pacific, these have remained growth poles to this day. They were joined for half a century by the Soviet Union. This has since collapsed, while notable also has been the growing productivity of Asian states other than Japan.

At present, growth is concentrated in three global regions, and it is no accident that there is now a regional organization committed to fostering each one. The regions are Europe, North America, and Northeast Asia, and the organizations are the European Union, the North American Free Trade Association, and the Asia Pacific Economic Community. So striking is this regionalization (and the marginalization at the same time, particularly of Africa but also of much of Central and South America, plus parts of Asia, too) that analysts talk, in geographic terms, of a contraction rather than an expansion of global productive marketeering (Overbeek 1994).

In liberal terms, it is largely up to marketeers to sort out the tensions between growth poles and the rest of the international political economy, and between growth poles in ascendancy and growth poles in decline. The free movement of the factors of production allows equilibrium to be maintained, it is argued, as capital and labor, commodities and technology, move in various combinations from countries in ascendancy to countries in decline. Market mechanics keep the system strife-free. In practice, however, state makers are called upon to intervene to protect those disadvantaged by the geographic disparities in patterns of growth and to expedite factor flows. As Gilpin (1987:99) observes, "In a world of nation-states and political boundaries capital and especially labor cannot migrate easily from declining to rising sectors to find new employment. As a consequence, interstate conflicts arise as individual states seek either to promote their expanding industries or to protect their declining ones." Leading countries that are moving down don't relinquish their dominance readily, while the competition from those on the rise can make for systemic crises that are commercially highly fraught.

In Marxist terms, the logic of geographic growth poles is usually expressed as "cores" and "peripheries," with some adding in a "semi-periphery" as well. Growth poles were a definitive feature of capitalism (in the Marxist sense of a specific mode of production) from the start. Capitalism was a European invention that Marx described, in the most graphic and dramatic of terms, as making the world over into a place of owners and workers, bourgeois accumulators and proletarians in despair. Most notable, even in his day and much more so in ours, is the highly uneven character of this make-over. In its simplest form the capitalist countries of the global North are seen as systematically underdeveloping those of the global South. The rising tide of world prosperity does not lift all the boats together, Marxists say. Rather, wealth rushes in to the world's centers, leaving those on the peripheries high and dry.

The notion of the world as constituted of independent cores and dependent peripheries was ostensibly discredited by the success of the East Asian countries that grew so rapidly in the 1970s and 1980s. How come, it was said, if they were being "underdeveloped" by capitalist neoimperialists, they could show such convincing evidence that they were becoming developed? A good question, but the way the issue of Third World debt was dealt with in the 1980s and 1990s made Marxists wonder if the notion of cores and peripheries did not still have considerable substance to it. When an impoverished global South could be shown to be subsidizing a much more well-off global North; when for every pound sterling Britain gave in foreign aid to Africa it got two pounds sterling in debt repayments in return; then it would seem, at least on the surface, that the "development of underdevelopment" was still a feature of global capitalist practice. It would seem that the concepts *core* and *periphery* still had analytic validity, though their meaning may have changed from a statecentric, geographic one (with global core states as opposed to dependent state peripheries) to a social and systemic one (with cores of capitalists and capital managers and peripheries of "relatively disposable short-term temporary, part-time subcontracting, putting-out, and underground economy producers," plus those unemployed) (Cox 1991).

Sectors

Growth poles and regions have invariably been built, as noted above, around leading productive sectors. In very general terms, the world political economy can be said to have seen the predominance in turn of the primary (agricultural) sector, then the secondary (industrial) sector, then the tertiary (service) sector. The changing international division of labor has meant, as noted earlier, the industrialization of parts of labor-poor countries (with new employment opportunities in "export-processing zones") and the deindustrialization of parts of labor-costly ones (with high unemployment in places that once had manufacturing plants). It has also meant knowledge-intensive service industries like computing restructuring global production, with "information and communication . . . replacing raw materials as capital assets" (Walker 1988:39). Members of cultures like that of Japan have adapted industrial capitalism in the process, evolving their own management techniques and combining them with extensive subcontracting and such innovations as "just-in-time" component delivery to produce in the process sophisticated, high-quality commodities at highly competitive prices (Jenkins 1984:4).

Social Aspects

In liberal terms, free marketeering is bound to have uneven social consequences, since those who command more of the factors of production to begin with will be able to use them to profitable advantage, and those who have none will find themselves under a competitive handicap. This is not supposed to matter, however, since the productive power of free market enterprise is such that everyone benefits, albeit some more than others.

In Marxist terms, this is self-serving nonsense, since it mystifies a process of patterned exploitation that Marxists believe is best described in terms of class conflict, and best explained in terms of the social relationships definitive of capitalism itself. The class conflict is not an acute one at this stage. While whose who own and manage the means of production may be said to show signs of cohering on a global scale, those who sell their labor for wages are hopelessly split into territorial and sociological fragments.

Cox (1987:358) defines the dominant social groups in contemporary capitalist society as "those who control the big corporations operating on a world scale, those who control big nation-based enterprises and industrial groups, and . . . locally based petty capitalists." As to the subordinate social groups, he identifies "tendencies," at best, toward class formation among the "new middle stratum of scientific, technical, and supervisory personnel . . . closely linked to the functions of industrial management; . . . established workers [in the advanced capitalist countries]; . . . nonestablished [workers] . . . in advanced capitalist countries; . . . new industrial labor forces in industrializing Third World countries; . . . and . . . marginal populations and so-called informal sector employ[ees]" in both the advanced capitalist countries and the Third World (Cox 1987:368).

The last group, the marginalized one, has grown quickly as populations themselves have grown, as people have spilled from the land, and as industries have proved incapable of employing more than a tiny fraction of all the displaced. It is this last group that might be considered to represent a threat to dominant groups, though this threat has not so far materialized. It is little wonder since the recently marginalized are most likely to be apolitical and preoccupied with having to cope, while the longer-term marginalized find the more dominant groups in society armed against them. The very fact that they exist is used to rationalize police and military repression (Cox 1987:389).

The other social unevenness that most characterizes contemporary growth is that of gender. The growth of the international political economy, as noted by the UN reports cited earlier, clearly benefits men more than women. Not to belabor the point, but global firms seeking cheap, formally free wage labor to do their work for them look for "unfree, 'femalized' . . . wage labour," that is, wage labor with "no job permanency, the lowest wages, longest working hours, most monotonous work, no trade unions, no opportunity to obtain higher qualifications, no promotion, no rights and no social security" (Von Werlhof 1988:169). They find women, but not so much in manufacturing as in service industries. Women have not, in other words, been taking men's jobs in manufacturing. In the service industries, however, "'women's' jobs have expanded in the past couple of decades, while traditional 'male' jobs have been disappearing" (*Economist*, March 5, 1994:61).

The informal world political economy, inhabited in the main by Cox's marginals, is not recognized as part of any global production chain. It is therefore largely ignored, except by Marxist scholars aware of the use of reserve labor armies to put the frighteners on wage laborers in established jobs. And yet even Marxists show little appreciation of the fact that "eighty to ninety per cent of the world population consists . . . of women, peasants, craftsmen, petty traders and such wage labourers whom one can call neither 'free' nor proletarian" (Von Werlhof 1988:171).

Though radically neglected, this massive group is immensely important. After all, it is "not the 10% free wage labourers, but the 90% unfree non-wage labourers [who] are the foundation of accumulation and growth . . . [who are, that is] the real 'producers'" (Von Werlhof 1988:173–174). It is the informal and largely invisible workers who form the base on which the capitalist world political economy is built. They are a kind of proletariat beyond the proletariat. They do the "part-time work, contract work, seasonal and migrant work, illegal work, 'borrowed' work, as well as [the] unpaid work like the so-called 'work for one's own' . . . , [the] 'shadow work' . . . , [the] subsistence work and, [the] mostly 'forgotten', housework" (Von Werlhof 1988:171).

Structure

Just as dramatic in productive terms as sectoral and social unevenness has been the growth of structural disparities between the relative mobility of finance capital and the relative immobility of labor. The mobility of finance capital is not absolute. State makers in richer countries have a wide range of policy instruments they can and do use to impede this mobility. The immobility of labor is also relative. The migration worldwide from the world's countrysides to the world's cities and towns may not cross state borders, but it represents nonetheless the greatest movement of peoples in the history of humankind. People do cross borders to look for work, too, despite policies to prevent them. Allowing a porous border can be a more attractive option than relocating a factory. A lack of local workers for fixed industries can make for lax border controls, and this applies not only to unskilled labor, like the Mexican agricultural workers in California, but also to skilled ones, like the "professional transients" in world advertising, management consultancy, or academia.

Liberals downplay structural disparities. Woodall (1994:20), for example, argues that, in terms of capitalists relocating factories to take advantage of cheaper labor, "a few drops do not make a flood." As the United Nations Development Programme also observes, "of the global flows of foreign direct investment, the developing countries have been getting a steadily smaller share" (UNDP 1992:52). What investment there has been has gone to only a handful of potential recipients (UNDP 1992:52), and as Woodall also points out, this has been in service or agricultural industries, not in industrial manufacturing.

The foreign direct investment (FDI) responsible for the new international division of labor, liberals say, has so far been relatively small. Certainly not enough, except in such industries as textiles and electronics, to account for the "hollowing out" of jobs in countries like the United States. FDI between the richer countries is still greater than that from the richer to the poorer ones. Indeed, "the entire net outflow of investment since 1990 has reduced the rich world's capital stock by a mere 0.5% from what it would otherwise have been" (Woodall 1994: 25). Woodall does not expect the relocation of factories to cheaper labor countries to increase dramatically in the future either, since the labor cost component of commodities is relatively low (and hence relatively little is to be saved by a move on these grounds alone), the infrastructural demands of post-Fordist production chains are relatively high (often too high for cheaper labor countries to meet adequately), and the low education standards of cheaper labor countries restricts the range of what can be relocated. She is wise enough to hedge her bets, however, observing that "you ain't seen nothing yet." As a good liberal, the "net result," she claims, "will, of course, be a more efficient international divison of labour." She also observes, however, that the transition from a less to a more efficient such division "could be painful" (Woodall 1994:26).

Nonliberals take a rather different view. They note, for example, the structural disparity in interest rates, which are higher for poorer countries than they are for richer ones (17 percent throughout the 1980s as opposed to 4 percent). They note the way global firms also tend to bypass poorer countries to invest in richer ones. Moreover, rich states keep tariffs high on those manufactured goods in which poorer countries do have a comparative advantage, such as clothing and shoes, and immigration laws are deliberately used to stop as many laborers as want to from moving from poorer countries into richer ones (stopping, in the process, the equilibrating mechanism of the world labor market from working the way classical liberals say it should) (UNDP 1992:48).

"No market is perfect," as the UNDP points out, "but the international market for labor is one of the most restricted of all. The supply is there. . . . And so could be the demand, if it were up to entrepreneurs only." However, international labor is "steered and controlled by the industrial countries," with the nonindustrial ones denied in the process both direct income and indirect income (such as remittance payments home) of "at least \$250 billion a year" (UNDP 1992:54, 58).

When this picture, and in particular the labor part of it, is put together with the facts that global unemployment is running at rates not seen since the Great Depression in the 1930s, that long-term unemployment has shown a "sharp increase" in Europe in particular (ILO 1994:1), and that the situation in poorer countries is now chronic (UNCTAD 1994:165), and the structural disparities of the global political economy begin to appear much more serious.

Add to this the concentration of finance capital in the hands of bankers and corporate managers (Sklar 1987), and the distance between these people and popular scrutiny and democratic controls (Cox 1992), and the structural situation looks even grimmer. Bankers and the heads of global firms are not hired and fired by those whose lives they have such influence upon. While democracy waxes globally as a governmental ideal, it wanes as a politicoeconomic reality. All of which is hopeful stuff for classical Marxists, for whom the "violent restlessness of capital is the clearest indication of the inadequacy . . . of capital's incapacity to subordinate the power of labour" (Holloway 1994:43). It is not so hopeful, however, for reformist Marxists, who worry that capital has the measure of labor, and that the best labor can expect is more or less of the same, namely, structural exploitation.

Environment

As the combined effects of population growth, resource depletion, and environmental degradation become more evident, it does become problematic how long these effects can be sustained. Simple extrapolation into the future from what prevails in the present is tempting, but it can be highly misleading as well. It can both overestimate and underestimate the magnitude of problems to come. Legitimate environmental concerns do exist, however, and they do generally get bigger as the globe's productive systems do.

It has been apparent for some time now that "growth" and "development" are not synonymous in socioeconomic terms. It is becoming apparent that they are not synonymous in environmental terms either. A world in dynamic equilibrium is not inconsistent with liberal ideals, and scenarios have been sketched of steady-state world political economies that would work along liberal lines. They would be worlds of permanent disparity, though, since liberalists rely on growth to provide for the less advantaged or less entrepreneurial. Redistribution requires governmental intervention, which classical liberals deplore and reformist liberals sanction very warily. Without growth, the market could still work—there would be supply, demand, price signals, and a burgeoning "environmental industry"—but there would be no overall expansion of the system to make the poor richer and keep the rich rich at the same time (Daly 1973). Marxists find this "zero growth" alternative completely unfeasible. Capitalism is a driven system, they say. The desire to accumulate capital, to maximize profits, is what motivates capitalists to expand their reach and increase their holdings, and there is no limit to such a motive except those set from without; for example, those set by some kind of environmental collapse. Implicit in classical Marxism is the assumption that capitalism itself will collapse before the environment does. Neo-Marxists are not so sure, hence the interest they show in ways of protecting those worse off in the here and now, and their concern that we may be developing ourselves to death (Trainer 1988).

Mercantilists are in somewhat of a bind. Some environmental issues are clearly international ones and can only be dealt with cooperatively. Acid rain from another country's factories, or radioactive emissions drifting down from a failed nuclear plant, or logged forests that jeopardize the stability of major atmospheric systems are all clearly threats to autonomy, self-sufficiency, and national strength. Dealing with such issues can require cooperative initiatives that compromise the very sovereignty mercantilists are supposed to defend, however.

Greens of various hue are likely to indict production for production's sake, though the more liberal of them are likely to see marketeering as able to provide the resources necessary to deal with production's worst environmental effects. The more radical of them, on the other hand, are likely to recommend much more localized production systems and much less of that long-standing mainstay of the global market, long-distance trade.

5

World Trade

❖ **Cheryl Payer (1974) "The Lawyer's Typist: Variations on a Theme by Paul Samuelson"**

Nora, who was Improving her Mind with a night school course in introductory economics, settled down to do her homework. That week's assignment was the chapter on international trade in the textbook for the course (which the instructor had assured the class was The Very Best, being the seventh edition of Paul Samuelson's *Economics: An Introductory Analysis*).

She found it difficult to follow, and therefore boring, until her attention was suddenly caught by a passage which seemed to make more sense than the rest:

> A traditional example used to illustrate this paradox of comparative advantage is the case of the best lawyer in town who is also the best typist in town. Will he not specialise in law and leave typing to a secretary? How can he afford to give up precious time from the legal field, where his comparative advantage is very great, to perform typing activities in which he is efficient but in which he lacks *comparative* advantage? Or look at it from the secretary's point of view. She is less efficient than he in both activities, but her relative disadvantage compared with him is least in typing. Relatively speaking, she has comparative advantage in typing.
>
> So with countries. Suppose America produces food with one-third the labour that Europe does, and produces clothing with one-half the labour. Then we shall see that America has a comparative disadvantage in clothing—this, despite the fact that America is absolutely efficient in everything. By the same token, Europe has a comparative advantage in clothing (Samuelson, p. 647).

Nora, you see, was in fact a typist, who worked for one of the partners in a law office. It was natural that she should perk up when she discovered that the difficult concept of comparative advantage in international trade was being explained with an example from her own life. Skipping briefly over the second paragraph, she returned to the first one to read it more slowly and carefully, for she felt an instant empathy with the secretary in the parable.

Too much empathy, perhaps. Her first reaction was an uneasy resentment at the idea that her boss might after all be superior to her in the realm of

121

secretary skills—the only marketable skill she had. It was bad enough, she thought, that he should know enough about the law to be able to command high fees and to pay her to do his office drudgery—but to deny that she had an absolute superiority in doing that kind of work, why, that was insult added to injury! Even though she kept reminding herself that it was just a story, the sense of humiliation lingered.

Nora turned back to study the paragraph again. "Or look at it from the secretary's point of view. She is less efficient than he in both activities . . . " At this point Nora snorted. Less efficient in law practice! Non-existent was a better word. How could one compare efficiency when she'd never even been to law school (even if she had picked up some of the techniques and the jargon through rendering assistance to Mr Woodbore, her boss).

She stopped laughing and began to think about it. Denigrating as the paragraph in the textbook was to her, it had stirred in her mind the first suggestion of the possibility that perhaps she ought to have the same skills which her boss was exercising, in order to make the example a fair test. What if (she choked with amusement at the idea) she turned out to be a more efficient lawyer than he?

That delicious idea brought a further problem to her mind. Just how could efficiency be tested in such occupations? There were typing and dictation tests, of course, which measured your speed in each of those activities. But that, she knew, was only a small part of the skills which a really good secretary was expected to have; and, confident as she was that she was a good secretary, intelligent and reliable and discreet, she had no idea of how such qualities could ever be quantified.

And how in the world, if she was a lawyer, could her efficiency in that activity be tested and measured against, say, that of Mr Woodbore? It just wasn't possible to time the preparation of legal briefs the same way one could clock typing speeds with a stopwatch, deducting errors from the total score.

From her previous lessons in the Samuelson textbook, Nora had learned however that there was supposed to be a direct relationship between *price* and efficiency. Perhaps the efficiency of lawyers could be measured by what they earned? But as she thought about Mr Woodbore, his partners, and the other lawyers that she knew, she was not really satisfied with this hypothesis. She was not convinced that Mr Woodbore, who was a senior partner and handled a lot of corporation work, was more efficient (for surely efficiency had something to do with intelligence and hard work) than the young lawyers she knew who preferred to handle draft and civil liberties cases—but he certainly earned a lot more. And as for what she knew about the earnings of *women* lawyers (she had met one or two)—well! she was not prepared to accept that as the measure of her efficiency when (if?) she became a lawyer.

She read the passage in the text again. It certainly did imply that Professor Samuelson was equating efficiency with the lawyers' earnings.

The first paragraph, however, really didn't go far enough to give her an idea of what comparative advantage would mean if she were a lawyer too, so she read the second paragraph carefully. Then she got out her paper and pencil and began to figure, muttering out loud as she did so:

"Now Mr Woodbore earns $120 a day while I earn $30. If I am only one third as efficient as a lawyer and only one half as efficient as a secretary, that means I could earn $40 a day as a lawyer and he could earn $60 as a typist. (That's ridiculous, even an efficient woman lawyer would earn more than an extremely efficient male typist the way things are set up now, but I don't know how else to figure it.) Well, obviously he'd be worse off to be a secretary—but *I'd* be better off to be a lawyer *even* if I was at a relative as well as an absolute disadvantage there!

"But if I have a *relative* advantage as a lawyer, being half as efficient as he is but only one third as efficient as a secretary, then I would be earning $60 as a lawyer while he earns $90 as a secretary (that's even more absurd, no secretary could possibly earn that much—I wonder why not?). I would be better off, but he certainly wouldn't be happy to take the cut in earnings. But Paul Samuelson seems to be saying he ought to! That is, he would have if he'd worked it out as I'm doing.

"But then he can't be correct when he argues that everyone would be better off to do what he or she has a relative advantage doing. Obviously anybody at all would be better off—personally speaking—doing what pays the best (which in this case is practising law), even if they're not as efficient as somebody else."

But if everybody were a lawyer and nobody did the typing, it would be an impossible situation. For the sake of argument Nora adopted an unselfish point of view and thought about the implications to National Income, rather than to her own salary, of the various combinations she had been playing with. Nora had learned enough economics by now to know that National Income equals the sum of everybody's earnings, so it was a simple exercise.[1]

She discovered that in the case where it was hypothesized that she had the relative advantage as a lawyer, it made no difference at all to the National Income if Mr Woodbore worked full time as a lawyer at $120 a day and she as a typist at $30 a day; if he worked full time as a typist at $90 a day and she as a lawyer at $60; or if both worked half a day at each task, in which case his daily earnings would be $105 and hers would be $45. The sum in all three cases would be $150.

When she worked out the sums on the opposite assumption—that her relative advantage was as a typist, not a lawyer—then the National Income would fall, if she insisted on working as a lawyer, from $150 a day to $100. But Nora was beginning to suspect by this time that this might have more to do with the absolute level of typists' salaries rather than with the inherent virtues of comparative advantage. After all, lawyers really couldn't produce any faster or more efficiently than the secretarial work relating to their work was done. And Nora did not forget that even when the National Income fell by one third *her* salary would have gone up by one third if she were a lawyer rather than a secretary.

Nora had decided by the end of the exercise that the absolute disadvantage of being a secretary was a lot more important than any relative advantage to be had doing it efficiently. But Mr Woodbore flatly refused to take a typing test when she showed her calculations to him the next day, and Nora applied to the local law school. She was accepted in the course because, under pressure of the women's movement, the law school had upped its quota of female students from 5 to 15 per cent. Since she has not graduated yet, we do not know whether she will find it to her advantage to hire a secretary to do her typing for her when she begins to practice law.

She will be eternally grateful to Professor Samuelson for showing her (albeit probably against his will) where her true interest lies. She has not, however, opened his textbook since that fateful evening and occasionally still wonders whether the truths she discovered apply also to trade between nations.

EXCHANGE AND GROWTH

The cornerstone of the liberal conception of long-distance trade is that of comparative advantage. As Payer shows, this may not offer as much support to market arguments as classical liberals typically suppose. Along with the growth in global production has gone growth in global trade, and whether it be comparative advantage or some less automatic mechanism that prompts it, goods and services are now moved in increasing quantities, often following land and sea routes that are thousands of years old.

Global Trade

The international trade of the mercantile era, as noted, is giving way to global trade within transnational firms. Goods and services cross state borders, but they do so under nonstate, suprastate auspices.

Global trade is moving from primary and secondary sector trade to tertiary sector trade as well. The world tourist trade, for example, discussed earlier, is one of the biggest industries in the world. The tangible component to this trade involves the moving and storing, in planes and hotels, of increasingly large numbers of people. These people are usually intent on consuming something less tangible, however, called a "holiday," which though it may have tangible components to it, like views of distant mountains or rides in fun parks, involves the subjective appreciation of a mood, sensation, or idea. This appreciation takes place in the context of a strict mental division between "work" and "leisure."

Global trade, in other words, is also becoming more abstract. This is very evident when we come to the trade in credit, national currencies, or in such financial instruments as derivatives. Here no transport is needed, only rapid and capacious channels of communication. The trade in national currencies alone is now forty times more valuable than the trade in commodities (Helleiner 1994:163). Contemporary technology and the capitalist pursuit of profit have fused to create a realm of "virtual" trading, or "hypertrade," which, as we shall see later, is one of the most compelling parts of the world political economy.

How can trade become "abstract"? To answer this question we need to look more closely at the phenomenon of trade itself.

Liberals will set up the analysis of trade in terms of autonomous states and firms, which exchange goods and services. International trade has been growing as such for several hundred years. In 1667, for example, over a hundred years before Adam Smith's classic articulation of the liberalist doctrine, we find John Dryden, the English poet, talking of the advantages of world trade in what are unmistakeably liberal terms. In his "Annus Mirabilis," he writes:

> Instructed ships shall sail to quick Commerce,
> By which remotest Regions are alli'd;
> Which makes one City of the Universe,
> Where some may gain, and all may be suppli'd.
> (McVeagh 1981:51)

Nations exchange goods in a market, Smith says, because of some comparative advantage they possess, or some comparative advantage they have been able to make for themselves. They trade between them the goods and services they make and do best. Even if one or more countries are good at making and doing everything, it is still more efficient, Ricardo went on to add, if they trade between them those goods and services they make and do best.

The notion of *efficiency* here is a restricted one, however, as Payer points out. The very definition of efficiency itself is restricted. It refers only to the "efficient allocation of resources," which is not a notion mercantilists would accept, since to mercantilists "efficiency" means "state survival." Open competition may work for those who set up the system in the first place. For the rest, mercantilists say, state regulation and protection is mandatory.

Mercantilists would rather that nations remained autonomous, since it is autonomy, they believe, that makes a state strong and most helps it endure. They eschew trade altogether as a pernicious source of "insecurity, dependence and vulnerability" (Gilpin 1987: 172). Or they conduct it along chains of vertically integrated production and distribution that maximize the returns to the core firm and country while minimizing the erosion of sovereign controls. (Vertically integrated firms, as mentioned earlier, organize the different parts of a production process, from the raw materials at one end to the sale of the finished goods at the other, in such a way as to minimize costs, maximize profits, and create "a kind of protective envelope" that "cushions" the firm from market forces [Caporaso 1987c:197]).

Marxists and neo-Marxists see trade as part of the capitalist process of value extraction. They see the whole trade system as skewed in favor of those with more capital against those with less. They find world trade as problematic as mercantilists do, in other words, though for very different reasons. The more extremist Marxists await a revolutionary outcome. The more reformist Marxists, on the other hand, less sure radical change will eventuate soon, seek meanwhile to protect the world's poor from the exploitative logic of international capitalism. Like mercantilists, they see the market as favoring those who built it and who benefited most from it first. Coming to interstate trade later, like most countries did in Africa, South and Central America, and Asia, meant coming to it, reformist Marxists say, at a distinct disadvantage. The only way to cope with this disadvantage was to implement policies to compensate for it. In reformist Marxist terms, this meant a country's getting special access for its exports to the markets of richer ones, getting special trade credits and trade aid, and putting up tariff and nontariff barriers against imports likely to destroy local industries. This was not a guarantee of prosperity, but as MacEwan (1992:29) argues (in distinctly illiberal terms),

> the idea that active political control of a country's foreign economic relations is necessarily destructive is about as silly as the idea that life is not worth living—though of course some government control can be very nasty and some lives are not worth living. Just because it is complicated and takes some effort to lead a worthwhile and happy life, this does not justify the simple solution of suicide. And just because it is complicated and takes some effort to forge a useful set of political controls of economic life, this does not justify the simple solution of free trade.

With such contending "truths" in mind, what can we say about world trade?

Trade starts with barter, that is, the direct exchange of goods or services for goods or services. Barter does not need, nor does it use, a medium of exchange like money. People barter whatever they have as surplus, whatever they have some advantage in producing, or, if they're desperate, anything at all. My father did the gardening for the osteomasseur who treated my mother's prolapsed spinal disc. Entrepreneurs in the eighteenth and nineteenth centuries traded guns and industrial trinkets for South Pacific bêche-de-mer and sandalwood. It's all barter. It's all trade.

The simple trade that barter entails is a feature of hard times. It is often the only alternative for the poor, which is why it's a feature of hard-sell industries, like the armaments one, where manufacturers use the fears and desires of poor state purchasers to do deals, even though the purchasers have only commodities, not lines of credit, with which to pay.

In the relatively more prosperous world, post–World War II, the more highly industrialized countries have traded multilaterally, using money. The bartering and the bilateralism that were a feature of the Great Depression period of the 1930s (liberals would argue they were key causes of that Depression and of the war that followed it) were kept on as a way to trade with the socialist bloc, which was a political economy apart. It was also used as a way of trading with and between the poorer countries of the so-called Third World. With the collapse of the socialist bloc, the reemergence of its component states as members of the impoverished part of the capitalist world political economy, and the ongoing decline of many of those already in that marketeering world, trade by barter remains an important aspect of world trade. Estimates range from 5 to 40 percent of all world trade (Grimwade 1989:261)—admittedly, a large margin for error, but even at the lower estimate of 5 percent we are still talking about a considerable volume of exchange.

"Counter trade," as barter is called, remains a popular option, then, referring in practice to a wide range of ways of doing deals, some of which even use money.

"Pure barter," as the label implies, involves the direct exchange of goods and services—oil for industrial machinery, perhaps, or dairy products for computing services.

"Balanced flow" barter ensures that trade between two countries works out at the same book value over a set period of time (say, three or five years). Accounts are established in each other's banks. These are denominated in monetary terms. In terms of the trade itself, however, no money passes between the countries concerned. It is "pure barter," but it uses monetary accounting systems to value and balance the international exchange.

"Counter purchase" barter (or "compensation trade," as it's also called) occurs where an importing country closes a deal because whoever is exporting to it agrees to buy back some other good or service as part of the deal. As Grimwade (1989:257) says, this usually involves two separate contracts. Under one, goods or services are sold to a buyer for a specified price in hard currency. Under the other, sellers are required to use part or even all of what they've earned to buy back goods or services from the buyer. Indeed, there is even a kind of counter purchase specifically called "buy-back," where sellers buy back from a plant they've just provided, part or all of that plant's output as part or whole payment for having supplied the plant in the first place.

"Coproduction" barter is more complex. It takes place between firms in different countries that have different technological capacities. Imagine, for example, a particular product assembled from a number of components of different technological complexity, a North-world firm making the advanced components and a South-world firm making the less advanced ones. If these firms swap components and assemble the finished products from the complete inventory, either at home or in some other place where assembly is cheaper, they both get to benefit.

"Offset" barter is a tight kind of coproduction barter, or it can be a counter purchase agreement. To close a deal, for example, a seller may specifically agree to take some part of what is being sold by the buyer. This offsets (reduces) for the buyer the cost of what is being bought (a coproduction deal). The seller may also accept entirely different goods and services, in payment or part payment for what is being sold (a counter purchase deal). An airplane manufacturer, for example, may use plane parts made by the buyer to offset the cost to that buyer of the finished plane he is buying. Or the manufacturer may accept something else in return, such as bananas or dairy goods.

"Switch trade" barter is where one country sells more to another country than it buys, building up over time a credit surplus with that other country. The first country then uses the credit surplus it's built up to buy goods from a third country. The third country takes this credit and uses it to buy goods from the second (deficit) country, goods that then act, in effect, as payment for those originally supplied to the first country (Grimwade 1989:260). No money changes hands and the system is infinitely expandable. Switch trading often involves, as a consequence, more than three countries, and discounts may be offered to get rid of unused credit. There are banks and trading firms that specialize in brokering such deals as a way of making a living for themselves.

Poor state traders like counter trade because it lets them trade when they otherwise couldn't. It lets them pay off debts, get around protectionist import quotas and tariff barriers, and diversify.

Free trade marketeers don't like counter trade, because it uses reciprocity rather than pricing. They see it being used for dumping and as leading to protectionism, even though it can be used in practice to get around protectionism. They think of it as a precapitalist hangover. It's too basic, too old-fashioned, and it doesn't provide for profit in monetary terms, profit that can then be used to store value and be invested, making for more enterprise and profit.

If we privilege free trade instead, as liberals recommend, then we can trade either what we have an absolute surfeit of (as Smith recommended) or we can trade what we have a comparative surfeit of (as Ricardo thought we should). Historically, absolute advantage was the basis of international trade. In some cases it still is. Oil, for example, can be exchanged for anything—gold-plated Cadillacs, desert robes by Yves St. Laurent, sophisticated weaponry. Given the global demand for it, oil confers upon those who own the source of its supply an abundance of finished goods and services. No one wants the desert sands above the Saudi fields in quite the same way, for example, though they conceivably might one day, given the march of technological innovation.

If, as a state-made citizenry, you don't have an absolute advantage in anything, you still have your labor power, and with it you can make a relative advantage by mixing your labor power with technical know-how, plus the entrepreneurial use of credit, management skills, and access to other resources. The consequence may well be highly marketable commodities that you can sell. By combining the factors of production in innovative ways, that is, you can make a comparative advantage of the sort Ricardo saw as the central inspiration for free trade.

Comparative Advantage

"Many have difficulty with this principle," Burningham (1991:320) notes, "although the idea is simple enough. Suppose," he says, "that a medical doctor can also type, file and take shorthand better than [her] secretary . . . " Despite such a plethora of talents the doctor will still opt to practice as a doctor rather than work as an office temp, since this is obviously where a doctor's greatest comparative advantage (and greatest earning power) lies. This is a commonsense decision, though as Payer points out, commonsense can mislead. Like the lawyer's typist in Payer's example, the doctor's typist is apparently less "efficient" in both professions. But don't we bias our example by taking only the doctor's or the lawyer's point of view? How fair are these comparisons, anyway? Aren't they skewed from the start? After all, while a doctor or lawyer may have learned some secretarial skills, their secretaries will rarely have done medicine or law. If they had, they might have found they are better doctors or lawyers than their bosses, in which case their bosses should be the secretaries and they should be doctors or lawyers (assuming they had no other choice). What, furthermore, as Payer asks, does that troubled word *efficiency* mean? Not only is it difficult to measure the efficiency of medical, legal, or secretarial practice, but if, for convenience, we do equate them in terms of their relative price ("wages"), then, as Payer (1974:47) points out, "anybody at all would be better off—personally speaking—doing what pays the best . . . even if they're not as efficient as somebody else." In other words, secretaries should be doctors or lawyers, even bad doctors or lawyers.

Since liberals often liken countries to the individuals in the example just cited, the same logic applies there, too, namely, that despite the seeming advantage of comparative advantage, this is only advantage for the higher-earning countries. For lower-earning countries the absolute disadvantage in being poor is greater than any relative advantage there might be in being poor "efficiently." The solution, then, is not to look for some relative advantage to sell, but to try to get an absolute advantage, which is exactly what a number of Asian nations (unimpressed by nineteenth-century English liberal logic) have chosen to do to become more "developed."

Though arguably flawed, the logic of comparative advantage is still widely prescribed. Thus we find Woodall, in her survey of the global economy in 1994, pointing out that a "bond dealer . . . is quite happy to pay a low-wage laundry worker rather than wash his own clothes," that "specialisation increases the living standards of both parties," and that the "case for free trade with China is no different" (Woodall 1994:5). She says nothing about the laundry worker, of course, who would clearly be better off learning to trade in bonds rather than washing bond dealers' clothes. She says nothing about China in this respect either.

As countries converge upon similar levels of development, the competition among them makes judgments of comparative advantage so fine that it is often hard to see what purpose can be served by their trade. What are we to make, for example, of the fact that more than 60 percent of international trade in the post–World War II period has been among developed countries, that these countries have very similar industrial structures, and that much of this trade has been "intraindustry," where one industrialized country exports cars to another, for example, and imports that other country's cars back again (Gilpin 1987:177)?

The value of comparative advantage has clearly declined as it has become more a thing of state and firm policy than of competing factors of production. Indeed, the explanatory value of comparative advantage has declined so far by now that even a staunch liberal like Gilpin concedes that as an argument for free trade, it has "necessarily . . . become less relevant" (Gilpin 1987:178).

All liberals are apt to rally at this point, however, as Gilpin quickly does, wagging his finger at nationalistic protectionists and arguing that free trade, while it won't help everyone, and won't provide equitable outcomes, will, if given time and the right attitude ("appropriate policies") benefit all in the end. What is more, it will benefit all "in absolute terms." (The notion that we have to wait for the long run in this regard is very similar to the Marxist notion that in the last instance there will be revolution and a new mode of production.) The implacable nature of liberal opposition to mercantilism was well expressed by key U.S. policymakers in the choice of epithet they used in condemning the first director-general elect of the World Trade Organisation. The unfortunate man, U.S. critics said, was a "protectionist," a term that according to the (classically liberal) periodical, the *Economist*, is "perhaps the most painful barb in the lexicon of trade politics." So bad was the candidate that Americans "stooped to the P-word," the *Economist* (March 25, 1995: 90) said, as the only way of expressing the depths of their disapproval.

To mercantilists, this is nonsense. The free trade that the use of comparative advantage requires favors the most developed, they say. It throws countries open to exploitation by those with politico-economic power. It promotes specialization, especially in commodities for export, and in doing so "reduces flexibility, increases . . . vulnerability, . . . threatens . . . national security," and otherwise rots the moral fiber of the state (Gilpin 1987:183). Rather than risk being subordinated by world capitalists, people need protection and a trade policy that builds up domestic industries capable of sustaining import substitution and a self-sufficient state. This was the view historically of German and U.S. analysts, who saw free trade as a cover for continued British trade supremacy. And it is the view of underdog traders today.

Mercantilists advocate a wide range of trade restrictions to frustrate liberalist resolve. These include tariffs (taxes on imports), quotas (specific limits on the quantity of imports or on their value), subsidies (made to particular industries to help them be competitive, such as depreciation allowances, cash grants, tax holidays, and the like), voluntary restrictions on imports (voluntary in name only and imposed by an exporting country under pressure from an importing country), currency controls (that limit the availability of foreign currency for the purchase of foreign goods), and administrative regulations (such as bureaucratic procedures, systems of advance payment, minimum domestic product content rules, special marketing standards, and special safety and health provisions) (Burningham 1991:324–325).

Unequal Exchange

In Marxist terms, capitalists make their money not from trade or the comparative advantages that liberals so prize, so much as from the laborers who make the commodities or provide the services that capitalists trade with. Capitalists are always seeking to minimize the costs of the factors of production they use, including the factor of labor power. They seek cheap, motivated, disciplined workers, who will exchange maximal value (in terms of their work) for minimal value (in terms of their wages). The more unequal this exchange, the higher the profit. The price of all the goods and services that capitalists trade will include this unequal exchange, and since workers of the sort capitalists seek are predominantly women, trade prices will be a statement about gender inequalities as well as class ones.

Growth

Strange (1988:162) cites the global growth in international trade over the last hundred years as the first, and arguably the foremost, of its definitive features. "During the whole of the present century," she says, "trade between countries has grown faster than their total production. That is to say, the proportion of production sold across state frontiers has steadily risen." Not only the proportion of production traded across state borders, but the total volume of trade across such frontiers has grown, too, with the exception of periods like that of the Great Depression in the 1930s, the recession of the early 1980s, or major wars. At these times it has declined or fallen (Green and Sutcliffe 1987:172).

One would expect such growth, given what has happened to the international political economy as a whole over this period. But it is still important to know how quickly world trade itself has grown. A scant forty years after World War II, for example, it was fifty-five times greater than it had been in 1945 (Strange 1988:162).

Since trade has been a feature of human society for as far back as we can reliably discern (people wanting what they don't make at home and exchanging what they do for commodities from afar), and since the number of people has been growing in the world, too, a change like this is hardly a surprise. It is still remarkable, however.

In valorizing marketeering, liberals automatically sanction exchange. The modern success of liberal doctrine has legitimized trading as a creative, affirmative, wealth-making, peace-making practice, and this, too, has promoted the growth of trade. The mercantilist attempt to restrict this legitimacy to those trading ventures that directly enhance state autonomy and strength has not been able to halt the process. Marxist criticism of the use of trade as an instrument of exploitation has had even less of an inhibitory effect. And though the growth of trade has been overshadowed in recent times by the international flows of short-term and long-term investment, and the building of "world factories," it remains a key and still expanding part of the world political economy.

Uneven Growth

Like the world political economy as a whole, trade has also grown unevenly—ideologically (in terms of the hegemonic as opposed to marginalized worldviews); temporally (in fits and starts); geographically (with some parts of the world trading more than others); sectorally (from raw materials to finished goods and services); socially (in terms of who participates); and structurally (in terms of the arguments about who benefits from the terms of trade).

Ideologies

The liberal, mercantilist, and Marxist ways of analyzing trade have all been discussed. The truths of the matter are no less significant as perceived by marginalized groups like environmentalists, indigenous peoples, or women, however. The success of the more orthodox perspectives on international trade as opposed to the less orthodox ones is the most notable unevenness in ideological terms.

The Cold War that followed World War II introduced another ideological unevenness into the growth of world trade, and that was an East-West one. The world trading system was in practice two systems, one marketeering and capitalist, the other committed to central planning and so-called socialism. On the one side the United States sought to restrain its traders from dealing with socialist states, while placing similar restrictions upon its various allies. On the other side the ruling regimes of the communist world placed restrictions on their traders, too. Though this ideological exclusivity was breaking down, in trading terms, long before the end of the Cold War, it remained a powerful inhibiting factor to the end, and it is obvious that the consequences of such a long ideological rift will be felt for a considerable time to come.

Temporal Aspects

The general growth trend conceals a host of particular irregularities. As the production system as a whole has boomed and busted, so has world trade. In the last century or so, for example, there have been three notable periods of rapid growth in world production—after the Great Depression of the 1870s until World War I; after World War I until the Great Depression of the 1930s; and after World War II until the recession of the 1970s and 1980s. These have been periods of rapid trade growth, too (Strange 1988:166–167).

It is interesting to note, Strange (1988:167) says, that the expansionary phases in world trade occurred despite the protectionist measures of a number of the main trading nations: "Before World War I, for instance, trade was growing rapidly, even though all the fastest-growing industrial countries—the United States, Japan, Germany and France—were . . . highly protectionist. . . . The forces of the market appeared to triumph over the policies of states." This seems paradoxical unless full measure is given to the fact that a double game was being played. None of these countries was an advocate of free trade at the time, though none of them eschewed it either.

After World War II the triumphant leaders of the United States planned to put in place a package of measures that would produce an open international political economy over which they could still have some control. The Marshall Plan was the basis of their postwar foreign policy. This plan was designed to ensure a stable system for exchanging currencies, and free trade. "Free trade," in relative terms at least, is what they managed to get, despite the protectionist proclivities of Japan, Germany, and even the United States itself.

Environment

There is one temporal dimension not covered above, and that is the future. The growing problems of pollution, resource depletion, and overpopulation portend a time of planetary ill-health that few in the years ahead may be able to escape. We can't know. What we do know, though, is that the human impact on the natural environment is immense.

Trade itself in not the cause of most environmental concerns. There are important issues, however, that link world trade to transnational pollution and to resource depletion in particular. One of these issues must surely be the extent to which what gets traded seems to be, in principle, redundant. Half of world trade, for example, consists of the importing and exporting of essentially the same goods (Low 1992).

The main question is whether freer trade would be worse for the environment than more-controlled trade. Would freer trade lead to competitive deregulation, for example, lower environmental standards, and "dirty" industries migrating to less-regulated places—"pollution havens," as they are called?

Freer trade could conceivably encourage production that is less damaging to the environment, rather than more damaging. Indeed, in liberalist terms, the demand for environmental repair industries should be met, once the price is right, by an efficient supply of them.

It is still feared, however, that lax standards do act as a pull factor for those industries that want to cut costs by not having to pay for pollution inhibition measures. Perhaps, therefore, we should regulate to control transnational pollution. Might this not act as a push factor, driving dirty industries out to produce and trade from somewhere else? Regulation could only work if it were universal, in other words, which in a state-made world would require agreement of a kind that is always going to be hard to get.

Marketeers show relatively little interest in environmental matters. They see increasing world trade as a result of increasing world commerce and as much to be desired. Both are part of a wealth-creating system that raises living standards in poorer parts of the world and provides the means to invest in a cleaner environment. They see the ideology of environmentalism, however, as an open-ended argument for restricting trade. They see it as a direct threat.

Environmentalists themselves, though more particularly the deep greens, see the planet being gutted by opportunistic entrepreneurs in the drive to industrialize. They place an absolute value on not damaging or destroying the world's ecosystems, large or small. They want green world trade, as they want green world production systems.

Whether we can get sustainable global development without an end to growth, and therefore an end to the world capitalist system (which Marxists see as predicated on growth), is still, of course, an unanswered question. Fortunately or unfortunately, it is one that will be answered definitively only by the future.

Geography

"To those who have shall be given more," it seems. Thus those parts of the world that mastered capitalist industrialism first were the parts that prospered first, and with their prosperity were able to buy the world's produce, either from each other or from elsewhere.

Most trade in finished products takes place today between the relatively rich countries. These are the ones who sell and can buy the most goods and services, simply because they have the means to do so. It is between the countries of the "developed" world, in other words, that we find the strongest growth in world trade. As to the relatively poorer ones, only 3 percent of the global trade total takes place between them (so-called South-South trade), while trade from South to North is now less than 10 percent of the total global sum.

Thus the "developing" countries enter the markets as unequal partners, leaving it again with unequal rewards (UNDP 1992:68). When they do try and trade they find themselves prevented from doing so by rich state protectionists. As they don't have the funds to wait and sell at the most profitable prices, they have to take "distress" ones, with the "disturbing result . . . that rich producers are paid more than poor ones for identical goods" (UNDP 1992:60).

The least well-off countries in the world have been the greatest losers, however. They suffer in a more serious form from all the liabilities mentioned above. As a result most sub-Saharan African countries, for example, have seen their trade share fall to a quarter of what it was thirty years ago. And though the poorest countries have nearly 10 percent of the world's population, they engage in less than one-half of 1 percent of the world's trade (UNDP 1992:48).

For the duration of the Cold War there was another notable geographic unevenness in the growth of world trade, and that was the East-West one discussed above in ideological terms, and earlier again in terms of the uneven growth of the world political economy as a whole. With the collapse of the Soviet Union, its rapid conversion to capitalism, and the beginnings of a similar conversion evident in mainland China, the grounds for this particular disparity have been or are in the process of being removed. The disparities remain, however. The catch-up task is enormous and despite notable change in China in particular, few expect the consequences of the Cold War to disappear in one or even two generations.

Strange points to another geographic unevenness, one that is a legacy of an earlier global system as well, namely, that of the great European empires of the nineteenth century. The investments that the imperial powers made in their colonies at that time, and in the first part of the twentieth century, had lasting effects on trade flows, she says, so much so that "trade figures for African countries thirty years after independence still show a marked partiality for trade with France, or Britain, as does Indonesian trade with the Netherlands" (Strange 1988:170).

A similar effect has followed upon U.S. investments in Latin America and Japanese investments in Southeast Asia. The local preponderance of these capitalist powers is reflected, Strange (1988:170) says, in trade flows "in both directions," flows that favor, as one would expect, the countries of the investors, not those of the investees.

Sectors

The uneven growth of the world trade system is also apparent in changes in the nature of the goods traded. Since trade patterns are a picture, in a sense, of the commodity preferences of those who buy and sell, and those doing most of the buying and selling are those who live in capitalist, industrialized countries, it is no surprise that most traded goods are secondary and tertiary rather than primary ones. Today it is factory-made finished goods, and services like education, entertainment, tourism, and insurance, that predominate. This is a marked change from the nineteenth century, when primary products accounted for two-thirds of world trade (Strange 1988: 167), though there is one glaring exception to this trend and that is oil, a commodity of no account last century, that in the twentieth became a kind of black, liquid gold.

Social Aspects

Who are the world's traders? In liberalist terms, they are the entrepreneurs who, risking ruin, bring goods between countries to sell in their markets, and who, in doing so, enrich some more than others, while enriching us all. Unevenness matters less to them than the growth they make possible for the system as a whole, though traders do, unequivocally, make for unevenness.

The ones who benefit most from world trade are the world's rich. Despite the industrial revolution and the capacity of our species to make food and other commodities on an unprecedented scale, the disparity between the world's rich and the world's poor is very great, and trade is one aspect of the global process that sustains that disparity.

In mercantilist terms, the world's traders are either traitors or licensed patriots. The latter create international industries that trade as much as possible to national advantage. Unevenness is not a problem, since only national vulnerability is.

In Marxist terms, the world's traders are capitalists who seek profits. They produce by exchanging. They are the creators of social classes whose interests are so divergent, so uneven, that only revolution can reconcile them. A revolution as such has not yet occurred, and unevenness prevails, which is why reformist Marxists want to act now. They want to alleviate the human suffering this entails.

"Both the state and the market," argues Sylvester, are masculinist communities that dominate those outside them, "those" in this case being specifically "women," and the domination being that conceptualized by labels like "free exchange, comparative advantage or division of labor" (Sylvester 1990:240). To focus only on what states and firms do, or on how the world capitalist system works, is to miss, she says, how social attitudes and social practices have gender-specific effects upon states, firms, and the world capitalist system itself. More particularly it is to miss the gender dimension of the trading arrangements that are made between states and firms and within the world capitalist system. It is to miss, in short, the female standpoint. It is to tell stories about how states and firms, the world capitalist system and world trade work, in ways that deny women "agency"; in ways that deny, that is, that women "do" anything. Which is nonsense, since women are traders, too, though reading the large literature on world trade one would hardly think so.

Structure

In practical terms all this unevenness means dire structural inequalities. If we look at the disparities between the richer and poorer states, we find that the poorer ones seek to trade in primary sector products, that is, mineral and agricultural ones. We find that as a consequence of recession, of the substitution of other materials, and of overproduction (as well as shorter-term factors like business cycles, speculation, and the weather) there has been a decline in prices for primary agricultural commodities like coffee, cocoa, sugar, and rubber, or primary raw materials like bauxite, tin, copper, lead, and zinc. We find a price squeeze on primary commodities, in other words (UNDP 1992:59). At the same time the pressures to make money remain unrelenting. It is in this light that we must read poor state needs to pay off international debts and to buy what they are not able to make and do. It is in this light that we can begin to see the extent of the structural disadvantages such countries face.

Poorer countries, acutely aware of their plight, have striven to diversify and industrialize. The depth of their dependence on particular primary commodities can be so great, however, they cannot—particularly with declining prices—readily overcome it. They may need the revenues from such commodities too much, however, to make any "fundamental structural changes" (UNDP 1992:62). As to industrialization, it is obvious that by processing and finishing goods, poorer countries can add value to them and can make much more money. What they find when they do try to manufacture and trade more finished goods, however, is a rising wall of rich world protectionism—tariff and nontariff barriers designed to keep them in their place. It remains to be seen how much the World Trade Organisation will be able to break down this wall.

Meanwhile trade in the most technologically innovative products and services remains a rich world monopoly. Here protectionism is at its most intense. The question, for example, of intellectual property rights, that is, the protection of patents, copyright, and trademarks, has become a pressing one for richer countries determined to keep their productive edge. Such determination is "in stark contrast," as the UNDP points out, to liberalist notions of openness and freedom, and betrays a structural disparity at the heart of the world trading system that no amount of poor world "development" has so far been able to undo (UNDP 1992:66).

Indeed, it has even been argued that we are entering a new trading era, that of "adversarial" trade, where the objective is to maximize market shares rather than to seek complementarities—as in Smith's day—or to compete—as, until recently, in our own (Drucker 1989:129). "Complementary trade," says Drucker (1989: 129–130), "seeks to establish a partnership. Competitive trade aims at creating a customer. Adversarial trade aims at dominating an industry. Complemetary trade is a courtship. Competitive trade is fighting a battle. Adversarial trade aims at winning the war by destroying the enemy's army and its capacity to fight."

Where adversarial trade prevails, mere competition is inappropriate. Other defenses must be found. Liberals eschew protectionism, so they seek other alternatives. One of these is regionalism, arguably a new kind of protectionism, one of a collectivist kind. Another alternative is "reciprocity," a concept that is set, Drucker says, to revolutionize the world trade system, since it is "clearly the only trade policy that can effectively work in a world . . . that features adversarial trade." It is this concept, he believes, that will integrate the world economy, just as competitive trade integrated the international economy (Drucker 1989:132). Clearly, structural changes are afoot, though they are not ones that would seem, in Drucker's scenario at least, to include the poorer countries at all.

RESTRUCTURING WORLD TRADE

The competitive trading order of the contemporary world was put together by capitalist, industrialist countries after World War II. The agreement to create a General Agreement on Tariffs and Trade (GATT) was meant to restructure world trade, and while "restructuring" may be too strong a word for what went on in practice, the GATT did become a key feature of the global political economy.

The General Agreement on Tariffs and Trade (GATT)

The GATT was established in 1947–1948 by twenty-three countries seeking freer and fairer international trading practices. The national protectionism common in the depressed 1930s was widely believed to have been the cause of a dramatic fall in exports from the main industrial countries at the time. The fall was indeed spectacular. In five years, from 1928 to 1932, world exports dropped from $33 billion to $13 billion (Moffitt 1984:16). The high unemployment and the balance-of-payments problems that followed, whether cause or consequence of this fall, were socially disastrous and were directly responsible, in part at least, for the subsequent success of fascism and World War II.

The GATT was designed, first to set rules for world trade, and second to keep those rules up to date.

Three basic rules were set. The first was the most favored nation principle, whereby GATT members agreed to treat all other GATT members in a nondiscriminatory way. A tariff on an import from a GATT member had to be placed on all GATT member imports, and vice versa (with the exception of customs unions, common markets, or free trade areas already in existence). Another exception was made later to provide a preference for manufactured imports from poorer countries. This was the generalized system of preferences. It was, in effect, a form of positive discrimination, since treating unequals equally was clearly unfair. In this case it was decided to trade a degree of freedom for greater fairness. Second, the GATT members agreed to restrict protection to the use of tariffs (dismantling import quotas, for example). Third, GATT members agreed that tariff rates should remain negotiable and that there should be no "free riding," that is, the getting of concessions without offering any.

There were also escape clauses and exceptions that could be used to safeguard countries suffering from balance-of-payments imbalances.

The whole agreement was voluntary, and though there were a disputes procedure and an organization that supervised the rules, the GATT had no powers of enforcement. The whole system ran on reciprocity and the willingness of the participants to abide by it.

Follow-up tariff reduction negotiations have gone on practically nonstop since the GATT was established. There have been eight rounds to date: Geneva (1947); Annecy (1949); Torquay (1950–1951); Geneva (1955–1956); Geneva (1960–1962, the so-called Dillon round); Washington (1964–1967, the so-called Kennedy round); Tokyo (1973–1979, the so-called Tokyo round); and Paris (1986–1994, the so-called Uruguay round).

The rounds have become longer as the size of the association has grown, and as the liberalist cause of nonprotectionism has become more popular. They have gotten progressively more ambitious, too. The Kennedy round, for example, resulted in an "across-the-board tariff cut of 35 percent on 60,000 products" (Gilpin 1987: 192). This was counted a considerable victory by marketeers, though it failed to deal with the growth of nontariff barriers, the needs of poorer countries, or the highly protected nature of agricultural trade; hence the Tokyo and Uruguay rounds.

Nontariff barriers have presented a particularly intractable problem. Statecentric protectionism is in practice a matter of infinite regress. "For the critics of GATT," Kahler (1993:2) argues, "its yeoman service in removing barriers to trade at national borders has only revealed countless other barriers and distortions behind those borders. The decades-long process of lowering trade barriers resembles the draining of a lake that reveals mountain peaks formerly concealed or (more pessimistically) the peeling of an onion of barriers that conceals innumerable layers."

Nontariff barriers have become progressively more complex, both technically and ideologically. As the United States has gone deeper into debt, for example, the country's state makers have begun looking for ways to trade their way out of it. Members of Congress have begun to favor "bilateral" solutions to what they have increasingly characterized as "unfair practices" on the part of other traders. In 1988 they passed the Omnibus Trade and Competitiveness Act, strengthening section 301 of a previous trade act and making it possible thereby for them to single out particular countries as protectionist or dishonest (for example, as violators of intellectual property rights). The preferred punishment was to close the U.S. market off to the supposed offenders. "These extensions of American trade law were controversial," as Kahler points out, since they allowed the United States unilaterally to determine whether there was any unfairness or not, as well as threatening extra-GATT countermeasures if its determinations were not accepted. This extended U.S. demands into policy areas and practices "in which there were not GATT obligations and in which the link to trade was arguable (such as denial of worker rights, export targeting, and anti-competitive business practices)" (Kahler 1993:23).

The U.S. attempt to widen the GATT agenda can be seen either as an attempt by U.S. state makers to break down nontariff barriers, or as a way of trying to compensate for the declining competitiveness of U.S. wealth makers. It depends on the national perspective one takes, and the ideological perspective one takes, too.

The U.S. attempt to negotiate a "structural impediments initiative" with Japan was an attempt to negotiate, bilaterally, a reduction in nontariff barriers. In mercantilist terms, it was marginally defensible. In practice, however, it placed "virtually any domestic practice or national policy on the table as [a] possible impediment . . . to international exchange" (Kahler 1993:24).

U.S. state makers wanted to reduce U.S. dependence on Japanese savings, savings that were used annually to cover the U.S. deficit. They wanted to see the Japanese—state makers and consumers alike—spending more, and spending more on U.S. goods, though in liberal terms this was utterly indefensible. The main U.S. bargaining card—increased protectionism on their part—was decidedly not a liberal one. And however much U.S. state makers argued their case in liberal terms (as a bid to free up trade with the Japanese, for example), liberals remained unconvinced that U.S. state makers weren't hypocrites; that they weren't being dishonest about their intentions. The Japanese were equally skeptical.

The Japanese have not been the United States' only target. Up to the very last moment, before the signing of the Uruguay round agreement in Marrakesh in 1994, U.S. (and French) negotiators were arguing for more of a link between the trade rules in the agreement and their non-GATT concerns for the labor standards and workers' rights in other member states. It's hardly surprising that industrial capitalist countries like this should discover a Marxist-like concern for the poor downtrodden workers of the world just when exporters from a number of countries, where these workers live, were beginning seriously to impinge upon U.S. markets. Called "social dumping," that is, competition deemed unfair because workers' basic rights have been denied and working conditions are poor, this concept represents either a genuine concern for human suffering or a particularly cynical form of protectionism. The timing would suggest the latter, that is, a material interest couched in terms of a moral interest convenient to its cause.

The World Trade Organisation (WTO)

Created by the Uruguay round GATT agreement negotiations, the WTO was a reincarnation of an original proposal by the Western allies who met in Geneva in 1947 to plan a world trading order. The original proposal envisaged an international trade organization akin to the current WTO (the change from "international" to "world" over the intervening years is saying much in itself). The charter that enshrined the original proposal, agreed to in Havana in 1948, was not ratified by the U.S. Congress. The notion that there should be an organization capable of overseeing world trade was not supported, since Congress was not prepared to grant a non-U.S. body control of any of its commercial policies.

Having prevented its formation the first time, the U.S. Congress did not do so the second. The WTO was ratified in 1994. Clearly, many things had changed in the interim, not least being the reduced significance of trade itself in the world political economy. Around the same time, however, the Congress voted into being a major regional trading bloc, the North American Free Trade Association (NAFTA)—originally, the United States, Canada, and Mexico. This would lead one to wonder which way the U.S. Congress saw the world going. Perhaps both ways at once, with tariff reduction between the NAFTA countries and other countries as a result of the GATT/Uruguay, and even higher tariff reductions between themselves as a result of NAFTA. This raises the question as to whether regional blocs inhibit or complement freer world trade.

The Uruguay round did resolve one long-standing issue in favor of a less bloclike, more open global system, and that was agriculture. Long-term resistance on the part of the European Union (EU), and particularly France, to cutting subsidies to farmers and to accepting the marketeering logic of the liberal globalizers was brought to an end, in token form at any rate. This was not before time. Many had noted the paradox of famine in Africa, for example, while European state makers spent billions of dollars annually stockpiling excess food for which they could find no buyers. European price support systems long sustained production at a rate the market, as a market (where food is for sale not use) could not absorb. The food could always have been given to those who most needed it, of course, but no marketeer would countenance a policy like that.

In getting a less bloclike world, notable persistence was shown by the Cairns Group of thirteen primary producing countries, a self-nominated group with members as diverse as New Zealand and Hungary. These countries tried hard for years to keep the issue of agriculture high on the GATT agenda. In practice, though, it was pressure from U.S. state makers, who saw U.S. wealth makers losing exports to the EU because of the protectionist policies of particular EU countries, that finally got the French to capitulate. The French trade-off was the right to protect themselves from the cultural onslaught of Hollywood. This was no small right. One-quarter of world trade is now in such service industries as entertainment, industries that have now become more important globally than commodity manufacture.

It was the United States that most wanted to move the GATT debate into the service domain, and for the first time a GATT round was dedicated to getting less state-made resistance to world trade in the tertiary sector. The reduction of protectionism in service industry areas advantages countries like the United States and the firms they harbor. This puts pressure on countries that want to protect themselves in this regard. Presumably the whole question of service sector protectionism will become more acute as the trade in services increases. It will also become more acute because of the move, not only on the part of richer countries into the services, but also on the part of poorer countries that opt for a more service-centered version of the East Asian development model.

The United States is also showing the way to a new model of development. For example, the most successful East Asian countries are currently seen as those that have eschewed the conventional import substitution model. They have specialized in higher value-added industries, using cheap labor and advanced technology, and they have exported their manufactures into high-spending markets while exploiting consumers at home.

From the U.S. experience, however, it is possible to envisage a model of development that bypasses the manufacturing stage and goes directly to the tertiary one instead. Countries adopting this model might choose to develop their education industries, for example, or to specialize in information superhighway construction, or to advertise themselves as tourist attractions—much as Fiji with its University of the South Pacific, India with its computer software companies, or Nepal with its mountain-trekking industry are doing. Such countries provide services rather than finished goods. They are harbingers of a world political economy that produces and trades more in "mental" commodities than "manual" ones. They also indicate where global investors are going and how far the circuits of world finance now reach.

NOTE

1. Another paradox of national income accounting is the example of the man who marries his housekeeper. Let us say that the man pays his housekeeper $3,000 a year for her services. When he does this, the national income grows by a like amount. But if he and the housekeeper marry, and she is no longer on salary, the national income is diminished by $3,000.

6

World Finance

❖ **R. A. Radford (1945) "The Economic Organisation of a P.O.W. Camp"**

Introduction

After allowance has been made for abnormal circumstances, the social institutions, ideas and habits of groups in the outside world are to be found reflected in a Prisoner of War Camp. It is an unusual but a vital society. Camp organisation and politics are matters of real concern to the inmates, as affecting their present and perhaps their future existences. Nor does this indicate any loss of proportion. No one pretends that camp matters are of any but local importance or of more than transient interest, but their importance there is great. They bulk large in a world of narrow horizons and it is suggested that any distortion of values lies rather in the minimisation than in the exaggeration of their importance. Human affairs are essentially practical matters and the measure of immediate effect on the lives of those directly concerned in them is to a large extent the criterion of their importance at that time and place. A prisoner can hold strong views on such subjects as whether or not all tinned meats shall be issued to individuals cold or be centrally cooked, without losing sight of the significance of the Atlantic Charter.

One aspect of social organisation is to be found in economic activity, and this, along with other manifestations of a group existence, is to be found in any P.O.W. camp. True, a prisoner is not dependent on his exertions for the provision of the necessaries, or even the luxuries of life, but through his economic activity, the exchange of goods and services, his standard of material comfort is considerably enhanced. And this is a serious matter to the prisoner: he is not "playing at shops" even though the small scale of the transactions and the simple expression of comfort and wants in terms of cigarettes and jam, razor blades and writing paper, make the urgency of those needs difficult to appreciate, even by an ex-prisoner of some three months' standing.

Nevertheless, it cannot be too strongly emphasised that economic activities do not bulk so large in prison society as they do in the larger world. There can be little production; as has been said the prisoner is independent of his exertions for the provision of the necessities and luxuries of life; the emphasis lies in exchange and the media of exchange. A prison camp is not to be compared with the seething crowd of hagglers in a street market, any more than it is to be compared with the economic inertia of a family dinner table.

Naturally then, entertainment, academic and literary interest, games and discussions of the "other world" bulk larger in everyday life than they do in the life of more normal societies. But it would be wrong to underestimate the importance of economic activity. Every one receives a roughly equal share of essentials; it is by trade that individual preferences are given expression and comfort increased. All at some time, and most people regularly, make exchanges of one sort or another.

Although a P.O.W. camp provides a living example of a simple economy which might be used as an alternative to the Robinson Crusoe economy beloved by the text-books, and its simplicity renders the demonstration of certain economic hypotheses both amusing and instructive, it is suggested that the principal significance is sociological. True, there is interest in observing the growth of economic institutions and customs in a brand new society, small and simple enough to prevent detail from obscuring the basic pattern and disequilibrium from obscuring the working of the system. But the essential interest lies in the universality and the spontaneity of this economic life; it came into existence not by conscious imitation but as a response to the immediate needs and circumstances. Any similarity between prison organisation and outside organisation arises from similar stimuli evoking similar responses.

The following is as brief an account of the essential data as may render the narrative intelligible. The camps of which the writer had experience were Oflags and consequently the economy was not complicated by payments for work by the detaining power. They consisted normally of between 1,200 and 2,500 people, housed in a number of separate but intercommunicating bunga-lows, one company of 200 or so to a building. Each company formed a group within the main organisation and inside the company the room and the messing syndicate, a voluntary and spontaneous group who fed together, formed the constituent units.

Between individuals there was active trading in all consumer goods and in some services. Most trading was for food against cigarettes or other foodstuffs, but cigarettes rose from the status of a normal commodity to that of a currency. RMk.s [Reichsmarks] existed but had no circulation save for gambling debts, as few articles could be purchased with them from the canteen.

Our supplies consisted of rations provided by the detaining power and (principally) the contents of Red Cross food parcels—tinned milk, jam, butter, biscuits, bully, chocolate, sugar, etc. and cigarettes. So far the supplies to each person were equal and regular. Private parcels of clothing, toilet requisites and cigarettes were also received, and here equality ceased owing to the different numbers despatched and the vagaries of the post. All these articles were the subject of trade and exchange.

The Development and
Organisation of the Market

Very soon after capture people realised that it was both undesirable and unnecessary, in view of the limited size and the equality of supplies, to give away or to accept gifts of cigarettes or food. "Goodwill" developed into trading as a more equitable means of maximising individual satisfaction.

We reached a transit camp in Italy about a fortnight after capture and received 1/4 of a Red Cross food parcel each a week later. At once exchanges, already established, multiplied in volume. Starting with simple direct barter, such as a non-smoker giving a smoker friend his cigarette issue in exchange for a chocolate ration, more complex exchanges soon became an accepted custom. Stories circulated of a padre who started off round the camp with a tin of cheese and five cigarettes and returned to his bed with a complete parcel in addition to his original cheese and cigarettes; the market was not yet perfect. Within a week or two, as the volumes of trade grew, rough scales of exchange values came into existence. Sikhs, who had at first exchanged tinned beef for practically any other foodstuff, began to insist on jam and margarine. It was realised that a tin of jam was worth 1/2 lb of margarine plus something else; that a cigarette issue was worth several chocolate issues, and a tin of diced carrots was worth practically nothing.

In this camp we did not visit other bungalows very much and prices varied from place to place; hence the germ of truth in the story of the itinerant priest. By the end of a month, when we reached our permanent camp, there was a lively trade in all commodities and their relative values were well known, and expressed not in terms of one another—one didn't quote bully in terms of sugar—but in terms of cigarettes. The cigarette became the standard of value. In the permanent camp people started by wandering through the bungalows calling their offers—"cheese for seven" (cigarettes)—and the hours after parcel issue were bedlam. The inconveniences of this system soon led to its replacement by an Exchange and Mart notice board in every bungalow, where under the headings "name", "room number", "wanted" and "offered" sales and wants were advertised. When a deal went through it was crossed off the board. The public and semi-permanent records of transactions led to cigarette prices being well known and thus tending to equality throughout the camp, although there were always opportunities for an astute trader to make a profit from arbitrage. With this development everyone, including non-smokers, was willing to sell for cigarettes, using them to buy at another time and place. Cigarettes became the normal currency, though, of course, barter was never extinguished.

The unity of the market and the prevalence of a single price varied directly with the general level of the organisation and comfort in the camp. A transit camp was always chaotic and uncomfortable: people were overcrowded, no one knew where anyone else was living, and few took the trouble to find out. Organisation was too slender to include an Exchange and Mart board, and private advertisements were the most that appeared. Consequently a transit camp was not one market but many. The price of a tin of salmon is known to have varied by two cigarettes in 20 between one end of a hut and the other. Despite a high level of organisation in Italy, the market was morcellated in this manner at the first transit camp we reached after our removal to Germany in the autumn of 1943. In this camp—Stalag VIIA at Moosburg in Bavaria—there were up to 50,000 prisoners of all nationalities. French, Russians, Italians and Jugo-Slavs were free to move about within the camp; British and Americans were confined to their compounds, although a few cigarettes given to a sentry would always procure permission for one or two men to visit other compounds. The people who first visited the highly organised French trading centre, with its stalls and known prices, found coffee extract—relatively cheap among the tea-drinking English—commanding a fancy price in biscuits or cigarettes, and some enterprising people made small fortunes that way. (Incidentally we found out later that much of the coffee went "over the wire" and sold for phenomenal prices at black market cafes in Munich: some of the French prisoners were said to have made substantial sums in RMk.s. This was one of the few occasions on which our normally closed economy came into contact with other economic worlds.)

The permanent camps in Germany saw the highest level of commercial organisation. In addition to the Exchange and Mart notice boards, a shop was organised as a public utility, controlled by representatives of the Senior British Officer, on a no profit basis. People left their surplus clothing, toilet requisites and food there until they were sold at a fixed price in cigarettes. Only sales in cigarettes were accepted—there was no barter—and there was no haggling. For food at least there were standard prices: clothing is less homogeneous and the price was decided around a norm by the seller and the shop manager in agreement; shirts would average say 80, ranging from 60 to 120 according to quality and age. Of food, the shop carried small stocks for convenience; the capital was provided by a loan from the bulk store of Red Cross cigarettes and repaid by a small commission taken on the first transactions. Thus the cigarette attained its fullest currency status, and the market was almost completely unified.

It is thus to be seen that a market came into existence without labour or production. The B.R.C.S. may be considered as "Nature" of the text-book, and the articles of trade—food, clothing and cigarettes—as free gifts—land or manna. Despite this, and despite a roughly equal distribution of resources, a market came into spontaneous operation, and prices were fixed by the operation of supply and demand. It is difficult to reconcile this fact with the labour theory of value.

Actually there was an embryo labour market. Even when cigarettes were not scarce, there was usually some unlucky person willing to perform services for them. Laundrymen advertised at two cigarettes a garment. Battle-dress was scrubbed and pressed and a pair of trousers lent for the interim period of twelve. A good pastel portrait cost thirty or a tin of "Ham". Odd tailoring and other jobs similarly had their prices.

There were also entrepreneurial services. There was a coffee stall owner who sold tea, coffee or cocoa at two cigarettes a cup, buying his raw materials at market prices and hiring labour to gather fuel and to stoke; he actually enjoyed the services of a chartered accountant at one stage. After a period of great prosperity he overreached himself and failed disastrously for several hundred cigarettes. Such large scale private enterprise was rare but several middlemen or professional traders existed. The padre in Italy, or the men at Moosburg who opened trading relations with the French, are examples: the more subdivided the market, the less perfect the advertisement of prices, and the less stable the prices, the greater was the scope for these operators. One man capitalised his knowledge of Urdu by buying meat from the Sikhs and selling butter and jam in return: as his operations became better known more and more people entered this trade, prices in the Indian Wing approximated more nearly to those elsewhere, though to the end a "contact" among the Indians was valuable, as linguistic difficulties prevented the trade from being quite free. Some were specialists in the Indian trade, the food, clothing or even the watch trade. Middlemen traded on their own account or on commission. Price rings and agreements were suspected and the traders certainly co-operated. Nor did they welcome newcomers. Unfortunately the writer knows little of the workings of these people: public opinion was hostile and the professionals were usually of a retiring disposition.

One trader in food and cigarettes, operating in a period of dearth, enjoyed a high reputation. His capital, carefully saved, was originally about 50 cigarettes with which he bought rations on issue days and held them until the price rose just before the next issue. He also picked up a little by arbitrage; several times a day he visited every Exchange or Mart notice board and took advantage of every discrepancy between prices of goods offered and wanted. His knowledge of prices, markets and names of those who had received cigarette parcels was phenomenal. By these means he kept himself smoking steadily—his profits—while his capital remained intact.

Sugar was issued on Saturday. About Tuesday two of us used to visit Sam and make a deal; as old customers he would advance as much of the price as he could spare then, and entered the transaction in a book. On Saturday morning he left cocoa tins on our beds for the ration, and picked them up on Saturday afternoon. We were hoping for a calendar at Christmas, but Sam failed too. He was left holding a big black treacle issue when the price fell, and in this weakened state was unable to withstand an unexpected arrival of parcels and the consequent price fluctuations. He paid in full, but from his capital. The next Tuesday, when I paid my usual visit he was out of business.

Credit entered into many, perhaps into most, transactions, in one form or another. Sam paid in advance as a rule for his purchases of future deliveries of sugar, but many buyers asked for credit, whether the commodity was sold spot or future. Naturally prices varied according to the terms of sale. A treacle ration might be advertised for four cigarettes now or five next week. And in the future market "bread now" was a vastly different thing from "bread Thursday". Bread was issued on Thursday and Monday, four and three days' rations respectively, and by Wednesday and Sunday night it had risen at least one cigarette per ration, from seven to eight, by supper time. One man always saved a ration to sell then at the peak price: his offer of "bread now" stood out on the board among a number of "bread Mondays" fetching one or two less, or not selling at all—and he always smoked on Sunday night.

The Cigarette Currency

Although cigarettes as currency exhibited certain peculiarities, they performed all the functions of a metallic currency as a unit of account, as a measure of value and as a store of value, and shared most of its characteristics. They were homogeneous, reasonably durable, and of convenient size for the smallest or, in packets, for the largest transactions. Incidentally, they could be clipped or sweated by rolling them between the fingers so that tobacco fell out.

Cigarettes were also subject to the working of Gresham's Law. Certain brands were more popular than others as smokes, but for currency purposes a cigarette was a cigarette. Consequently, buyers used the poorer qualities and the Shop rarely saw the more popular brands: cigarettes such as Churchman's No. 1 were rarely used for trading. At one time cigarettes hand-rolled from pipe tobacco began to circulate. Pipe tobacco was issued in lieu of cigarettes by the Red Cross at a rate of 25 cigarettes to the ounce and this rate was standard in exchanges, but an ounce would produce 30 home-made cigarettes. Naturally, people with machine-made cigarettes broke them down and re-rolled the tobacco, and the real cigarette virtually disappeared from the market. Hand-rolled cigarettes were not homogeneous and prices could no longer be quoted in them with safety: each cigarette was examined before it was accepted and thin ones were rejected, or extra demanded as a make-weight. For a time we suffered all the inconveniences of a debased currency.

Machine-made cigarettes were always universally acceptable, both for what they would buy and for themselves. It was intrinsic value which gave rise to their principal disadvantage as currency, a disadvantage which exists, but to a far smaller extent, in the case of metallic currency—that is, a strong demand for non-monetary purposes. Consequently our economy was repeatedly subject to deflation and to periods of monetary stringency. While the Red Cross issue of 50 or 25 cigarettes per man per week came in regularly, and while there were fair stocks held, the cigarette currency suited its purpose admirably. But when the issue was interrupted, stocks soon ran out, prices fell, trading declined in volume and became increasingly a matter of barter. This deflationary tendency was periodically offset by the sudden injection of new currency. Private cigarette parcels arrived in a trickle throughout the year, but the big numbers came in quarterly when the Red Cross received its allocation of transport. Several hundred thousand cigarettes might arrive in the space of a fortnight. Prices soared, and then began to fall, slowly at first but with increasing rapidity as stocks ran out, until the next big delivery. Most of our economic troubles could be attributed to this fundamental instability.

Price Movements

Many factors affected prices, the strongest and most noticeable being the periodical currency inflation and deflation described in the last paragraphs. The periodicity of this price cycle depended on cigarette and, to a far lesser extent, on food deliveries. At one time in the early days, before any private parcels had arrived and when there were no individual stocks, the weekly issue of cigarettes and food parcels occurred on a Monday. The non-monetary demand for cigarettes was great, and less elastic than the demand for food: consequently prices fluctuated weekly, falling towards Sunday night and rising sharply on Monday morning. Later when many people held reserves, the weekly issue had no such effect, being too small a proportion of the total available. Credit allowed people with no reserves to meet their non-monetary demand over the weekend.

The general price level was affected by other factors. An influx of new prisoners, proverbially hungry, raised it. Heavy air raids in the vicinity of the camp probably increased the non-monetary demand for cigarettes and accentuated deflation. Good and bad war news certainly had its effect, and the general waves of optimism and pessimism which swept the camp were reflected in prices. Before breakfast one morning in March of this year, a rumour of the arrival of parcels and cigarettes was circulated. Within ten minutes I sold a treacle ration, for four cigarettes (hitherto offered in vain for three), and many similar deals went through. By 10 o'clock the rumour was denied, and the treacle that day found no more buyers even at two cigarettes.

More interesting than changes in the general price level were changes in the price structure. Changes in the supply of a commodity, in the German ration scale or in the make-up of Red Cross parcels, would raise the price of one commodity relative to others. Tins of oatmeal, once a rare and much sought after luxury in the parcels, became a commonplace in 1943, and the price fell. In hot weather the demand for cocoa fell and that for soap rose. A new recipe would be reflected in the price level: the discovery that raisins and sugar could be turned into an alcoholic liquor of remarkable potency reacted permanently on the dried fruit market. The invention of electric immersion heaters run off the power points made tea, a drop on the market in Italy, a certain seller in Germany.

In August 1944, the supplies of parcels and cigarettes were both halved. Since both sides of the equation were changed in the same degree, changes in prices were not anticipated. But this was not the case: the non-monetary demand for cigarettes was less elastic than the demand for food, and food prices fell a little. More important however, were the changes in the price structure. German margarine and jam, hitherto valueless owing to adequate supplies of Canadian butter and marmalade, acquired a new value. Chocolate, popular and a certain seller, and sugar fell. Bread rose; several standing contracts of bread for cigarettes were broken, especially when the bread ration was reduced a few weeks later.

In February 1945, the German soldier who drove the ration waggon was found to be willing to exchange loaves of bread at the rate of one loaf for a bar of chocolate. Those in the know began selling bread and buying chocolate, by then unsaleable in a period of serious deflation. Bread, at about 40, fell slightly; chocolate rose from 15; the supply of bread was not enough for the two commodities to reach parity, but the tendency was unmistakable.

The substitution of German margarine for Canadian butter when parcels were halved naturally affected their relative values, margarine appreciating at the expense of butter. Similarly, two brands of dried milk, hitherto differing in quality and therefore in price by five cigarettes a tin, came together in price as the wider substitution of the cheaper raised its relative value.

Enough has been cited to show that any change in conditions affected both the general price level and the price structure. It was this latter phenomenon which wrecked our planned economy.

Paper Currency—Bully Marks

Around D-Day, food and cigarettes were plentiful, business was brisk and the camp in an optimistic mood. Consequently the Entertainments Committee felt the moment opportune to launch a restaurant, where food and hot drinks were sold while a band and variety turns performed. Earlier experiments, both public and private, had pointed the way, and the scheme was a great success. Food was bought at market prices to provide the meals and the small profits were devoted to a reserve fund and used to bribe Germans to provide greasepaints and other necessities for the camp theatre. Originally meals were sold for cigarettes but this meant that the whole scheme was vulnerable to the periodic deflationary waves, and furthermore heavy smokers were unlikely to attend much. The whole success of the scheme depended on an adequate amount of food being offered for sale in the normal manner.

To increase and facilitate trade, and to stimulate supplies and customers therefore, and secondarily to avoid the worst effects of deflation when it should come, a paper currency was organised by the Restaurant and the Shop. The Shop bought food on behalf of the Restaurant with paper notes and the paper was accepted equally with the cigarettes in the Restaurant or Shop, and passed back to the Shop to purchase more food. The Shop acted as a bank of issue. The paper money was backed 100 percent by food; hence its name, the Bully Mark. The BMk. was backed 100 percent by food: there could be no over-issues, as is permissible with a normal bank of issue, since the eventual dispersal of the camp and consequent redemption of all BMk.s was anticipated in the near future.

Originally one BMk. was worth one cigarette and for a short time both circulated freely inside and outside the Restaurant. Prices were quoted in BMk.s and cigarettes with equal freedom—and for a short time the BMk. showed signs of replacing the cigarette as currency. The BMk. was tied to food, but not to cigarettes: as it was issued against food, say 45 for a tin of milk and so on, any reduction in the BMk. prices of food would have meant that there were unbacked BMk.s in circulation. But the price of both food and BMk.s could and did fluctuate with the supply of cigarettes.

While the Restaurant flourished, the scheme was a success: the Restaurant bought heavily, all foods were saleable and prices were stable.

In August parcels and cigarettes were halved and the Camp was bombed. The Restaurant closed for a short while and sales of food became difficult. Even when the Restaurant reopened, the food and cigarette shortage became increasingly acute and people were unwilling to convert such valuable goods into paper and to hold them for luxuries like snacks and tea. Less of the right kinds of food for the Restaurant were sold, and the Shop became glutted with dried fruit, chocolate, sugar, etc. which the Restaurant could not buy. The price level and the price structure changed. The BMk. fell to four-fifths of a cigarette and eventually farther still, and it became unacceptable save in the Restaurant. There was a flight from the BMk., no longer convertible into cigarettes or popular foods. The cigarette re-established itself.

But the BMk. was sound! The Restaurant closed in the New Year with a progressive food shortage and the long evenings without lights due to intensified Allied air raids, and BMk.s could only be spent in the Coffee Bar—relic of the Restaurant—or on the few unpopular foods in the Shop, the owners of which were prepared to accept them. In the end all holders of BMk.s were paid in full, in cups of coffee or in prunes. People who had bought BMk.s for cigarettes or valuable jam or biscuits in their heyday were aggrieved that they should have stood the loss involved by their restricted choice, but they suffered no actual loss of market value.

Price Fixing

Along with this scheme came a determined attempt at a planned economy, at price fixing. The Medical Officer had long been anxious to control food sales, for fear of some people selling too much, to the detriment of their health. The deflationary waves and their effects on prices were inconvenient to all and would be dangerous to the Restaurant which had to carry stocks. Furthermore, unless the BMk. was convertible into cigarettes at about par it had little chance of gaining confidence and of succeeding as a currency. As has been explained, the BMk. was tied to food but could not be tied to cigarettes, which fluctuated in value. Hence, while BMk. prices of food were fixed for all time, cigarette prices of food and BMk.s varied.

The Shop, backed by the Senior Officer, was not in a position to enforce price control both inside and outside its walls. Hitherto a standard price had been fixed for food left for sale in the shop, and prices outside were roughly in conformity with this scale, which was recommended as a "guide" to sellers, but fluctuated a good deal around it. Sales in the Shop at recommended prices were apt to be slow though a good price might be obtained: sales outside could be made more quickly at lower prices. (If sales outside were to be at higher prices, goods were withdrawn from the Shop until the recommended price rose: but the recommended price was sluggish and could not follow the market closely by reason of its very purpose, which was stability.) The Exchange and Mart noticeboards came under the control of the Shop: advertisements which exceeded a 5 percent departure from the recommended scale were liable to be crossed out by authority: unauthorised sales were discouraged by authority and also by public opinion, strongly in favour of a just and stable price. (Recommended prices were fixed partly from market data, partly on the advice of the M.O.)

At first the recommended scale was a success: the Restaurant, a big buyer, kept prices stable around this level: opinion and the 5 percent tolerance helped. But when the price level fell with the August cuts and the price structure changed, the recommended scale was too rigid. Unchanged at first, as no deflation was expected, the scale was tardily lowered, but the prices of goods on the new scale remained in the same relation to one another, owing to the BMk., while on the market the price structure had changed. And the modifying influence of the Restaurant had gone. The scale was moved up and down several times, slowly following the inflationary and deflationary waves, but it was rarely adjusted to changes in the price structure. More and more advertisements were crossed off the board, and black market sales at unauthorised prices increased: eventually public opinion turned against the recommended scale and authority gave up the struggle. In the last few weeks, with unparalleled deflation, prices fell with alarming rapidity, no scales existed, and supply and demand, alone and unmellowed, determined prices.

Public Opinion

Public opinion on the subject of trading was vocal if confused and change-able, and generalisations as to its direction are difficult and dangerous. A tiny minority held that all trading was undesirable as it engendered an unsavoury atmosphere; occasional frauds and sharp practices were cited as proof. Certain forms of trading were more generally condemned; trade with the Germans was criticised by many. Red Cross toilet articles, which were in short supply and only issued in cases of actual need, were excluded from trade by law and opinion working in unshakable harmony. At one time, when there had been several cases of malnutrition reported among the more devoted smokers, no trade in German rations was permitted, as the victims became an additional burden on the depleted food reserves of the Hospital. But while certain activities were condemned as anti-social, trade itself was practised, and its utility appreciated, by almost everyone in the camp.

More interesting was opinion on middlemen and prices. Taken as a whole, opinion was hostile to the middleman. His function, and his hard work in bringing buyer and seller together, were ignored; profits were not regarded as a reward for labour, but as the result of sharp practices. Despite the fact that his very existence was proof to the contrary, the middleman was held to be redundant in view of the existence of an official Shop and the Exchange and Mart. Appreciation only came his way when he was willing to advance the price of a sugar ration, or to buy goods spot and carry them against a future sale. In these cases the element of risk was obvious to all, and the convenience of the service was felt to merit some reward. Particularly unpopular was the middleman with an element of monopoly, the man who contacted the ration waggon driver, or the man who utilised his knowledge of Urdu. And middlemen as a group were blamed for reducing prices. Opinion notwithstanding, most people dealt with a middleman, whether consciously or unconsciously, at some time or another.

There was a strong feeling that everything had its "just price" in cigarettes. While the assessment of the just price, which incidentally varied between camps, was impossible of explanation, this price was nevertheless pretty closely known. It can best be defined as the price usually fetched by an article in good times when cigarettes were plentiful. The "just price" changed slowly; it was unaffected by short-term variations in supply, and while opinion might be resigned to departures from the "just price", a strong feeling of resentment persisted. A more satisfactory definition of the "just price" is impossible. Everyone knew what it was, though no one could explain why it should be so.

As soon as prices began to fall with a cigarette shortage, a clamour arose, particularly against those who held reserves and who bought at reduced prices. Sellers at cut prices were criticised and their activities referred to as the black market. In every period of dearth the explosive question of "should non-smokers receive a cigarette ration?" was discussed to profitless length. Unfortunately, it was the non-smoker, or the light smoker with his reserves, along with the hated middleman, who weathered the storm most easily.

The popularity of the price-fixing scheme, and such success as it enjoyed, were undoubtedly the result of this body of opinion. On several occasions the fall of prices was delayed by the general support given to the recommended scale. The onset of deflation was marked by a period of sluggish trade; prices stayed up but no one bought. Then prices fell on the black market, and the volume of trade revived in that quarter. Even when the recommended scale was revised, the volume of trade in the Shop would remain low. Opinion was always overruled by the hard facts of the market.

Curious arguments were advanced to justify price fixing. The recommended prices were in some way related to the calorific values of the foods offered: hence some were overvalued and never sold at these prices. One argument ran as follows:—not everyone has private cigarette parcels: thus, when prices were high and trade good in the summer of 1944, only the lucky rich could buy. This was unfair to the man with few cigarettes. When prices fell in the following winter prices should be pegged high so that the rich, who had enjoyed life in the summer, should put many cigarettes into circulation. The fact that those who sold to the rich in the summer had also enjoyed life then, and the fact that in the winter there was always someone willing to sell at low prices, were ignored. Such arguments were hotly debated each night after the approach of Allied aircraft extinguished all lights at 8 PM. But prices moved with the supply of cigarettes, and refused to stay fixed in accordance with a theory of ethics.

Conclusion

The economic organisation described was both elaborate and smooth-working in the summer of 1944. Then came the August cuts and deflation. Prices fell, rallied with deliveries of cigarette parcels in September and December, and fell again. In January, 1945, supplies of Red Cross cigarettes ran out: and prices slumped still further: in February the supplies of food parcels were exhausted and the depression became a blizzard. Food, itself scarce, was almost given away in order to meet the non-monetary demand for cigarettes. Laundries ceased to operate, or worked for pounds or RMk.s: food and cigarettes sold for fancy prices in pounds, hitherto unheard of. The restaurant was a memory and the BMk. a joke. The Shop was empty and the Exchange and Mart notices were full of unaccepted offers for cigarettes. Barter increased in volume, becoming a larger proportion of a smaller volume of trade. This, the first serious and prolonged food shortage in the writer's experience, caused the price structure to change again, partly because German rations were not easily divisible. A margarine ration gradually sank in value until it exchanged directly for a treacle ration. Sugar slumped sadly. Only bread retained its value. Several thousand cigarettes, the capital of the Shop, were distributed without any noticeable effect. A few fractional parcel and cigarette issues, such as one-sixth of a parcel and twelve cigarettes each, led to momentary price recoveries and feverish trade, especially when they coincided with good news from the Western Front, but the general position remained unaltered.

By April, 1945, chaos had replaced order in the economic sphere: sales were difficult, prices lacked stability. Economics has been defined as the science of distributing limited means among unlimited and competing ends. On 12th April, with the arrival of elements of the 30th US Infantry Division, the ushering in of an age of plenty demonstrated the hypothesis that with infinite means economic organisation and activity would be redundant, as every want could be satisfied without effort.

CURRENCY AND CREDIT

Radford's account of the use of cigarettes as currency in a prisoner of war camp suggests that where goods are scarce and a measure and store of value do not exist, people will make one. They will invent money. Even under conditions as restricted as a prison camp, where one would expect barter alone to be the main means of exchange, the flexibility, the sheer usefulness of a unit of account will make some form of money indispensable.

The world political economy is not a prisoner of war camp. In the "outside world," as Radford points out, there is production. Unlike prisoners, most people in the world do not have their basic needs met for them, either. Trade is a much more comprehensive activity.

The role that money plays is the same, however. Hence the intriguing character of the story Radford tells.

Though the role money plays in the world market may be basically the same, it has been growing in importance. So much so that it is argued that finance has been "decoupled" now from production to become a power in itself; an "autocrat," in Cox's (1992) words, that rules over rather than moving within the world political economy. What is the substance of such a claim? What is the role that money plays in the capitalist world market?

The contemporary foundations for the international flow of finance capital were laid at Bretton Woods in 1944, in the concluding stages of World War II. Since then capitalists have built a vast superstructure of global credit, with corporate and noncorporate private capital being moved from one country to another, in ever-increasing amounts and to more and more countries worldwide. International financial flows via corporations and banks—the main transmission belts—now tower over those of trade. So marked has been this development that Gilpin (1987:119) calls it a "virtual revolution" in world affairs.

Consider, for example, FDI flows. In the first half of the 1980s less than one-third of the total long-term capital from private sources (excluding nonguaranteed credit) that was moved into ninety-three capital-importing countries was made up of FDI. By the second half of the 1980s, however, it was three-quarters (Neyer 1994:6).

Short-term capital flows have also shown marked increases. The global returns from portfolio investments (stocks and shares), for example, were ten times higher in 1992 than they were at the end of the 1970s.

The increase was most dramatic in the area of foreign exchange, that is, currency transactions. To quote Neyer (1994:12):

> Beginning with the formation of the euro- or offshore markets in the late sixties, continuing with the growing volatility of exchange rates in the seventies and leading to the deregulations of the national stockmarkets in the U.S., the U.K., and later in Japan and the rest of Europe, the international trade in currencies is growing . . . ever faster. . . . The daily turnover at the ten largest stock markets is now estimated to amount to US$1,000 billion. This is . . . twice the total of all the currency reserves of the OECD countries.

Compare this with worldwide exports, which on a daily basis amount to less than U.S.$10 billion, or 1 percent of foreign exchange transactions.

FDI is increasingly short-term, and increasingly self-referential. So much so that the speculative play on financial asset prices has displaced the raising of capital as the chief task of the great financial houses. In addition, the use of computers, plus contemporary telecommunications, has created a hyperspace for money that has made a hyperspace for capitalism, too.

Because of the speculative nature of so many FDI transactions today, derivatives have proliferated. *Derivatives* as a term is used to describe a range of financial instruments—futures, options, and the like—that are valued in terms of (derived from) other assets, such as equities or bonds. They are useful as insurance. They provide the chance to hedge bets, such as the risks incurred in speculating on changes in the relative value of different currencies. As the world market grows, currency speculation has grown with it, and so has the use of derivatives. The number of contracts in derivatives doubled, for example, between 1988 and 1992, by which time they were running at the rate of 143 contracts a second (Neyer 1994:13). It is now at the point where derivatives have a life of their own, and they are able to drive the system in opportunistic ways.

In practice they are a kind of gambling, and as such they magnify market uncertainty by multiplying the (debt-based) buying capacity (leverage) of insurance funds (hedge funds) and other speculative financial instruments. The business is dominated by some of the world's biggest banks.

There is risk in that the failure of one derivatives firm could cause others to default in a cascade, threatening in turn the integrity of the whole world political economy. Derivatives tie banks and other financial houses together in complex global webs that can quickly transmit a local crisis to the system as a whole. This risk is well defined by now, however, and major traders have learned to manage it as part of their everyday business.

In classical liberal parlance, this kind of free market behavior can only be beneficial. As short-term money is sent from countries of low short-term returns to those where higher short-term returns are available, it is supposed to balance the different national rates of interest. This is supposed to stabilize the market system as a whole. Everyone ostensibly benefits, albeit some more than others, and since prosperous people tend to prefer peace, the outcome is said to promote harmony as well as opulence.

What about currency changes that halve the value of a farmer's crop before he or she harvests it, however, or that drive an exporter out of business? What about the takeovers, engineered for financial gain alone, that cost workers jobs? What about the young derivatives trader, caught short in a gamble on the stability of the Tokyo stock market, who attempts to buy enough options to force that market up, and when the market falls instead, manages to bring down with it one of Britain's oldest banks (Baring's)? If what gets decided in the interests of short-term profit in the office blocks of the world's financial centers, in other words, has such sudden, unpredictable, and unavoidable effects (Strange 1986), in what way can we say that the system works, and for whom?

The more extreme liberals would maintain that market "punishment" is the price we pay for the superior benefits of having the market as a whole. Finance capitalists are mostly liberals of this sort. They are not concerned with the concrete needs of known people but with abstract calculations of profit and loss, and this, they believe, is as it should be. After all, it is profit that makes such a productive system possible, and it is this system that, in classical liberal terms, provides "most of the Western proletariat and most of the millions of the developing world" with their very existence. It is this system, and the socially heedless, self-maximizing, short-term, profiteering strategies used by the "advanced" members of it, that creates the opportunities for poor people to survive (Hayek 1988:131). Take away the rewards for entrepreneurial opportunism, classical liberals say, and the system would collapse. There would be no incentive to produce, and the poor would suffer first. And anyway, how else are we to motivate the world's marketeers? How else are we to eliminate the weak and the inefficient? How else to make for prosperity and peace, unless by promoting the pursuit of profit, accepting the pain of "adjustment," and appreciating the consequences?

For empirical support liberals like these need turn no further than the United Nations Children's Fund's (UNICEF) "progress of nations" report. In this report the Deputy Executive Director notes how, over the last fifty years, average life expectancy in the developing nations has risen from forty to over sixty years, child death rates have fallen from three hundred to one hundred per thousand births, and adult literacy rates have doubled to run now at 70% (UNICEF 1995a). Then there is UNICEF's "state of the world's children" report, which documents a global reduction in malnutrition, maintenance or the increase of immunization levels, success in the war against polio, elimination of iodine and vitamin A deficiencies, and progress in primary education (UNICEF 1995b).

More generally they have the World Bank's report for 1994 on the "social indicators of development." The aggregate statistics used there from 192 countries suggest that the global picture is one of improvement. Indeed, the World Bank concludes that trends over the last twenty years describing life expectancy and gross national product (GNP) per capita are going up, while those describing infant mortality and the percentage of poor in the world are going down.

At the same time, however, by the World Bank's own reckoning, the actual number of the poor is continuing to increase. An estimated 1.1 billion people in the world currently subsist on the equivalent of U.S.$1 a day, and this number, they say, grows daily (World Bank 1994b).

> In the last 10 years, in particular, falling commodity prices, rising military expenditures, poor returns on investment, the debt crisis, and structural adjustment programmes [austerity measures required by the IMF in exchange for debt relief], have reduced the real incomes of approximately 800 million people in some 40 developing countries. . . . For many millions of families in the poorest villages and urban slums of the developing world, the daily consequences of these economic forces over which they have no control, is that they are unable to put enough food on the table, unable to maintain a home fit to live in, unable to dress and present

themselves decently, unable to protect their health and strength, unable to keep their children in school (UNICEF 1995b:2).

The World Bank's and other reports, therefore, contain both good and bad news. They can be used to justify the status quo. They prompt cause for concern as well. It is because of the concern that reformist liberals worry whether global capital flows have not become too big, too fast, and too detached to be sustained without doing significant damage to the social consensus that makes societies possible and to the natural environment as well. They recommend regulation. Can marketeers afford not to have controls, they say, if the marketeering system is to survive?

Because of their own experience with the downside of the global market system, for example, the heads of governments at an EU summit meeting in 1994 decided that the unemployment that accompanies free marketeering had become too problematic an issue for European finance ministers to solve alone. They began looking at revising tax policies to reward firms for employing people and to punish them for doing environmental damage. At the same time, and for the same reason, they commended EU moves to oblige multinational companies to consult EU staff on strategic corporate decisions.

Classical Marxists, like classical liberals, approve of the free movement of capital, though for very different reasons. The sooner the class conflicts such movements create turn revolutionary, they say, the sooner socialism will ensue and conditions will improve. Since "neither the global economy . . . nor government," Sweezy (1994:11) declares, "can deliver what the great majority of the people in the world need—decent jobs, security, livelihood—it seems clear that they have no choice but to challenge the structure itself." And he is confident that they will—"eventually."

Reformist Marxists, long witness to the proven capacity of capitalists to perpetuate their system, and less sure as a consequence that conflict will turn revolutionary, want to mitigate the worst of its exploitative effects. They decry international capital flows that, directly or indirectly, establish more wage labor relationships (like FDI, or international bank lending to industrial capitalists) because these flows create more exploited workers, more alienation, more capitalism. They also decry the success of those financial speculators who, in circulating fictitious capital in the form of derivatives, for example, further empower the global bourgeoisie.

Members of diverse social movements note the differential gender effects of FDI, for example, or the relative impoverishment of indigenous people, or the negative effects on the environment, or the erosion of spiritual awareness brought about by the consumerism and the materialism that FDI helps foster. They note the relative absence of women or indigenous people or environmentalists or the devout among those making these investments, and the relative presence of men, members of hegemonic cultures, planet poisoners, and secularists.

Money

I've talked above as if we all know what "finance" means. One of the benefits of reading Radford, however, is the way we are reminded by what he has to say of how much we take for granted when we use money as finance. We take money for granted in a cash economy. What is it, however, what does it do, and how does it do it?

The goods and services that producers make and perform are traded wherever a market is found for them. This trading can be done in barter form, as most was until recent times. Or it can be done using independent units of value against which the worth of the goods and services to be exchanged can be measured. Independent units of value can be used to store value, too. This is money. It can have intrinsic worth of its own (like gold) or it can have symbolic value only (like paper notes). It doesn't matter, as long as it is durable, portable, and its unit value is agreed.

While barter trade is still common, monetized trade is said to be more efficient (in the liberal sense of allowing the optimal combination of the factors of production). Monetized trade is also said to be more effective (in the same liberal vein—it supposedly gives people more choices, that is, a wider selection of goods and services and the chance to consume these things now or later). More critically, monetized trade is said to concentrate power in the hands of a small number of capitalist accumulators, without democratic controls over what they choose to do.

Production and trade systems that use an independent measure and store of value, like money, can be infinitely more complex than ones that don't. Strange (1988:89–90) likens money to the blood supply of the human body, which has to be kept staunch, sound, and within specific limits, but which flows through every part of the whole being and makes it possible for us to survive and thrive. So widespread has the use of money become that one is tempted to assume that if we didn't have it, like Radford's prisoners, we'd soon have to invent it, as indeed people have done at many different times, in many different places, and in many, often quite striking ways. There are alternatives to money, of course, though imagining a world that functions in terms of reciprocal social obligations, for example, or spiritual transcendence, is more the stuff of science fiction or prayer than international political economy.

Production or trade using money is not as common as production or trade per se, but it is as ancient as the organized conduct of them both. Whether it be great stone wheels as on the island of Yap, long strings of feathers as in the northern Solomons, coins, notes, or numbers in computers, it's all money. It's all a matter of nominating relative worth, moving its measure from place to place and from the past to the future, in reified forms.

Early forms of money did have intrinsic worth—"merchandise" money, Amin (1993:6) calls it. They were items valued in and of themselves, often for their aesthetic appeal. Strings of feather and shell, or pieces of silver and gold, were considered decorative and were desired for their visual or tactile qualities alone. "In the gloom the gold gathers the light against it," says one of the earliest English poems, capturing in a single line a clear sense of the perennial appeal of this much prized metal.

Money need have no specific use or appeal in itself, however, to function as a medium of exchange. It is, after all, only a representation of value or worth. Indeed, this process of representation has become progressively more attenuated over time, so that notes and coins need only now be strips of plastic or alloy slugs, or glowing figures on a computer screen, to perform their symbolic task.

It has been noted already that money flows now dwarf trade flows, and that money flows have become a major feature of the international political economy. Liberals see money, and the "international monetary system," as separate from the social order of which it is a part. Money is used in an "economy" separate from, and at most resting upon, a particular "political order" (Gilpin 1987:119). Marxists, by contrast, do not separate "economy" and "polity" in this way, and as a consequence, money for them has a much more profound social meaning. Their talk of "capital," for example, is of monies that make for "wage labor relationship[s]," classes (McIntyre 1992:236), and ruling-class power.

In discussing money flows, in other words, liberals detach "economics" and "politics" from the social context in which such practices take place. This social context they detach in turn from the material means used to make the goods and services that people use. Having separated economics from politics, liberals posit specific "economic" arrangements (such as monetary ones) that can be presumed in turn to "rest"—to use Gilpin's word—on particular political arrangements.

For liberals, the key issue is the extent to which money flows make for human freedom.

Whatever the virtues of this analytic language, its great vice is how it accounts for money flows in terms of power structures that only have "states" or "firms" in them; that have "the United States" doing this and "Mitsubishi" doing that as reified, unitary entities. As a consequence liberals miss the way money maps material power in terms of a world society "conditioned" or "determined" (the verbs do matter) by world capitalism; where "economics" and "politics" only have meaning as aspects of such a society; where capitalists use money flows to defend and extend capitalism (and the social relationships definitive of it); and where state makers participate, wittingly or unwittingly, in this defensive/extensive process. They miss, in a word, the way "international financial markets and institutions stand at the center of contemporary class restructuring" (McIntyre 1992:243).

They miss what Marxists see first, that is, the extent to which money makes, or fails to make, for social equality and well-being.

Credit

A thousand years ago there were no patterns of human behavior we can categorize as a world political economy. The most prominent productive systems were the great imperial jurisdictions of Near, South, and Far East Asia. By the sixteenth century, however, the Ottoman and Indian empires were in decline and the Manchus were turning away from the world. Meanwhile, European explorers were looking for new trade routes for European merchants, and as it happened, they were the first drops in a subsequent deluge.

A movie film of what Euoropeans were to build over the next five hundred years, taken from space and speeded up, would show roads and railways, power lines and telephone lines, sprouting prodigiously. It would show enormous cities, assembled at extraordinary speed. Forests and fish, birds and beasts would be erased only to reappear, as different species, in singular profusion.

The world political economy described in genesis above would not have been possible without money as a way of storing value. What people value can be stored in the form of land, tools, skills, but the most convenient such store is a symbolic one—money. All these stores of value are called *capital*. They can all be loaned on the understanding that the loan will be returned, and a loan like this creates credit. Since "every materialist society . . . has to have a system for creating credit," and because money is so durable, portable, and flexible, this is one of the main things money is used to do (Strange 1988:89). Money, in other words, is the most popular way of making loans, that is, of creating credit.

Money is pooled and loaned in institutions called banks. Bankers store the money that people want to save, and entrepreneurs rent this—plus money that does not materially exist—to fund their commercial projects, paying rent for the loan from their profits. This sustains banks and bankers as businesses, making them in turn major players in any complex political economy.

The portability of money is most evident where it has been rendered in electronic form inside computers, as symbols, that is, of what is already a symbol. This is "pure" money as it were; number without form. It only has a function, and as such can be used, in ways completely detached from production or trade, to facilitate its own production and supply. By placing these symbols of a symbol in strategic relationships, what is more, highly abstract profits (and highly abstract losses) can be made—practically instantaneously—half a world away from whoever is doing the relating. These profits and losses are respected because of what they represent. No matter how abstract they are, they can be downloaded from their glowing screens into named accounts. The figures in these accounts can be converted into concrete national currencies, or in the case of losses, into legitimate claims for currency. The currency in these accounts can then be withdrawn as hard cash and used to buy goods and services. The losses can be converted into debt, default, bankruptcy, unemployment, and if serious enough, into the collapse of the system as a whole.

How are we to understand stored value and credit creation when it takes such an attenuated form? What does money mean when it is used in such an abstracted way?

In mercantilist terms, capital as portable as money, and more particularly, as cybermoney in computers, enhances state vulnerability. Any state vulnerability, to any kind of mercantilist, will be intolerable. Mercantilism as a concept was coined to account for the defensive way in which European state makers of the seventeenth and eighteenth centuries sought to consolidate their sovereign autonomy by building up trade surpluses and storing what they had earned in precious metals of maximum intrinsic value. (This is no different from people without debts who prefer others to be beholden to them and who put their savings in bullion under the bed.) The mercantilists of today may not believe any longer in hoarding gold, but they do retain a deep suspicion of money and credit that isn't nationally controllable and controlled.

Those who have historically argued against mercantilism have tried to show how countries that hoard precious metals and that run a balance-of-trade surplus as a way of not depleting their hoard (exporting more, that is, than they import) act in self-defeating ways. Adam Smith's close friend, David Hume, was one such antagonist. In his discussion "Of Money," for example, he declared "the absolute quantity of . . . precious metals" to be a matter of "great indifference." "There are," he said, "only two circumstances of any importance [with regard to precious metals], namely, their gradual increase, and their thorough . . . circulation" (Hume 1955:46). Hume's liberalism was also apparent in his trade theory, where, as in his analysis "Of the Jealousy of Trade," he argued that interstate commercial rivalries were understandable but wrong. We "daily adopt," he said,

> in every art, the inventions and improvements of our neighbours. The commodity is first imported from abroad, to our great discontent, while we imagine that it drains us of our money. Afterwards, the art itself is gradually imported, to our visible advantage. Yet we continue still to repine, that one neighbour should possess any art, industry, and invention; forgetting that, had they not first instructed us, we should have been at present barbarians.

Thus did he, "as a BRITISH subject," pray for the "flourishing commerce" of "GERMANY, SPAIN, ITALY, and even FRANCE" (Hume 1955: 78–79).

State makers persuaded of the benefits of liberal doctrine aren't about to surrender all control over the material practices that make them powerful, however. So those who endorse the idea of free trade still keep control of money and credit. Indeed, they keep too much control of it, the more extremist liberals say. Because state makers can print notes and mint coin, they can physically make more money and extend more credit than there are goods and services for the buying. Too much money chasing too few goods is inflation, and this has, indeed, been the general effect, liberals say, of having state makers controlling money supply. It's too tempting to print and mint what you want when it's your main medium of exchange and your main store of value. It's too tempting, for example, to "money" your way out of debt. For this reason liberals have historically argued for limiting governmental controls over market activity, including the monetary flows used to facilitate market activity. Liberals, and particularly classical liberals, prefer money policies that operate with minimal governmental intervention and with maximal regard to supply and demand.

The laissez-faire system of the nineteenth century was based on gold. Gold was bought and sold freely, though the main national banks did so at a set price in sterling. This was supposed to make for stable national currencies and steady flows of money that, in the absence of a world bank or a world government, allowed marketeers to generate and utilize credit in a balanced way. In practice it did do this, but as Marxists have long pointed out, it did so only by skewing the system as a whole. The state makers of rich countries like Great Britain were able to rely on their capitalist marketeers to work the system to the national advantage. As the leading imperialists of the day, British state makers and wealth makers were able to ensure that "free trade" took place in the context of monopolistic money markets, controlled in turn by the City of London. So when there were problems, then as now, "the poorer nations and poorer classes within societies . . . paid the price of adjustment through higher rates of unemployment and decreased welfare" (Gilpin 1987:126).

A good deal of human suffering is summarized by the concept of a "price of adjustment." Stable dealings for capitalists were possible, it seems, but only because the masses didn't know their Marx, and accepted as inevitable or ordained their collective degradation.

With the advent of World War I the global monetary system, such as it was, fell apart. After that war was over an attempt was made to rebuild a system based on gold-backed currencies like sterling, but Britain was in debt and decline. The United States was not yet interested in running the world capitalist system by itself. So state makers reverted to mercantilism. The British had their sterling bloc. The United States made a dollar bloc. The French made a gold one. Meanwhile, the German, Italian, and Japanese state makers went for "autarkic empires," that is, for self-sufficiency by imperial means. Another war ensued.

Debt

The decades of high growth in finance capital flows that followed World War II were also decades of growing debt. By the 1980s the most indebted country was the United States. Because the U.S. dollar was used as the world currency, however, U.S. state makers were able to maintain a standard of living higher than U.S. productivity warranted by the simple device of printing money. This reduced the value of each unit of currency, but as long as the country remained productive, the dollar remained sufficiently valued to be in demand. Those holding U.S. dollars in reserve sought to protect the value of their reserves by investing in U.S. production and property, but they never seriously contested the continued use of U.S. currency as the de facto world one.

No other indebted country could do what the United States did, however. The crunch for many of the others came in the early 1980s.

By the end of 1981, for example, "of the total debt of $271 billion owed to commercial banks by twenty-one major LDCs [less developed countries], almost one-half . . . was due to be repaid in a year or less" (Edwards 1985:188). Declining prices for LDC exports, caused in turn by decreased demand on the part of "developed" countries (because of recession and rising interest rates) caught most debtors without the capacity to pay. In August 1982 Mexican state makers were forced to suspend their country's foreign exchange dealings, signaling thereby an incapacity to meet the nation's debt repayments. Other countries' leaders followed suit, calling for debt rescheduling and the deferral of repayments.

Rising interest rates were the immediate trigger. In the early 1970s the oil-producing (OPEC) countries quadrupled the price of oil. This not only caused severe adjustment problems (including recession) throughout the world, but the windfall profits the OPEC countries made were put back into the world's banks and used to provide cheap credit for developing countries in Latin America, Africa, and Eastern Europe. These were largely short-term loans and they were mostly made by commercial banks, who in their desire for profits had built for themselves huge capital overhangs. In 1981, for example, the nine largest U.S. banks had "nearly 300 per cent of their capital exposed in loans to developing and east European countries" (Edwards 1985:190), and "the ratio of the banks' own capital to total assets was around 4 per cent. . . . [By comparison] in the early nineteenth century the ratio had been about 40 per cent."

In Marxist terms, what had happened was only to be expected. Rates of profit were declining, an effect Marx had anticipated and one he considered a definitive feature of capitalism. Since rescue could only entail further exploitation, classical Marxists saw the situation as potentially revolutionary. Reformist Marxists were not so sure. The whole picture they found depressing in the extreme. Living standards for much of Latin America and sub-Saharan Africa were falling to those of the 1970s and 1960s. Debt restructuring seemed mostly to involve a massive transfer of wealth from the poor in poor countries to the rich in the poor and the rich ones. And there seemed nary a revolution in sight.

The basic cause of the debt crisis in classical liberal terms could only be a distorted market. The cure was to allow self-equilibrating responses on the part of the buyers and sellers of credit themselves. Bank stockholders, managers, and debt-burdened regimes should all pay the price of their inefficiency and go to the wall.

To reformist liberals, it was not so much a matter of market distortion as market "mismanagement," both on the part of the creditors and on the part of the state makers of the countries in debt.

And in the event it was reform liberalism that prevailed. The debts were restructured and the bankers were saved. Many people, living at a considerable sociological distance from those who had originally made the contracts, were not.

In the longer term the debt crisis depressed productive activity, employment capacity, and living standards in a large number of countries that could not pay interest. None defaulted, however, because of the costs that delinking from the world market were supposed to carry. Since many in a position to authorize default were corrupt, with a profound commitment to their own privileged lifestyles and with foreign bank acounts to feed, they were not about to bite the hands that ultimately fed them. Despite odd noises to this effect, they were more interested in complying with the IMF's classical liberal deregulation requirements for debt rescheduling than trying anything more radical, like default.

"Never before," observed one analyst (George 1988:44), "have so few been so wrong with such a devastating effect on so many." Just how devastating can be judged from the fact that "in spite of total debt service . . . of more than 1.3 trillion dollars from 1982–90, the debtor countries as a group began the 1990's fully 61 percent more in debt than they were in 1982." Moreover, "the debt burden of the very poorest . . . was up by 110 per cent [and in these same eight years] the poor [had] financed [the equivalent of] six Marshall Plans" (George 1992:xvi).

In Marxist terms, the elite few had merely been promoting their class interests. It was only to be expected. This was at the workers' expense, but this too was only to be expected. Capitalism is about the creative use of credit. Credit is an incentive to capitalists to expand production. Expanding production means further exploiting the labor power of the workers, making credit, in Marx's words, the "purest and most colossal form of gambling and swindling."

Bretton Woods: Currency Convertibility

Out of World War II the U.S. state makers emerged triumphant, determined to make the world "safe for democracy" and determined to capitalize on their productive edge. At the same time Europe and Japan, two centers of the prewar industrial world, were in ruins. "Millions of people were on the move; occupying troops, defeated troops, evacuees, slave laborers, those expelled as borders were redrawn; refugees of every description. Food was hopelessly insufficient. The military administrations were ill-equipped to deal with huge civilian problems. Civilian administrations were . . .

disorganized and often without much authority" (Armstrong 1991:3). These once highly productive regions were a mess. And yet out of their ashes was built "the greatest boom in the history of capitalism" (Armstrong 1991:6). The question is, how?

The postwar situation was not as bad as it might have first appeared. The widespread destruction of the means of production brought about by the war was not as great as the chaos at the time seemed to suggest. Indeed, most capitalist countries were producing as much or more by the end of the war as they had been at the beginning (Armstrong 1991:7). Moreover, many capitalists like war. Wars present all kinds of profitable opportunities. World War II was no exception, and at the end of it the same capitalists were just as keen to make profits out of postwar reconstruction as they had been out of wartime destruction.

State makers were quick to curb the potentially assertive power of organized labor as well. Capitalists saw a potential threat to their profits and feared that in having to pay for too many concessions a slump would ensue, even perhaps one serious enough to cause revolts. With the advent of the Cold War the state makers of the major democracies concurred, and they moved to contain the strength of labor and to augment that of capitalists. In the United States, for example, a postwar law designed to endorse the right to work was made into one enjoining the federal government "to . . . promote free enterprise . . . under which there will be afforded useful employment for those who are willing and seeking to work"; a law, in other words, that promised "anyone needing a job" the right to "go out and look" for one (Armstrong 1991:14).

Since capitalists do, on balance, prefer an orderly international environment, free-flowing trade, and an organized payments system, there is a need for appropriate mechanisms to help ensure them. As representatives of the major capitalist postwar power, and as point riders for a country bursting with individuals with a basic interest in "the largest possible markets for . . . exports and freedom to invest abroad wherever [it] was most profitable" (Armstrong 1991:27), U.S. state makers were well placed and very willing to oblige.

The reconstruction of the postwar world, and the installation of the appropriate mechanisms, began at Bretton Woods, New Hampshire, in 1944. At a meeting there of forty-four different countries—the United Nations Monetary and Financial Conference—arrangements were made for a postwar monetary and trading order that not only allowed for sovereign autonomy, but also fixed exchange rates, that is, a means whereby one currency could be reliably converted into another. It was an order articulating comparative advantage.

The first twenty-five postwar years were boom years. The availability of large pools of credit made possible rapid growth in production and trade, particularly for the wealthier states, who quickly assembled themselves into an Organization for Economic Cooperation and Development (the OECD). Global firms were established in growing numbers to take advantage of the new opportunities. Capital, moving from one country to another, incorporated labor into globally integrated structures of mass production. Growth rates soared.

It is interesting to note in retrospect how U.S. greediness in the immediate postwar period nearly scuttled the whole recovery process. The disabled production systems of Europe and Japan were still prostrate, and yet they needed commodities, which Americans were only too pleased to provide. In making such provision, however, the Americans took in exchange what little foreign currency Europeans and Japanese had left. The point was ultimately reached where the countries concerned had no more money.

Not only did this portend the potential disappearance of what were major markets, posing a serious threat to U.S. exports and industries; there were also plenty of European and Japanese—workers in particular—who were prepared to strike out on their own on a permanent basis, and they were not talking of doing so along capitalist lines. The need to kick-start European and Japanese production systems became acute, not only to preempt a disaster for the U.S. one, but also, as the Cold War confrontation with Soviet state makers grew more acute, to keep the capitalist world "safe." So the Americans abandoned classical liberalism and actively embraced the need for reformist liberal intervention instead, instituting as a consequence the Marshall Plan for Europe and the Dodge Plan for the Far East to fund the respective attempts at recovery .

With the U.S. Federal Reserve as the "world's banker," and the dollar the de facto currency internationally, it was U.S. state makers who determined how many dollars came out of that country to invest in production around the world. And come out they did, in a seemingly never-ending stream. The U.S. state makers were seeking to contain what they construed as communist expansionism worldwide, and they were prepared to pay handsomely in Europe and Japan to construct bulwarks against the Soviets. They fought two major proxy wars, one in Korea and one in Vietnam, in the process, to the considerable material benefit of countries like South Korea and Japan.

U.S. spending overseas was not U.S. saving at home, however. A United States providing dollars for global use was a United States running a chronic balance-of-payments deficit, which is not something that can be done indefinitely, as anyone knows who has spent all they have and all they can borrow, and then looks around for someone to express confidence in the value of their IOUs. The United States was able to live beyond its means longer than most by the time-honored expedient, already mentioned, of printing money, and paying for imports in depreciated "greenbacks." Since the dollar was the key currency in the capitalist world market and the one that other countries saved their money in, the U.S. state makers were able in this way to pass on the cost of these wars and the country's domestic living standards to the rest of the world. Because the increase in U.S. currency was not matched by an increase in U.S. production, however, the Americans were in effect exporting inflation. Their alternative was a less expensive foreign policy and standard of living, neither of which they wanted or were prepared to implement.

Under the Bretton Woods agreements the dollar was backed by gold at $35 an ounce. Over time, however, no one believed that U.S. state makers had the requisite gold to cover all the dollars they had printed. Lack of confidence in the dollar became acute.

The French were the first to ask for gold and the first to be refused. Indeed, the United States had not had the requisite gold for some time. To deal with the growing lack of confidence in the U.S. dollar, U.S. state makers had either to slow the flow of their dollars into the world pool, and with it the growth of the world political economy, or find a new way of putting money into the global system. In the event it did neither. Japanese and German state makers decided to buy the U.S. deficit instead, allowing U.S. state makers to repudiate the original Bretton Woods agreement outright.

The rescue of the U.S. dollar by the Japanese and the Germans was seen by liberals as a kind of swap. U.S. state makers printed dollars. They and their capitalists spent them on wars on behalf of "world security" and in productive global enterprises. Each year the Japanese and the Germans bought large amounts of U.S. government securities to cover the national budgetary shortfall.

In liberal terms, the Germans and the Japanese were in effect making the United States loans, albeit depreciating ones, since they held the securities they bought from the United States in dollars, and these securities were quickly worth less than their face value. (This wasn't all bad since dollars worth less than their face value are also, from a foreign perspective, overvalued dollars, and this made the United States easier to sell against.) In return the United States didn't oppose Japanese and German tariffs on U.S. goods, or oppose as much as it might have done growing Japanese or German export competitiveness.

Marxists, by contrast, saw all this in terms of U.S. hegemony, that is, in terms of U.S. state makers, as the world's bankers, indirectly taxing the world, enabling the U.S. well-to-do to live beyond their means. To Marxists, the whole project was highly exploitative, since the ones ultimately paying were those earning less because of the decline in the real value of their wages, or those earning nothing at all because they had been made redundant.

In 1971 U.S. President Richard Nixon cut the link between the dollar and gold. He abandoned the gold standard, that is, and announced at the same time temporary controls on imports. In 1973 the decision was taken to "float" exchange rates altogether. Rather than adapt to the changes that had occurred in the world political economy, in other words, and accept a shift in the world's center of gravity from the Euro-Atlantic rim to the Asia-Pacific; rather than share control over the central institutions of global monetary control; U.S. state makers and wealth makers chose to abandon the principles on which the whole system was based. The dollar continued as the world currency, for lack of a globally acceptable alternative, but major currencies were no longer tied to each other in any kind of predictable relationship. State makers and wealth makers, under pressure to earn more to pay for rising oil prices, started "dirty" floating, that is, deliberately undervaluing their currencies to make their exports more competitively priced abroad, or overvaluing them to control inflation at home. Groups of states, like those in Europe, started setting up their own monetary arrangements. It was the beginning of a sustained recession.

The instability of the 1970s continued through the 1980s and into the 1990s. The Soviet empire collapsed. Oil profits from the price hikes of the 1970s, recycled through the world's banks to poor state regimes hungry for credit, aggravated a massive debt crisis that had begun well before but came to a head when interest rates soared. Though a range of rescheduling arrangements were made, it was estimated by 1991 that the poorer states, through their debt repayment commitments, were subsidizing the richer ones at a rate of $60 billion a year (Vickers 1991:4). A new equilibrium was being established, to use liberalist language, though it was not one where the costs and benefits were equally shared. In the richer countries, for example, there was unemployment, a concerted attack on the value of working wages, cutbacks on government spending, and the wholesale "abandonment" of regions and peoples that did not fit the "new patterns of international production" (Walker 1988:40).

Despite its downside, the current monetary system is considered by liberals to be basically beneficial. A more global political economy needs constant fine-tuning anyway, the reformists among them say. The "trickle down" of new wealth does continue, they argue, despite inequalities and disparities. And this still provides the most "natural" solution, in their opinion, to problems of "adjustment."

To Marxists it is more a matter of "flood up," not trickle down. Not only does the current system create poverty as well as wealth; it also carries with it the promise of "complete exclusion" for those made "dispensable" to the "functional needs of the world [political] economy as a whole" (Walker 1988:42). The more ambitious of the poorer state wealth makers, driven into more capital- and technology-intensive production, have found richer states complaining that their unemployment is being caused by the export of jobs to cheap labor states. Some rich world state makers have even staged their own revolt by "deregulating," which in Marxist terms is a preemptive ploy by state makers desperate to protect themselves from the electoral consequences of recurrent market crises. Classically liberalist deregulation policies allow state makers to put at an electoral distance a whole process they have failed to control. This, they hope, will allow them to escape blame.

The basic problem, in Marxist terms, is that the capitalist system is organized only indirectly to meet human needs. It is simply not planned.

If it were planned, liberals say, people wouldn't be so entrepreneurial, since there'd be no incentive for them to produce. Capitalism provides incentives in the form of profits for capitalists and money to live on for workers. It's a very dynamic system because it's built upon strong human predilections. These are not necessarily our highest predilections. This is why Marxists say that while a lot gets done by capitalist means, because it gets done for largely selfish reasons a lot of people don't get a lot.

After Bretton Woods

After the U.S. repudiation of the Bretton Woods arrangements the global monetary system came to be dominated by three market groups—international bankers, foreign exchange dealers, and international portfolio dealers.

International bankers serviced the needs of foreign direct investors, moving around the world as investors did, striving all the while to minimize the effects of local financial regulations. It was the bankers who decided, in effect, what was to be developed and how it was to be developed, both decisions with important social consequences. They did very large deals in a relatively limited way, however. This had everything to do with profitable returns in the medium to long term. It had much less to do with the kind of planning that development often requires.

Foreign exchange and international portfolio dealers were even freer agents. Their activities were even shorter-term and less institutionalized than those of the bankers. Their speculative use of "footloose money," for example, their use of special havens around the world designed to "shelter" money as capital, bore witness to both the regulated and deregulated nature of the world money market. Again, the sums were very large. "In April 1989," for example, "foreign exchange trading in the world's financial centers averaged about $650 billion a day, equivalent to nearly $500 million a minute and to forty times the amount of world trade a day" (Frieden 1991:427).

This was not what was envisaged at Bretton Woods. More accurately, it was envisaged with some apprehension, and deliberately opposed (Helleiner 1994:163). The agreement at Bretton Woods was designed to make for world trade in commodities, but not for world trade in money. In commodity terms, in other words, the postwar order was meant to be a classically liberal one. In monetary terms, however, the Bretton Woods planners wanted (liberally speaking) a much more reformist one, with state controls on money flows, that is, fixed exchange rates. Speculators moving large amounts of capital from country to country were likely, it was felt, to cause "adjustment" problems, such as unemployment, loss of social morale, and crime. In a bid to minimize these effects state makers were likely to become protectionist, which was not something those with vivid memories of both the Great Depression of the 1930s and the subsequent world war were about to countenance. Hence their emphasis on the need for capital controls, in the first place on legal transactions (with state makers taking "cooperative initiatives" to this effect) and in the second place on illegal ones (with state makers keeping a very close check on currency dealing) (Helleiner 1994:166).

In the event capital controls were not implemented. The state makers of the United States, to maintain their country's postwar dominance, vetoed suggestions that would have provided cooperative ways of doing so. A strong putsch by capitalists also frustrated moves to implement controls over currency exchange. As part of the putsch a Eurodollar market was established in London. This was a "kind of 'adventure playground'" for bankers (Helleiner 1994:169). It also brought some prestige to the hard-pressed British, who had decided by this stage to opt for the chance to maximize their own share of what was happening rather than fight for any preeminence themselves. Competitive deregulations quickly followed throughout the capitalist industrial world.

Classical liberals approve of deregulation because it gives free rein to entrepreneurial opportunists, who can then test the limits of state makers' controls and push beyond them to look for creative ways to make profits that, quite fortuitously, benefit us all. Money, Hayek says, is "indispensable for extending reciprocal cooperation beyond the limits of human awareness." And while

> producers, traders, and financiers are not concerned with the con-
> crete needs of known people but with abstract calculation of costs
> and profit . . . concern for profit is just what makes possible the
> more effective use of resources. . . . [Hence] disdain of profit is due
> to ignorance, and to an attitude that we may if we wish admire in
> the ascetic . . . but . . . is selfish to the extent that it imposes asceti-
> cism and indeed deprivations . . . on others (Hayek 1988:104–105).

Issues like capital strike, capital flight, tax evasion, the social costs of reductions in "welfarism," and diminished capacities for politico-economic planning are all brushed aside by liberals under the heading of "adjustment."

All of which is highly desirable as far as classical Marxists are concerned as well, since the "spontaneous extended human order created by a competitive market," which liberal utopians like Hayek envisage, is not, classical Marxists say, what we get in practice. What we do get is much less fortuitous and much more exploitative and therefore much more likely to result in revolution. They observe how the "world monetary system has always corresponded strictly to the organizing structure of the world order: to each phase of the history of capitalism there has been a particular monetary counterpart" (Amin 1993:2). And out of the current phase they envisage capitalism's collapse. We must anticipate that day, they say, because it is only then that we will be able to provide something more sensibly designed; something more explicitly concerned with moral principles; something more explicitly democratic and conscious of basic human needs.

Reformist liberals, who are more wary than classical liberals of the dangers of unsupervised speculation, along with reformist Marxists, who are more concerned than classical Marxists to do something now rather than wait for capitalism to collapse, recommend regulation. Both are adamant that world movements of money are well within the power of state makers to control, and what is more, that state makers should control them. That state makers have not chosen to exercise such controls, they say, has more to do with either the degree of their acceptance of classical liberalism or the degree of their collusion with their capitalist classmates.

Members of social movements articulate their own accounts of the world's financial vagaries. Bolivian housewives, for example, are reported as asking: "What have we done to incur . . . foreign debt? Is it possible that our children have eaten too much? Is it possible that our children have studied in the best colleges? Or do they wear the best clothes? Have we improved our standard of living? Have our wages become so great?" (Vickers 1991:9). Even the Marxist concern for the way that money made from credit or currency is money made by exploiting people's labor power, fails to account, many feminists say, for the fact that the "people" in question are more male than female, for the extent of women's contribution to the world's finances, or the extent of the plight, especially, of poor state women.

One of the strengths of postmodernist political economics is the way in which it demonstrates how issues like these are rendered largely invisible; how the invisibility is made to seem a normal, natural, and therefore uncontroversial state of world affairs; and how skewed a purpose is served in the process.

The IMF

Unlike the Bretton Woods plan for the overall control of world credit and currency exchange, the International Monetary Fund, which was also a child of this key conference, has survived. With the radical changes in the world monetary system since 1944, however, what the IMF does has also changed, as has its systemic significance. Originally made up of only thirty-nine countries, for example, it now has a membership of 180. Along with the growth in membership has gone expanded responsibilities. Originally designed as having a supervisory role, it has taken on a more interventionist one, and it now directs money flows to purposes never envisaged by those at Bretton Woods.

The Articles of Agreement at Bretton Words established "fixed but adjustable" exchange rates between national currencies. It also established the IMF to promote the stability of the global currency exchange system. In doing so it provided money to countries suffering short-term balance-of-payments problems. Promoting stability meant constantly surveying what was happening in the system, identifying problems in this regard, and supplying temporary loans and advice to countries trying to reduce budget imbalances. The money for such loans came from "quota" contributions from member countries. Countries granted loans drew them down in other currencies and made repayments in their own. This made it possible not to default on debts they lacked the currency to pay.

The voting rights of members in the IMF are proportional to the size of their quota contributions. Since the largest contributors are capitalist industrial countries, like those of Europe and the United

States, the IMF is controlled by these countries. Its concerns are accordingly those of the capitalist industrial world.

In the 1950s and 1960s these concerns were reformist liberal ones, with the IMF intervening to mediate and to help preserve the integrity of a "liberal internationalist" order (Pauly 1994:294). With the monetary troubles of the 1970s and the expansion of private credit flows the IMF began to lose its capacity to control currency exchange and correct member state imbalances. It retained a role, however, as a lender to poorer states in serious debt, and in the 1980s it found much to do managing and helping fund the debt reschedules negotiated between countries on the brink of default and private banks. Special Drawing Rights were created in the process as a "minor" kind of "international monetary issue" (Amin 1993:7).

When the Soviet Union collapsed, the IMF was drawn into the process of integrating the new states that formed into the capitalist world political economy. Indeed, the IMF has lasted so long by now that it has become "the only nearly universal forum for the discussion of global monetary issues" (Pauly 1994:207). The reformist liberals of the capitalist industrial world, in particular, see it continuing to serve a useful purpose in this regard.

Today's IMF promotes a range of highly specific prescriptions for sustainable development, prescriptions that reflect "decades of debate on the normative core of modern capitalism" and that include a "number of 'ought' statements of sweeping character: national policies ought to encourage expanding volumes of trade on a non-discriminatory basis; payments balances ought to tend towards equilibrium; stability ought to be the norm in exchange markets; policies ought to promote economic growth; . . . price stability ought to be achieved"; and "economic policies" ought to be "sound" (Pauly 1994:211). For "sound," of course, read "reformist liberal," since this is the ideology such prescriptions serve.

Classical liberals see no reason for any of this, of course. The recent revival of classical liberalism among the state makers and wealth makers of the industrial capitalist world has seen, as a consequence, a new emphasis on market "efficiency" and market "discipline" as the preferred means of dealing with monetary imbalances, and a new acceptance of the idea that free currency exchange, and free trade and investment, are compatible practices, not contradictory ones. There is nothing that the IMF can do, they argue, that private entrepreneurs and the "hidden hand" cannot.

Classical Marxists concur, though for very different reasons. Capitalism must rot, in classical Marxist parlance, before it is likely to be replaced. Meddling in national monetary concerns, the way the IMF does, can only delay matters. Classical Marxists, in other words, like all Marxists, see the IMF in terms of the accumulation of capital on a world scale and the globalization of production. Foreign exchange crises appear, to them, to be a matter of bringing the state makers into line with what global producers want. The IMF appears as villainous; as a capitalist plot; and what is more, given the preeminence of the United States as the dominant fraction of world capital, as a U.S. capitalist plot. Part of the plot is to get the makers of indebted states to impose "wage freezes, devaluations, public sector cut-backs, strike bans, privatisation and de-regulation" policies, rather than provide social welfare support. The point is to renationalize monetary risks and to protect the ruling-class interests of state makers and international bank managers.

Reformist Marxists prescribe other sorts of intervention, ones that they see as being more conducive to social justice and equity. They urge debtor governments to default, for example, rather than "structurally adjust"; to use their labor policies and their power to regulate money flows to foster local markets and local mixtures of factors of production; to legislate redistribution; and to protect the environment regardless—all initiatives the IMF, as currently constituted, is never likely to take (Pauly 1994:211).

Mercantilists, meanwhile, seem to be reconstituting themselves at the regional level, arguing for monetary arrangements and exchange rate coordination among blocs of states. It is at this intermediate level, rather than a global or a local one, they say, that states can now best promote their production and trade and best protect themselves from the "monetary terrorism" of global speculators. This, too, is a retrograde step in IMF terms. The liberal internationalism of the IMF is still "masked" by the "technical mysticism of Fund economists" but it is one that articulates deep liberal ideals (Pauly 1994:212).

The World Bank and Regional Banks

The other institutional child of the Articles of Agreement at Bretton Woods was the International Bank for Reconstruction and Development (the IBRD), later to be known as the World Bank. While plans for the IMF were well in hand long before the Bretton Woods meeting, those for a world bank were not. Indeed, it was only the persistence of the British political economist John Maynard Keynes that ensured a world bank was discussed there and finally accepted as such. In principle, Keynes wanted a world bank that could issue world money. In practice he was trying to defend the interests of the British, the by-then-defunct imperial hegemon. In the event he got only what the United States, as the new dominant power, was prepared to accept.

The World Bank was set up as a source of development funds for member states. Over time the Bank's focus shifted from the postwar reconstruction of Europe (a task performed by the Marshall Plan rather than the Bretton Woods agreements) to the development of the world as a whole. This meant in practice a major emphasis on North-South relations, a role the World Bank now plays largely alone, given the gap left by the "near-total absence of [a] coherent North-South strategy formulated by anybody else" (George 1994:1).

While largely alone at the global level, the World Bank is not alone at the regional level. It is only one now of a global consortium of public international financial institutions that includes the Inter-American Development Bank, the Asian Development Bank, the African Development Bank, and the European Bank for Reconstruction and Development. These institutions are all modeled on the World Bank. The first three were set up in the 1960s to make medium- to long-term loans to fund large-scale development projects in their respective regions. The last was set up in the 1990s to provide loans to the new nations of the former Soviet Union and Warsaw Pact.

The World Bank was originally established to provide funds at market rates to member countries, to allow them to implement infrastructural schemes and projects that had some promise of a nationally significant yield. Over time, however, and particularly after the "lending crisis" of the 1980s, private banks became reluctant to make long-maturing loans to South-world states for developmental purposes. The World Bank then began to use its authority to coax such banks into cofinancing deals. By offering loans itself, it was able to encourage private banks and North-world governmental aid agencies to provide monies, too.

Like the IMF, the World Bank also became involved in nonproject loans to countries with serious deficits in their balance of payments. These loans were made on the same sort of conditions as the IMF ones, obliging borrowers to make the same sort of "structural adjustments" and drawing the same charges of neoimperialism (for having forced states to accept global firms, for example, or to accept cheap prices for their raw materials) as those leveled at the IMF.

The World Bank borrows the capital that it lends on the world's private money markets. As security it offers the subscriptions made to the Bank by its member states. Because security of this sort is considered to be extremely sound, it has no trouble raising the money it wants. The confidence of those lending to the Bank is raised even further by the Bank's highly conservative policy of only lending what it borrows. The Bank's capital/loans ratio of 1:1 is in marked contrast to the same ratio commercial banks use, which is usually more like 1:10. The Bank also earns interest on what it lends, and these profits become part of its capital stock, too. High market confidence also accrues from the fact that, like the IMF, the World Bank is governed by its members; that large subscribers have a proportionately large say in how the Bank is run; and that the United States, as the dominant country in subscription terms, has a dominant role in Bank governance as well. The president of the Bank, for example, has always been an American, and in the case of the Banks's fifth president, Robert McNamara, a highly proactive one.

The Bank also provides technical advice to countries preparing loan applications, and it assists client states to use the loans that they receive to best effect. In the process of providing such advice the Bank has cultivated a development discourse characterized by one critic as "strangely featureless" in its account of the world. The Bank talks of "disembodied forces" such as "debt, adjustment, poverty, and the environment." Where something "bad" happens, the Bank calls it a "trade-off." The "fundamental solution to nearly every problem," the Bank says, is "growth," and growth has to be "sustainable" (Rich 1994:18). Language like this is meant, in part, to allow Bank members to talk about painful human problems without wincing. Its critics say such language impoverishes even further those the Bank would assist.

The Bank remains a highly controversial institution.

Defenders like Steer point to what has been achieved in developmental terms in the last twenty-five years, and by implication, they laud the Bank's beneficial effects. They highlight, for example, a "doubling of food production, a halving of infant mortality, a doubling of secondary school enrollment rates, a doubling of real incomes, and a sharp move toward democracy in developing countries" (Steer 1994:49). Admittedly, they say, structural adjustment has created problems, but those countries that do not adjust, that do not make a meaningful attempt to live within their means, have fared worse than those that have. Moreover, World Bank help must be seen in the context of the fact that in poorer states the Bank accounts for only "2 percent of total investment" (Steer 1994:49).

Critics like George and Sabelli see Bank-promoted development in a very different light. The word *development* itself they define as "programmed and violent change through outside intervention"; change that marginalizes people on a scale "previously unheard of, while simultaneously undermining their political capacity to fight back" (George and Sabelli 1994:56). Furthermore, any statistical summary of developmental success has to be seen, they suggest, in the context of an absolute increase in the numbers of the poverty-stricken worldwide. It must also be seen in the context of the Bank's own Wapenhans Report, made in 1992, that found that a "large and increasing number of Bank projects are failing, even when assessed only on narrow economic criteria." One in five of nearly two thousand projects in more than one hundred countries, the report said, "presented major problems," a proportion that in the early 1980s was only one-tenth overall, but in some sectors was up to two-fifths of the total by the time the report was compiled. Only two-fifths of the Bank's borrowers, furthermore, complied with their loan agreements, and against those three-fifths that didn't, there were "no discernible sanctions" (George and Sabelli 1994:223–224).

Is the Bank the "cornerstone of the house of development" or the "visible hand" of free market capitalism? Is it the leading advocate of a free global market or the interventionist promoter of predetermined change? Is it the secular defender of rationalistic modernism or the high priest of liberal redemption? To answer questions like these we need a better idea of what "development" means, and I turn to this topic next.

Radford observes at the end of his essay on money in prison that where there are "infinite means economic organisation and activity" become "redundant." By his reckoning, plenty would dispense with any need for trade flows or financing. With "every want . . . satisfied without effort," there would be no IMF or World Bank.

World trade and finance flows are indicative, then, of a world where goods and services are notably less than infinite. Our world is one where strictly limited means must still be distributed among "unlimited and competing ends," and where opulence is to be found only in planetary pockets. Why, then, with the productive powers now at the disposal of our species, are we not closer than we are to having something like general largesse? That is the question.

7

World Development?

❖ **M. Atterbury (1964) "Depression Hits Robinson Crusoe's Island"**

"Friday," said Robinson Crusoe, "I'm sorry, I fear I must lay you off."

"What do you mean, Master?"

"Why, you know there's a big surplus of last year's crop. I don't need you to plant another this year. I've got enough goatskin coats to last me a lifetime. My house needs no repairs. I can gather turtle eggs myself. There's an overproduction. When I need you I will send for you. You needn't wait around here."

"That's all right, Master, I'll plant my own crop, build up my own hut and gather all the eggs and nuts I want myself. I'll get along fine."

"Where will you do all this, Friday?"

"Here on this island."

"This island belongs to me, you know. I can't allow you to do that. When you can't pay me anything I need I might as well not own it."

"Then I'll build a canoe and fish in the ocean. You don't own that."

"That's alright, provided you don't use any of my trees for your canoe, or build it on my land, or use my beach for a landing place, and do your fishing far enough away so you don't interfere with my riparian rights."

"I never thought of that, Master. I can do without a boat, though. I can swim over to that rock and fish there and gather sea-gull eggs."

"No you won't, Friday. The rock is mine. I own riparian rights."

"What shall I do, Master?"

"That's your problem, Friday. You're a free man, and you know about rugged individualism being maintained here."

"I guess I'll starve, Master. May I stay here until I do? Or shall I swim beyond your riparian rights and drown or starve there?"

"I've thought of something, Friday. I don't like to carry my garbage down to the shore each day. You may stay and do that. Then whatever is left of it, after my dog and cat have fed, you may eat. You're in luck."

"Thank you, Master. That is true charity."

"One more thing, Friday. This island is over-populated. Fifty percent of the people are unemployed. We are undergoing a severe depression, and there is no way that I can see to end it. No one but a charlatan would say that he could. So keep a lookout and let no one land here to settle. And if any ship comes don't let them land any goods of any kind. You must be protected against foreign labour. Conditions are fundamentally sound, though. And prosperity is just around the corner."

Whatever else "development" might mean, the growing disparities in the world's wealth suggest that it is a "more or less" concept. Even in the two-man case Atterbury describes, there is overproduction and mass unemployment, great wealth and absolute poverty, overpopulation and severe depression.

These disparities are so deeply entrenched that the concept of *development* alone cannot explain them. Something more radical and structural is needed that can account for them. Hence the concept of *imperialism* with its connotations of oppression and exploitation. It's clear that on Atterbury's version of Crusoe's island, for example, Friday is free, but that his freedom allows him only to beg or starve. Any attempt to do more than that, to provide for himself, for example, is inadmissible. He can carry Crusoe's garbage but he can't fish or farm. He can provide Crusoe with labor, however. He can even be recruited to help hold off those who would want to come and share Crusoe's bounty, to trade with Crusoe or to work as garbage carriers, too. But he can't copy Crusoe. Were he to try we can be certain he'd be imprisoned or killed, since Crusoe has not only wealth, he has coercive power.

MEASURE FOR MEASURE

How are we to assess the comparative well-being of earth's peoples? What measure will show us most clearly, concisely, and comprehensively the distribution of wealth in the world?

The most common measure of comparative well-being is a statecentric one. "States" loom large in world political economy, which is why it still makes sense to talk of an international political economy as well. The state is not all that looms large in the world political economy, which is why so much attention gets paid today to transnational firms, global nongovernmental organizations, and various social movements. The common choice of a statecentric measure of development, however, does directly reflect the ongoing significance of "the state."

This measure is made by dividing what each country earns as a whole, that is, its gross national product (GNP) by the number of people the latest census shows to be living there. This provides a single figure for each country, which can be readily compared with that of others, allowing us to assess which countries in the world are more developed, that is, earn more per head; and which are less developed, that is, earn less per head.

GNP per capita figures can also be assessed over time to provide a quantitative measure of any particular country's "progress." An upward trend in this line is considered to be progressive. A downward trend denotes "de-development." The steeper the trend line, the more or less progress we are supposed to see.

While GNP per capita figures provide a simple, supposedly highly effective measure of one kind of developmental change, it is also very crude. It reduces progress to a single material dimension. It provides an average figure only, which says nothing about the distribution of earnings within any particular country. And it paints the whole picture in statecentric terms.

In an attempt to provide a more nuanced measure of development than just GNP per capita, analysts at the United Nations Development Programme (UNDP) have been trying, since 1990, to devise what they call a "human development" index (HDI). The HDI is a composite measure of "longevity" (life expectancy), "knowledge" (adult literacy plus mean years of schooling, weighted two to one), and "standard of living" (that is, purchasing power, or gross domestic product per head, adjusted to allow for the local cost of living) (UNDP 1994:91).

UNDP analysts say that the lack of reliable statistics makes any more comprehensive index impossible to construct. Adding more indices to the list would not necessarily make the index any more accurate either, given the overlap between the various indicators. UNDP analysts are also aware that an HDI score can still hide other disparities not included. Switzerland, for example, is second on the HDI list of countries, but is twenty-first when it comes to ranking countries in terms of tertiary enrollments.

Those countries with a high GNP per capita do, as one might expect, have a high HDI as well. The most notable feature of the HDI, however, is the number of countries where this correlation does not hold. Some countries like Angola, Gabon, Guinea, Namibia, Saudi Arabia, and the United Arab Emirates have a much higher GNP per capita than their HDI one. Gabon is the most conspicuous in this regard. For other countries it is the opposite: their relative HDI ranking places them well above their relative GNP per capita. Examples here are China, Colombia, Costa Rica, Cuba, Guyana, Madagascar, and Sri Lanka, with China the most conspicuous in this regard.

Also notable is the way over time all the countries for which data exist have made "substantial progress" in human development. Moreover, while GNP per capita may go down, the HDI for a country never does, indicating, UNDP analysts claim, that "human capital, once it is built up, is more likely to be sustainable" (UNDP 1994:96).

Data exist for the UNDP time frame (1960–1992) for only 114 countries. Given that there are currently more than 185 countries in the world and that the missing seventy or so are presumably among the less well-organized and well-to-do ones, the fact that these missing countries do not and cannot appear in the UNDP's tables does rather compromise the general picture they provide. Coming to broad conclusions about the "progress" and "development" of the world, when more than a third of the countries in it are not part of the analysis on which such statements are made, would seem premature at best and misleading at worst. This is particularly so when the missing countries are ones that are highly likely to pull the progressive trend line down. They might conceivably even reverse it. If we were able to include these missing countries we might well find not global improvement overall, as UNDP analysts currently claim, but global de-development and decline. We might also find that the growing disparity between countries might be much greater than the HDI suggests.

While seemingly oblivious to the limits set by their overall data, the analysts at the UNDP are aware that average figures do conceal disparities within countries as well as revealing disparities between them. Their calculations show, for example, how "different population groups in the same country seem to be living in different worlds" (UNDP 1994:90), and they nominate ethnic groups, regional groups, social classes, and women and men, in this regard.

Ideally, they argue, different indices should be devised for each major subnational group. They have begun as a consequence to disaggregate the HDI, and by using specific HDIs for "gender" and "income distribution" they have been able to adjust the overall HDI to get a more accurate comparative picture. The data collection exercise is even harder here, since the statistics that state makers collect do not usually include such categories as "men" and "women."

From the statistics they have been able to collate, however, UNDP analysts have read a "startling" picture of discrimination, and particularly gender discrimination. For example, in the forty-three cases where there are data (twenty-four industrial; nineteen not) "all countries" apparently "treat women worse than men." In the industrial ones this is most notable in terms of employment and wages. In the nonindustrial ones this is most notable everywhere, that is, in employment, wages, education, nutrition, and health.

The UNDP analysts say this is simply "unconscionable," particularly after "so many years of debate on gender equality, so many changes in national legislation and so many years of struggle" (UNDP 1994:97). And so it is, though the picture is not all one of

gloom. Brighter spots do appear. Adjusting the HDI scores for gender disparity, for example, we find Canada going from first to ninth
and Japan going from third to nineteenth in the overall rankings.
Finland, however, goes from sixteenth to third and New Zealand
from eighteenth to eighth. This is evidence of very different national
projects at work, and a prima facie argument for policies that specifically try and redress gender imbalances.

Adjusting for the extent of income disparities also affects HDI
scores. When egalitarian as opposed to nonegalitarian income structures are accounted for, countries like Brazil and Botswana go down
the ladder, while China and Sri Lanka and Jamaica go up. This
suggests that policies can make for more fairness in terms of income, too.

In-country disparities have been the focus of a number of UNDP
studies, and the results further confirm the commonsense expectation that developmental progress within a state can be more problematic than developmental progress between one state and another.
Of the nineteen provinces in Nigeria, for example, the one with the
highest HDI is on a par with Sri Lanka. The lowest, on the other
hand, has an HDI below Guinea, which is the worst of all the listed
states. Within these regions are further disparities, of course. These
show up in gender terms, most notably, and in terms of income, too.

The UNDP is not alone in trying to provide a more nuanced
measure of development, though its efforts in this regard have been
the most influential so far. Since 1993 the United Nations Children's
Fund, for example, has been developing an annual "progress of nations" report in its bid to measure how well countries have complied with the goals agreed to in 1990 at the United Nations' World
Summit for Children. "National performance gaps" have been identified between the actual level of progress in child survival, nutrition,
and primary education statistics, and the level one would "expect"
given a country's GNP per capita (UNICEF 1995a).

Why is it that all of the above has a vaguely denigratory air
about it, however? Despite the clear concern being shown for global
underdogs, the UNDP's HDI and UNICEF's progress of nations
measure share with their GNP per capita cousin a sense of remote-
ness from the world. The quantities seem disconcerting. The qualitative experience of what is being described has been filtered out.
This serves UNDP's and UNICEF's research purposes well enough,
but it's hard not to be somewhat cynical about how well the result
represents reality. Compare my account of UNDP's HDI, for example, with Atterbury's account of Crusoe's island. The point becomes
plain.

One reason for the feeling of distance has been attributed to U.S.
state makers. After World War II, the United States was seeking to

cement the capitalist world's sense of U.S. preponderance. A part of the process is the appropriation of the concept of *underdevelopment,* which created a two-part model of the world—one of haves and have-nots, with nothing in between and nothing of each in the other. U.S. state makers were not, as they saw it, creating world poverty where none had been before. Rather, they were putting themselves at the apex of the postwar world.

Thus when Truman chose to label "underdeveloped" people as such, in his inaugural speech on January 20, 1949, "two billion people," Esteva argues, "became underdeveloped." They stopped, in effect, "being what they were, in all their diversity" and became an "inverted mirror of others' reality: a mirror that belittle[d] them and sen[t] them off to the end of the queue. . . . Today, for two-thirds of the peoples of the world, underdevelopment is a threat that has already been carried out; a life experience of subordination and of being led astray, of discrimination and subjugation" (Esteva 1992:7).

By posting development as a goal, Esteva says, U.S. state makers and U.S. "development specialists" were making a radical assault on the self-confidence of the poor. For those less well-off in the world, Esteva argues, using the language of development itself "impedes thinking of one's own objectives, . . . undermines confidence in oneself and one's own culture, . . . clamours for management from the top down [and] converts participation into a manipulative trick to involve people in struggles for getting what the powerful want to impose on them" (Esteva 1992:8).

To be "developed" is not, in this light, to cease being "underdeveloped." It is to accept the ideologies of the West and to copy the ways of living that these ideologies prescribe. It is to accept as definitive such concepts as *economic growth* and the universality of *scarcity.* It is to emulate the desire to evolve toward the "ever more perfect forms" of the mercantilist, the socialist, and especially the liberal dream (Esteva 1992:10, 23). In every case these are borrowed dreams and they are contested from the margins. They remain the dominant dreams of the day, however, and if it can be said, as Lewis Mumford once did, that every culture lives within its dream, then this fact about the world political economy deserves the closest possible attention.

IMPERIALISM

How did such dreams become hegemonic? The first step in defining what the world deems worth doing was the assertion, by European princes in the seventeeth century, of the primacy of the sovereign state. The curious construct these princes made is now universal, and how it became so is a story in itself.

Though they started commandeering other people's resources from the start, European capitalists and European state makers became involved, in the nineteenth century, in an extraordinary grab for land. For example, in 1800 European countries controlled 30 percent of the earth's surface. By 1914, however, this figure was nearly 85 percent. This was imperialism at its most naked. Europeans present on such a scale in the world meant the unprecedented presence of their thought forms as well. These included the ideology of statism itself, that is, the idea that people should live in territorially bounded, centrally governed, nominally equal jurisdictions called states.

The European empires of the nineteenth century were mostly destroyed by two twentieth-century wars between lesser but highly ambitious powers and greater, dominant ones. After these wars, the administrative territories that made up the European empires, or more exactly, key elites within them, were inspired to claim "state" status themselves. "States" subsequently proliferated, and as the leaders of new states, these elites were all keen to demonstrate how independent they had become.

The suggestion that imperialism (in the sense of one country overtly dominating another) should still be prevalent became highly provocative under such circumstances. Moreover, it didn't seem to fit the facts. As a consequence those who wanted to talk about the phenomenon found a very small audience. Michael Barratt Brown (1974:17) notes, for example, how an attempt to hold a seminar on "imperialism" at Oxford University in the late 1950s drew only four participants.

The success of U.S. state makers in building a postwar order to their own design did not go entirely unremarked, however, since their design did seem to have some notable imperial features, and particularly when U.S. state makers became engaged, in the 1960s, in an expensive land war in Vietnam. This had a politicostrategic component to it, as manifest in the land war part. But it also had politicoeconomic and politicocultural components. It became less and less clear at this time, for example, whether the ideas Americans had about "development" did much more than act as a gloss on the U.S. drive to stay at the top.

Meanwhile, the Soviets were intervening in Hungary and Czechoslovakia. A conference by Barratt Brown, held at this somewhat later date and on the same theme of imperialism, drew over a hundred participants, all of whom seemed quite keen to dust off the concept and to retest its explanatory value.

In the 1990s imperialism is once again in eclipse, and another conference on it would probably be down to four people again. So why discuss it here? Simply because it is still worth asking, as Atterbury suggests, whether the contemporary eclipse of the concept of imperialism is due to imperialism itself having come to an end, or whether it is more a matter of the widespread perception of imperialism as having come to an end. Or both.

It might be that the old, territorially tangible, politicostrategic form of imperialism is indeed no longer much apparent, but that imperialism does exist in the form of politicoeconomic and politico-cultural practices. The lack of tangibility of these other ways of imposing the human will may make it harder to appreciate their contemporary significance. That doesn't mean they don't matter, though. There may well, in other words, still be dominance and subordinance in the world of an imperialistic kind, but we don't see it as such because we still expect to see it in terms of held ground, directly governed, rather than in material and mental terms that allow for much more indirect and diffuse chains of command.

To a mercantilist in particular, preoccupied with state autonomy, imperialism retains strong, traditional, territorial associations. Mercantilism is a strategy that makes for statist autonomy and self-reliance. In all forms of mercantilism, this is done by promoting a clear version of what is "outside" and "inside" the state. In the inward-looking form, autarky is preferred. In the outward-looking form, mercantilists try to make others subordinate to themselves.

Historically, Brown says, mercantilists saw "trade and the flag moving together" as far as this could be arranged. "Modern states, [however, fight] for control over shares in total world economic activity" (Brown 1974:27). Finance is directed toward home investments and to foreign investments that promote statist self-sufficiency. In terms of the capitalist world system, this means dominating markets.

For liberals, nationalistic/imperialistic behavior of this sort is an unwelcome rock in the road toward the liberal free market utopia. Since liberals make an ideological distinction between "economics" and "politics" as well, an "imperialistic" rock is going to be construed by liberals in terms of either "political" imperialism or "economic" imperialism, or both.

Political imperialism is usually attributed to a "general impulse to dominate," that is, to the "power-hungry or . . . irrational group psychology" people supposedly manifest, and more particularly "the cultivation of nationalism which combines both" (Brown 1974:23). Joseph Schumpeter, for example, saw imperialism largely in this light. He called it the "objectless disposition on the part of a state to unlimited forcible expansion." In a capitalist world system like that of today, "imperialism" seemed to him to be an "atavism"— a relic from the past (Schumpeter 1951:85). It was a precapitalist phenomenon of little relevance to contemporary times. A completely capitalistic world would be one, he believed, that had no imperialism in it. Since capitalism relies on free exchange, and since any attempt to expand territory by force will disrupt that freedom and be bad for business, capitalists will eschew it. They will be much more likely to set up disarmament and arbitration systems rather than imperial ones.

Economic imperialism, in liberal language, is imperialism that occurs for economic reasons. In classical liberal terms, the movement of goods, capital, and labor should be unrestricted, and state controls over such movements should be abolished. In practice economic nationalists (mercantilists) find myriad ways to frustrate what is seen to be an otherwise straightforward, developmentally advantageous, and universalizing process. Free marketeering can even be frustrated by the workings of capitalism itself. John Hobson argued as much at the turn of the century, maintaining that capitalists save in the good times, investing their savings in expanded production, thereby flooding the market with too many goods (Hobson 1988). Rather than lower prices or raise wages, capitalists then look for markets for their surplus goods elsewhere. If need be, they call on their home state armies to force these markets open. Which is why, Hobson believed, you get imperialism under capitalism. It has nothing to do with feudal "hangovers," he argued. It has everything to do instead with the policies state makers pursue in capitalism's defense.

To a Marxist, it is capitalists who are responsible for imperialism in the industrial capitalist era. Capitalists compete to increase productivity and create new markets, and this has imperializing effects. They also compete to reduce their labor costs, and the most cursory reading of the world labor market quickly demonstrates how imperialistic this process has been as well.

The primitive accumulating that European protocapitalists did in the fifteenth and sixteenth centuries not only meant developing trade, for example. It also meant driving European peasants from the land and appropriating by violent means the precious metals and the labor power of the Americas (Potts 1990:9). After an initial period of plunder (estimated by Las Casas to have cost, in the Caribbean alone, 15 million lives) the conquistadors realized the value of Indian labor power and turned to slavery as well. Indeed, "Indian slavery was the first large-scale system in the history of capitalism to exploit the workers of conquered territories outside Europe to any great extent" (Potts 1990:16).

The more advanced accumulating that European capitalists did in the nineteenth and twentieth centuries also required labor power. Luxemburg, following Marx, specifically notes this point, arguing that "capitalist production . . . can[not] manage with white labour alone. . . . It must be able to mobilise world labour power without restriction in order to utilise all the productive forces of the globe" (Luxemburg 1951:362). Which is why, especially to an early Marxist like Luxemburg, imperialism was not a matter of political or nationalistic purpose of the sort Hitler, for example, was to indulge in. It was much more a matter of the "extension by industrial capitalists of that form of commodity production in which labour becomes itself a commodity" (Brown 1974:50–51).

That's clearly a very different view of imperialism from either of the liberalist ones. Driven by the need to compete, that is, to "expand or die," capitalists create a system whose logic allows only forward momentum. Like runners leaning forward and having to run faster and faster so as not to fall flat on their faces, successful capitalists have to beat the competition or surrender the field. Imperialism, in this respect, is simply what capitalists do when they try to beat the competition, or not have it beat them. It involves the (extremely profitable) use of colonized and neocolonized labor power. Thus Potts (1990:223–224) concludes that "in the final analysis it is debatable whether the world market for labour power has contributed more to the development of the metropole or to the underdevelopment of the colonised territories," since the "losses incurred by the colonies and countries still today not permitted to develop as a result of slavery, coolieism, colonial forced and migrant labor, the brain drain and labour migration . . . must surely be many times greater than the huge profits which the metropole drew from these forms of exploitation" and which, as a "permanent and integral part" of Western European and North American development, she considers to have been the basis for the development of those parts of the world to date.

To Lenin, imperialism was not so much about exploiting foreign workers, though he did note that imperialists did this, but about capitalists exporting capital. "Typical of the old capitalism," Lenin (1973:72) said, "when free competition had undivided sway, was the export of goods. Typical of the latest stage of capitalism, when monopolies rule, is the export of capital."

Imperialism, in this regard, is the capitalism of countries that have become "overripe" (Lenin 1973:73). It features large global firms, the merging of bank and industrial capital to create finance capital, the export of that capital in the form of loans to governments, direct investment in production in amounts greater than trade in commodities, and the territorial division of most of the world among the biggest capitalist powers. This territoral division came to an end when the great European empires collapsed. The last of these empires was the Soviet one. The other features of imperialism that Lenin identified do not disappear just because the territorial ones do, however. All of them, in reformist Marxist parlance, remain key features of the global political economy.

Most colonies became territorially independent in the twentieth century. Though armed intervention in these new states in support of capitalist concerns was hard to justify because of the importance all state makers placed upon sovereignty as such, armed intervention did not cease; nor did nonarmed intervention. What can self-determination mean, for example, when state makers are sold cheap international credit that ends up costing them dear, and when the IMF then tells governments to structurally adjust, that is, to privatize their enterprises, reduce their budget deficits, devalue their currencies, eliminate their subsidies and price controls, dismantle their trade and investment barriers, and cut or restrain wages, or they can't qualify for balance-of-payments relief? How relevant is territorial sovereignty when behind the map of high politics lies the map of world capitalism—a map that is becoming progressively harder to obscure.

From the above we can see that Marxist ideas about the development of capitalism, and of imperialism as well if we accept the connection Marxists see between the two, generally emphasize the way capitalists exploit some areas of the world at the expense of others. Critics of the Marxist approach highlight the fact that these exploited areas are marginal to modern capitalism. Most capitalist trade and investment, they say, is among the highly capitalized and industrialized areas of the world. It is not between these areas and those less "developed" in this regard (Reynolds 1981:105). And this is so. The relative insignificance of marginal domains does not mean, though, that they are not exploited. It is not enough, Marxists reply, to cite lack of centrality as proof of the absence of imperialism.

While Marxists like Lenin and Bukharin saw the world in terms of imperial centers and imperialized peripheries, they also saw the national identity of capitalists as being of paramount concern. Kautsky (1988) disagreed, since he saw the international coherence of the capitalist class as being greater, and he saw this coherence as being more significant than the statecentric incoherence of the world. Kautsky was more interested in what he called "ultra-imperialism," which was, as he saw it, a new phase of capitalism, dominated by a singular, unitary, global bourgeoisie. Lenin and Bukharin, however, saw the internationalization of capitalism not only as necessary to its sustained growth but as heightening the competition between national fractions of capital; between state-based traders and investors, that is (Bukharin 1925).

While Kautsky and his concept of a world class of capitalists that rules the world is at odds with those who believe in the continuing sovereign significance of states, Kautsky's concept may not be so controversial when we think of that superimperialist class in more cultural terms—as one sharing a common "consciousness," that is, and as one that shapes "popular" consciousness worldwide (Petras 1993:139). This class would be doing much more than maximizing its market shares. They would be pursuing their profits and accumulating their capital by exporting "culture," that is, by exporting such cultural commodities as package tours, educational services, computer software, or movies.

This is partly what Marx meant, no doubt, when he said that the ruling ideas in the world were likely to be those of the ruling class. Exporting culture is highly profitable. "The export of entertainment commodities," as Petras points out, "is one of the most important sources of capital accumulation and global profits," with an increasing proportion (currently about 20 percent) of North America's richest capitalists getting their wealth from mass media (Petras 1993:139, 141). The reformist Marxist, Antonio Gramsci, also made much of the notion that ruling ideas have a life of their own (Gill 1993). They play a "major role," such reformist Marxists say, in "dissociating people from their cultural roots and traditions of solidarity, replacing them with media-created 'needs.'" Thus workers are encouraged to make invidious comparisons between each other and those "below" them in "life style . . . race and gender" terms. The gap between workers and those "above" them is then made to seem innocuous and even necessary (Petras 1993:139).

Thus while the corporations purveying "Hollywood, CNN, and Disneyland" may have taken over today from the state and church missionaries of old, the imperialistic intention, in Marxist terms, is exactly the same. This includes the silencing of dissent by the provision of escapist fantasies (Petras 1993:141). And it involves blaming victims for their own poverty, and making change seem a personal rather than a collective affair.

Exporting culture, in other words, is part and parcel, in Marxist terms, of coordinating and consolidating global market capitalism. Gill (1990:296) identifies not so much a global capitalist class at work here as an "intersecting set of establishments." He cites in this regard the Trilateral Commission, which was a reformist liberalist group of Americans, Europeans, and Japanese who in the wake of President Nixon's classical liberal solutions to the United States' financial problems of the 1970s sought to legitimize a more reformist liberal alternative of the sort Bretton Woods was supposed to provide. There is a rich selection of liberal fora of this sort, sharing and seeking to disseminate the same liberalist vocabulary that Marxists consider culturally imperialistic.

THE "ASIAN ALTERNATIVE"

If imperialism persists, albeit in nonterritorial forms, then how come countries not already industrialized, "modernized," and developed have become so? How come Taiwan, Hong Kong, Singapore, and South Korea (the newly industrialized countries, or NICs) have become so successful in GNP per capita terms? And how come other Asian countries, like Indonesia, Thailand, and Malaysia (the newly industrializing economies, or NIEs), as well as parts of China and India, are joining them now? Should we proclaim as a consequence, as Tsuru (1993:219) does in his discussion of Japanese capitalism, that the "era of imperialism is now a thing of the past"? Might it not seem churlish to ask if such attempts to get out from under the imperial weight of the West, especially such seemingly successful ones as these, are less than proof of Tsuru's assertion? What, by contrast, of most of the countries of Africa and Latin America? What if the end of imperial dependency actually means what Marx thought it would, namely, more capitalism, not less? And what if more capitalism and more capitalists means more social distress, not less; that is, greater wealth but greater poverty, too, a planet gutted and poisoned in the drive to industrialize, and a kind of imperialism less territorially grounded and statecentric but still pervasive and exploitative in politicoeconomic and politicocultural terms?

Liberals would say that marketeering, even governmentally regulated marketeering, has made for genuine progress by any measure except perhaps those of environmental well-being and female liberation. Certainly something has been happening in these countries, and something notable, too, but what is it? And is it "development" and "anti-imperialism"?

The regional model was Japan, whose state makers began what they called the "catch-up" process after the Meiji Restoration in 1868. Their motives were clearly mercantilist, and they caught up so well that they were able to emulate in the East the imperial land grab of the European powers in the West. Decisively defeated in World War II, their territorial empire at an end, they resolved to catch up a second time. Having lost World War II, they resolved to win the second world peace. This they dutifully did, by blending ∨ governmental planning and highly disciplined marketeering in a kind of corporate capitalism peculiarly their own.)

This was not a particularly liberal model (Sharma 1995). It was very far from Adam Smith's laissez-faire notion that "little else" is required to become prosperous as a nation other than order, low taxes, and the "tolerable administration of justice." For the Japanese, development required a "governed market," a system of private enterprises "cooperating and competing under state supervision," and a "heavy investment in education" (Wade 1992:315). There was a strong element of necessity in all of this, since Japan had no apparent comparative advantage except the will to make one. They made many, and as a consequence were able to sustain for more than a decade growth rates in the order of 10 percent.

The Japanese model, though notably illiberal, was extraordinarily successful and one that other capitalists and state makers in the region wanted to be able to copy. Four countries did. These countries not only had the will to industrialize, and the Japanese example to follow, they had U.S. capital and a lot of cheap labor power. To these "situational" factors some add a cultural component, namely, "industrial neo-Confucianism." Vogel says this means meritocratic elites selected by rigorous examination procedures, group loyalty used to foster worker fidelity to their employers, and a culture of self-cultivation used to improve work skills (Vogel 1991:101). All these factors, plus large internal markets, intense competitiveness, and close attention to quality control, ultimately made it possible to outproduce and outsell those who had built the system in the first place. This list of factors is not exhaustive, however. Others would add to it the authoritarian nature of the national governments concerned, high domestic savings (which helped to generate capital at home), a consistent focus on value-added manufacture for export, familial coherence, and cultural homogeneity.

"It is hard to remember," as Schlossstein (1991:9) points out, that in the 1960s "nobody expected Asia to do well." And yet by the end of the 1980s four seemingly insignificant Asian states were able to account for two-thirds of the export of all manufactured goods, and two of them, together with Japan, held half of all the world's foreign exchange reserves.

In the light of the arguments above about cultural imperialism it is interesting to note how some in the NICs now claim that their high rate of development has been due not to their embrace of the Western idea of rationalistic, individualistic progress but to their own "affective" model of change. This model emphasizes, they say, "human emotional bonds, group orientation, and harmony" (Tai 1989:7). It consciously rejects liberalist rhetoric. And it is fair to say that NIC cultures do not place as high a priority on self-interest as North American or European ones do, though this is notably changing as more people in the NICs "develop."

What, if anything, is "Asian" about Asian capitalism, then? Are there differences between the Japanese, for example, and the Americans that matter in this regard? Are there differences between their capitalist practices that reveal different ways of doing capitalist industrialism in practice? Japanese state makers, wealth makers, and mind makers certainly took from the modernizing West in a highly selective way, retaining many premodernist characteristics in the process. As an island culture, which cut itself off from the rest of the world for four hundred years, this is hardly surprising. Are the premodernist elements they retain of any great significance, however, given the power of the modernist capitalist ones to produce not only industrial change but intellectual change as well?

One element of premodernist Asianism that has remained relatively strong is the concern for family. A sense of family is still clear throughout Pacific Asia, with the possible exception now of Singapore. It is part of the way East Asian workers are supposed to feel about the companies that employ them. The ethos still requires workers to sell not just their labor for a wage. It requires active participation in a paternalistic community, that expects long hours and loyalty. In Marxist language this only masks the underlying process of exploitation. Asianists generally accord it greater cultural significance than that, however.

Apart from the pervasiveness of familial feeling, we also find a profound respect for education. This has deep roots in the Chinese mandarin tradition, and has proved an important cultural asset. A respect for education makes easier the task of acquiring the knowledge-intensive base that contemporary development is built upon. Societies that value learning school their young to the standards that capitalist industrialism requires. While knowledge alone will not result in development, knowledge is a key factor of production. Developed countries are technologically complex countries, and such complexity cannot be sustained without skilled people to sustain it. Skilled people can be imported if a country has the means to pay. Oil-rich countries in the Middle East do just that. Poorer societies have to train their own, and those with a cultural inclination toward doing so clearly have an advantage in this regard.

There seems little else that can meaningfully be said about Asian capitalism beyond the above. Saying any more starts arguments that are impossible to finish, anyway. Westerners have been criticized for having assumed that they are rational and therefore virtuous and mature, while Orientals (those born east of Suez) are irrational, lazy, and corrupt (Said 1978). The notion of an Asian capitalism sometimes comes close to turning this old prejudice on its head, replacing former "bads" with contemporary "goods." In resisting such a move, we must be wary, nonetheless, of not excluding an important aspect of the Pacific Asian political economy from analysis, just because it is a relatively contentious and intangible one.

Is the success of the NICs likely to continue? While liberals will concede that the NICs have succeeded in mobilizing their resources, liberals can be pretty grudging in this regard. Krugman, for example, claims that this extraordinary mobilization effort was "no more than what the most boringly conventional economic theory would lead us to expect" (Krugman 1994:78). He is prepared to see such growth continuing in the future, but only if priority is placed on marketeering, not state intervention. If this is not done, he says, then the NICs can anticipate "diminishing returns." Mercantilists, on the other hand, see intervention as essential to continuing success. Classical Marxists, meanwhile, discern the seeds of class conflict in what has been happening and hold out for revolution. Reformist Marxists focus on the Asian embrace of capitalism, but are less convinced revolution will or even can be the historical result. Social movements mobilize on the margins.

Is the success of the NICs likely to be repeated throughout the rest of the nonindustrialized world? Even if it is, though ecological limits alone will probably preclude it, how are we to explain such success, at the same time as explaining the way the poorest quarter of the world's countries have seen their share of world income decline? One-fifth of the world's population, we should remember, currently shares less than 1.5 percent of it (UNDP 1994:64).

For some time analysts have wondered whether the "absorptive capacity of industrial country markets" was "infinite" or not, and some have concluded that it probably is not. As a result, a sharpening of "protective resistance" is anticipated, as state makers seek ways of dealing with surges of exports from the NICs and the NIEs (Cline 1982:81–82). To liberals, protectionism can only punish the aspiring poor by blighting their developmental prospects. They see the plight of the destitute fifth of the global population in this light. To mercantilists, this kind of protectionism would still be warranted, however, since it's always a matter, in their view, of "every state for itself."

Marxists, and particularly reformist Marxists, would say that development and underdevelopment can and do occur at the same time. Indeed, most would argue they are causally linked. Certainly any facts about the growing disparities of wealth in the world—like the one cited above, or the fact that the poorest fifth of those who live in the 44 poor and the 20 rich countries for which the World Bank could find statistics share only 5 percent now of the national income, while the richest fifth in those countries share 40 percent to 60 percent—would come as no surprise to them whatsoever (World Bank 1994b:220).

REGIONALIZATION

Development in conventional terms (high GNP per capita; high HDI ranking) is not something that can be taken for granted, in other words. Atterbury's Crusoe is acutely aware of this fact, which is why he tells Friday to "keep a lookout and let no one land." Once won, development can also be lost, and much of the story of postwar development is just that. It is as much a tale, in other words, of the rich striving to maintain their status, as it is of the poor seeking to elevate theirs.

The agreement at Bretton Woods was designed to reconstruct the West and to affirm the role of U.S. state makers as global guardians, U.S. wealth makers as global rent takers, and U.S. mind makers as arbiters of global liberal belief. The more of a material success they made of the reconstruction of the West, however, a category that did have one honorary member in the East, namely Japan, the more difficult it proved for the United States to sustain any sort of global primacy as policeman, profit maker, and paradigm sheriff.

The reconstruction of Europe did result in material success. With it went a regional attempt to construct a European common market, and more. The most forward-thinking Europeans, harboring fond memories of former glories but fully aware that these were not to be had again in the same way—and certainly not in single-nation terms—sought a collective base on which to rebuild their presence in the world. They created first a European Economic Community (the EEC). They then tried to turn this into something more integrated, that is, a European Union. The latter culminated in an attempt under the Maastricht Treaty to provide for a single European currency and a more collaborative foreign policy. The queue of countries wanting to join the EU was seen as evidence of the popularity of the overall approach, with regional state makers who were not already members fearing the consequences if they failed to join.

An ambitious attempt was also made to pool state sovereignty. Since sovereignty was being pooled to a sovereign purpose, the principle was generally acceptable, though the British in particular found it hard to think of using non-British money, and getting a common foreign and defense policy continued to present difficulties. The "willingness among most member states to deepen integration" (Murray 1993:2) in Europe was relatively high from the start, however, if only because what member states stood to lose in having to conform to EU agreements, they saw bringing gains in terms of other national interests.

The EU is very curious. It is a paradoxical mixture of intergovernmentalism and supranationalism, of interdependence and stubborn difference, that is unique to this association and reflects the fact "that it was not founded exclusively to provide a higher level of production, industrialisation and prosperity among the member states. It also had the aim of the creation of a high authority above the nation state" (Murray 1993:11).

Analysts differ in their assessments of how far the process of creating such a "high authority" has gone. Some see European states as still largely untouched by the confederal initiatives of the last forty years. Others see European state sovereignty as under siege. It is still of significance, they say, that state makers talk of national commitments abroad, on a single-state basis. Others again believe that a European "overstate" is already extant, and they complain about its bureaucratic and undemocratic character.

In practice we find a European-level no-man's-land, with state makers continuing to argue about how far to surrender what and how much sovereign power. Meanwhile, capitalists seem to be using every opportunity the EU framework provides to cash in. At the same time they seek to confound the construction of a more fully developed version of a "social Europe" with a European minimum wage, employment protection, common ecological policies, and living and working standards leveled up rather than down (Lambert 1991:12–15).

In practice we find a "two-speed Europe" with "rich and poor regions, and poor people (Turks, North Africans . . . women) in the rich regions to serve the rich." We find, critics claim, a "soulless hypermarket," and liberal productivism at an "impasse" (Lipietz 1992: 135, 143).

This is a far cry from a Europe able to offer creative developmental alternatives. But then, what ought we reasonably to expect from that part of the world that gave us the nation-state and capitalism in the first place? Should we anticipate the active repudiation of state making and wealth making in either of these forms? Do we dare hope for a luminous example of human community and planetary care instead? Even Eurotopians don't think so. So far, in fact, it has been arguably the opposite. Europeans in the EU have continued to show us how not to provide a "lighthouse for nations and a hope for peace" (Lipietz 1992:143). Europeans have, of course, given the world a lot over the last few hundred years. They also have a "lot to answer for" (Lambert 1991:9).

With all this and with the collapse of the Soviet Union, which brought to an end the U.S. rationale for maintaining a significant military presence in Europe, the United States found itself completely eclipsed there. It hung on, though, seeking to use its postwar politicostrategic alliance, NATO (the North Atlantic Treaty Organization), plus a web of corporate connections, as the basis for doing so.

In their own hemisphere U.S. state makers, in 1987, negotiated a liberal trade and investment arrangement with their Canadian counterparts. The U.S. state makers were seeking greater access to the Canadian market, and Canadian state makers were afraid of the consequences of being denied greater access to the U.S. one. Changes in production methods, from Fordist to post-Fordist ones, also made U.S. and Canadian state makers disposed to accept a Mexican proposal for a North American free trade zone. The Mexican state makers promised a large pool of cheap labor for the low-skill, manufacturing part of North America's progressively more disaggregated factory lines. The framework for a free trade zone was formulated in terms of a North American Free Trade Association (NAFTA). This was the first step in a larger strategy designed to include many more Central and South American countries in a U.S.-dominated regional association capable of rivaling that of Europe, and more lately, that of Asia, too.

NAFTA clearly had corporate sanction as well. Several thousand corporations mounted a multimillion-dollar campaign to lobby on NAFTA's behalf (Cypher 1993). Corporate publicists argued that tariff-free exports to the new consumer markets in Mexico would create jobs for U.S. workers and that the influx of competing firms there would be the key to Mexican development. The hidden agenda was access to Mexican oil.

The campaign budget of the U.S. corporations was matched by that of the Salinas government in Mexico City, which had staked its political credibility on getting NAFTA agreed to. Not that the Salinas government was renowned for letting critics undermine its "credibility," given its local reputation for breaking strikes, abolishing unions, and murdering members of the opposition Partido Revolucionario Democrática (*Latin America Report*, January/March 1994:1–2).

In a campaign with such high stakes it is "not surprising," however, "that the corporate sector and governments in each country . . . used their enormous financial resources and influence to shape the public policy, and academic debates" (Grinspun and Cameron 1993:15).

Signed in December 1992, NAFTA is the world's largest free trade zone. It has an estimated 370 million consumers and provides for the elimination of tariffs between Canada, the United States, and Mexico over a period of fifteen years, a free flow of investment across NAFTA-state borders—but not, predictably, a free flow of labor—an $8 billion North American Development Bank, and tripartite environmental and labor commissions. It is also the "first comprehensive trade agreement between developing and industrialised countries on essentially equal terms" (Thakur 1994:9).

Equal terms between unequals is not a recipe for fair outcomes, however, a point not lost upon Mexican workers. Despite predictions that NAFTA would create hundreds of thousands of jobs, they actively resisted it. So did small farmers who saw their livelihoods being eliminated by corn imports from the United States. The Zapatistas, for example, who subsequently took arms against the Mexican government in the southern state of Chiapas, specifically cited NAFTA as a key reason for their revolt. Resistance came also from U.S. workers, especially those destined to lose their jobs in industries where plants were transferred to labor-cheap, environmentally more lax Mexico. U.S. unions claimed that hundreds of thousands of jobs had been transferred to Mexico even before the agreement was signed.

Undaunted, liberals continued to anticipate enhanced development for all. The basic promise was always greater productivity and rising wages.

Marxists, who saw NAFTA as merely providing an "additional pathway . . . to capital mobility on the part of TNC's [transnational corporations]" and as part of a process—in train since the mid-1970s—of "global structural adjustment" (Ranney 1993:8, 11), anticipated its collapse. Under the gloss of free trade, they said, associations like NAFTA actively eschew social democracy. They promote the global reach of private companies and transnational capitalists; help undermine state capacities to intervene to public purpose; push monetarist macroeconomics, privatization, and deregulation; underwrite reduced standards of occupational and environmental care; marginalize unions; exploit labor; and drive development along "outward-oriented, natural resource–based, and TNC-driven" lines.

The negative effects of the developmental model that NAFTA represented were felt, Marxists said, not only by Mexicans but by

Americans and Canadians, too. The "de-industrialization" that followed the relocation of plants in the export-processing *(maquiladora)* zones along the U.S.-Mexican border resulted in regional U.S. and Canadian unemployment. In liberal terms, this was not supposed to matter. National growth was supposed to create more jobs for the unemployed to take. In practice, the "adjustment" process for the more developed United States and Canada was painful, too, and particularly so for the underdeveloped peoples within those countries, namely, women, African-Americans, and Latinos.

None of this deterred countries in East and Southeast Asia, who as they grew began to make efforts to explore regional free trade associations as well. There was a distinctly protectionist feel about these efforts. While successive GATT negotiations had succeeded in sustaining the growth in world trade at a higher rate than regional ones, the end of the boom of the 1950s and 1960s led to a regional defensiveness in Asia that struck analysts as mercantilistic (Dolan 1991:14). These efforts were also fostered by U.S. state makers, who were eager not to be eclipsed in Asia as they had been in Europe. U.S. state makers began to play up the need for regional free trade cooperation, and a fledgling Asia-Pacific Economic Cooperation (APEC) association was formed.

However it is defined, the Asian region is the most dynamic of the world's politicoeconomic zones. Since the end of World War II a number of its most successful members have been moving from the global margins into the global core, where they now account collectively for more than half of the global GNP (Bollard and Mayes 1992).

Industrialization seemed to spread in a wave from Japan, first to the NICs and later to the NIEs and beyond. The region became a major manufacturing one. Instead of exporting primary commodities and importing finished goods, it began to export finished goods. Even the oil price hikes of the 1970s, the consequent downturn of the 1980s, and the combined effects of appreciating currencies and Western protectionism were not enough to stop the growth process.

As they grew in volume, Asia's manufacturing exports began to diversify. The United States, for example, became progressively less important as an Asian export market. Asia, for example, became Japan's largest export market. One-third of its exports went there as opposed to just over one-quarter to the United States. Japan also replaced the United States as Asia's most important source of foreign direct investment, and the Asian NICs and NIEs became major investors in their own region (Kwan 1993:1–6).

Over the same time Asia became more important for the United States, absorbing a third of its exports and employing in the process

2.6 million U.S. workers. Since a 1 percent increase in the United States' market share in Asia was equivalent to several hundred thousand more U.S. jobs, there was clearly an incentive for the United States to stay engaged with the region. And engage it did, aggressively advocating open markets, promoting the presence of U.S. companies, and pursuing the sort of policies one would expect from a state that saw itself as an Asian as well as a European and an American power.

From the NICs and NIEs, the developmental frontier moved on to southern China. In October 1992, at its fourteenth national congress, the Chinese communist party authorized the idea of a "socialist market economy" and an "open-door" policy for trade and investment. After China, Asian analysts began seeing commercial success stories everywhere. A Northeast Asian zone (northern China, Japan, South Korea, and the Russian Far East), a South China zone (Hong Kong, southern China, and Taiwan), a Greater ASEAN zone (the Association of Southeast Asian Nations—Indonesia, Malaysia, Singapore, Brunei, Thailand—plus the socialist countries of Indochina), two growth triangles—Singapore and its neighboring provinces in Indonesia and Malaysia, and a northern triangle that included those provinces of Thailand, Malaysia, and Indonesia that border the Straits of Malacca, the overseas Chinese—there seemed no end to the list. These zones were also pictured as forming interlocking "networks of cooperation," arrayed along a Western Pacific corridor. Since each had its own extraregional connections, any notion of the Asian region as closed off from the world, or subordinated to some regional hegemon like Japan, seemed singularly far-fetched (Elek 1993:5).

Formal attempts to integrate new frontiers into the region have always been relatively limited. The longest-standing local organization is ASEAN, though not until recently was it thought opportune to use it to foster politicoeconomic cooperation. Fears that the EU or NAFTA might start closing off markets or diverting investment funds elsewhere, to Eastern Europe and to South America, for example, prompted such thinking. An ASEAN Free Trade Area (AFTA) was proposed to provide for a Common Effective Preferential Tariff (CEPT) scheme between ASEAN nations, capable of progressively reducing tariffs. An East Asia Economic Caucus (EAEC), which included Japan but excluded the United States, was proposed by Malaysian Prime Minister Mahathir Mohamad in an unsuccessful bid to head off a much more significant attempt to make regional arrangements for trading and investment purposes, namely, the Asia-Pacific Economic Cooperation association (APEC).

Initiated in 1989 by the ASEAN countries, plus Australia, New Zealand, China, Japan, Canada, and the United States, this was the first major attempt formally to arrange the flow of goods and money in the region. More of an Asian/Pacific Rim organization than one confined to Asian countries only, APEC was the "governmental arm" of the Pacific Economic Cooperation Council (PECC)—the two other arms being the Pacific Basin Economic Council (PBEC—the business organization) and the Pacific Trade and Development Conference (PAFTAD—the academic arm).

The pattern apparent from all the regional initiatives discussed above is claimed by analysts like Dolan to support the idea that the world political economy is regionalizing. Over the decade of the 1980s, Dolan says, trade within the European and North American areas grew more quickly than trade between them, and trade within North America and Asia did likewise. The exceptions were Asia and Europe, where trade between these domains grew more quickly than trade within them—though Dolan sees this as due "in part to the low amount of trade at the outset of the 1980s" and also (though he doesn't provide a figure) as due to the very high rate of growth of intra-Asian trade (Dolan 1991:15).

All this would seem to support the idea of "three blocs, centred around the leading economies, U.S., Japan, and Germany," using "intraregional trade as a source of power and interregional exports as a weapon against external competitors" (Hessler 1994:3). It would seem to suggest, in other words, that regionalization is being used by the main developed states as one way to stay developed.

There is a counterposition here, however. Hessler, for example, who takes a three-decade rather than a one-decade time frame (1960–1988), a much more comprehensive set of "regions," "subregional clusters," and "mega-regions," and a much bigger data base, concludes that the "'new regionalism' of the 1980s is a fiction" (Hessler 1994:10). According to him, the empirical evidence suggests that "regionalization in international trade patterns was stronger during the 60s, followed [because of the oil price hikes] by a decade of stagnation and de-regionalization," and then a decade of reintegration up to the level of 1970 (Hessler 1994:9). What seems to be regionalization, in other words, is only a process of "normalization" after the slow years of the 1970s.

Hessler notes a growing integration of "various Pacific clusters" during the 1980s, a result roughly comparable with Dolan's, though this was not, he says, of significance compared to the trade between the countries of the Pacific Rim as a whole. It was this that grew most markedly over the period, particularly as compared to the integration process in Europe—which was a comparatively "indifferent" one—and the integration process in the Western Hemisphere as a whole, which was falling apart rather than coming together.

As a consequence Hessler (1994:1) sees "American attempts to reinforce intraregional trade" as offering "no practicable alternative to the multilateral perspective in trade policy." The comparison with the 1930s, he argues, simply does not hold. Not only does the contemporary pattern of regionalization fail to provide the appropriate parallels, but the pattern of trade is no longer matched (unlike that of the 1930s) by the pattern of long- and short-term capital movements. The world's currency regions are not the same as the world's trading regions any more, and given the size and reach of the contemporary flows of global finance, trade regions have become less significant anyway. "Financial markets do not follow the rules of regional trade patterns," Hessler concludes. Indeed, "normally," he says, "they work against regional markets" (Hessler 1994:1). They favor globalizing ones, which does not bode well for developed states trying to stay that way. Unless they can keep their currencies from pricing their trade goods too high and can make their own share of profits from speculative capital flows, they are likely to see corporations trading intrafirm to escape tariffs, moving capital to escape taxes, and leaving them the poorer for it. Like Atterbury's Crusoe, it's always a struggle to stay ahead.

8

World Development:
Unmaking the Environment

❖ **Jonathan Swift (1729) "A Modest Proposal for Preventing the Children of Ireland from Being a Burden to their Parents and Country"**

It is a melancholy Object to those, who walk through this great Town or travel in the Country, when they see the Streets, the Roads and Cabbin-doors crowded with Beggars of the Female Sex, followed by three, four, or six Children, all in Rags, and importuning every Passenger for Alms. These Mothers instead of being able to work for their honest livelyhood, are forced to employ all their time in Strolling to beg Sustenance for their helpless Infants, who, as they grow up, either turn Thieves for want of Work, or leave their dear Native Country, to fight for the Pretender in Spain, or sell themselves to the Barbadoes.

I think it is agreed by all Parties, that this prodigious number of Children in the Arms, or on the Backs, or at the Heels of their Mothers, and frequently of their Fathers, is in the present deplorable state of the Kingdom, a very great additional grievance; and therefore whoever could find out a fair, cheap and easy method of making these Children sound and useful Members of the Commonwealth, would deserve so well of the publick, as to have his Statue set up for a Preserver of the Nation.

But my intention is very far from being confined to provide only for the Children of professed Beggars, it is of a much greater Extent, and shall take in the whole Number of Infants at a certain Age, who are born of Parents in effect as little able to support them, as those who demand our Charity in the Streets.

As to my own part, having turned my Thoughts, for many Years, upon this important Subject, and maturely weighed the several Schemes of other Projectors, I have always found them grossly mistaken in their computation. It is true, a Child just dropt from its Dam, may be supported by her milk, for a Solar Year with little other Nourishment, at most not above the Value of two Shillings, which the Mother may certainly get, or the Value in scraps, by her lawful Occupation of Begging; and it is exactly at one Year Old that I propose to provide for them in such a manner, as, instead of being a Charge upon their Parents, or the Parish, or wanting Food and Raiment for the rest of their Lives, they shall, on the Contrary, contribute to the Feeding and partly to the Cloathing of many Thousands.

There is likewise another great Advantage in my Scheme, that it will prevent those voluntary Abortions, and that horrid practice of Women murdering their Bastard Children, alas! too frequent among us, Sacrificing the poor innocent Babes, I doubt, more to avoid the expence than the Shame, which would move Tears and Pity in the most Savage and inhuman breast.

The number of Souls in this Kingdom being usually reckoned one Million and a half, of these I calculate there may be about two hundred thousand Couple whose Wives are Breeders; from which number I substract thirty Thousand Couples, who are able to maintain their own Children, although I apprehend there cannot be so many, under the present Distresses of the Kingdom; but this being granted, there will remain an hundred and seventy thousand Breeders. I again Substract fifty Thousand, for those Women who miscarry, or whose Children die by accident, or disease within the Year. There only remain an hundred and twenty thousand Children of poor Parents annually born.

The question therefore is, How this number shall be reared, and provided for? which, as I have already said, under the present Situation of Affairs, is utterly impossible by all the Methods hitherto proposed; for we can neither employ them in Handicraft or Agriculture; we neither build Houses, (I mean in the Country) nor cultivate Land: They can very seldom pick up a Livelyhood by Stealing till they arrive at six years Old; except where they are of towardly parts; although, I confess, they learn the Rudiments much earlier; during which time they can however be properly looked upon only as Probationers; as I have been informed by a principal Gentleman in the County of Cavan, who protested to me, that he never knew above one or two Instances under the Age of six, even in a part of the Kingdom so renowned for the quickest proficiency in that Art.

I am assured by our Merchants, that a Boy or a Girl before twelve years Old, is no saleable Commodity, and even when they come to this Age, they will not yield above three Pounds, or three Pounds and half a Crown at most, on the Exchange; which cannot turn to Account either to the Parents or Kingdom, the Charge of Nutriment and Rags having been at least four times that Value.

I shall now therefore humbly propose my own Thoughts which I hope will not be liable to the least Objection.

I have been assured by a very knowing American of my acquaintance in London, that a young healthy Child well Nursed is at a year Old a most delicious nourishing and wholesome Food, whether Stewed, Roasted, Baked, or Boiled; and I make no doubt that it will equally serve in a Fricasie, or a Ragoust.

I do therefore humbly offer it to publick consideration, that of the Hundred and twenty thousand Children, already computed, twenty thousand may be reserved for Breed, whereof only one fourth part to be Males; which is more than we allow to Sheep, black Cattle, or Swine, and my Reason is, that these Children are seldom the Fruits of Marriage, a Circumstance not much regarded by our Savages, therefore, one Male will be sufficient to serve four Females. That the remaining Hundred thousand may at a year Old be offered in Sale to the Persons of Quality and Fortune, through the Kingdom, always advising the Mother to let them Suck plentifully in the last Month, so as to render them Plump, and Fat for a good Table. A Child will make two Dishes at an Entertainment for Friends, and when the Family dines alone, the fore or hind Quarter will make a reasonable Dish, and seasoned with a little Pepper or Salt will be very good Boiled on the fourth Day, especially in Winter.

I have reckoned upon a Medium, that a Child just born will weigh 12 pounds, and in a solar Year, if tolerably nursed, encreaseth to 28 Pounds.

I grant this food will be somewhat dear, and therefore very proper for Landlords, who, as they have already devoured most of the Parents seem to have the best Title to the Children.

Infant's flesh will be in Season throughout the Year, but more plentiful in March, and a little before and after; for we are told by a grave Author, an eminent French Physician, that Fish being a prolifick Dyet, there are more Children born in Roman Catholick Countries about nine Months after Lent, than at any other Season; therefore reckoning a Year after Lent, the Markets will be more glutted than usual, because the Number of Popish Infants, is at least three to one in this Kingdom, and therefore it will have one other Collateral advantage by lessening the Number of Papists among us.

I have already computed the Charge of nursing a Beggar's Child (in which List I reckon all Cottagers, Labourers, and four fifths of the Farmers) to be about two Shillings per Annum, Rags included; and I believe no Gentleman would repine to give Ten Shillings for the Carcass of a good fat Child, which as I have said will make four Dishes of excellent Nutritive Meat, when he hath only some particular Friend, or his own Family to dine with him. Thus the Squire will learn to be a good Landlord, and grow popular among his Tenants, the Mother will have Eight Shillings neat Profit, and be fit for Work till she produces another Child.

Those who are more thrifty (as I must confess the Times require) may flay the Carcass; the Skin of which, Artificially dressed, will make admirable Gloves for Ladies, and Summer Boots for fine Gentlemen.

As to our City of Dublin, Shambles may be appointed for this purpose in the most convenient parts of it, and Butchers we may be assured will not be wanting; although I rather recommend buying the Children alive, and dressing them hot from the Knife, as we do roasting Pigs.

A very worthy Person, a true Lover of his Country, and whose Virtues I highly esteem, was lately pleased, in discoursing on this matter, to offer a refinement upon my Scheme. He said, that many Gentlemen of this Kingdom, having of late destroyed their Deer, he conceived that the Want of Venison might be well supply'd by the Bodies of young Lads and Maidens, not exceeding fourteen Years of Age, nor under twelve; so great a Number of both sexes in every Country being now ready to Starve, for want of Work and Service: And these to be disposed of by their Parents if alive, or otherwise by their nearest Relations. But with due reference to so excellent a Friend, and so deserving a Patriot, I cannot be altogether in his Sentiments; for as to the Males, my American acquaintance assured me from frequent Experience, that their Flesh was generally Tough and Lean, like that of our Schoolboys, by continual exercise, and their Taste disagreeable, and to fatten them would not answer the Charge. Then as to the Females, it would, I think with humble Submission, be a Loss to the Publick, because they soon would become Breeders themselves: and besides it is not improbable that some scrupulous People might be apt to Censure such a Practice, (although indeed very unjustly) as a little bordering upon Cruelty, which, I confess, hath always been with me the strongest Objection against any Project, how well soever intended.

But in order to justify my Friend, he confessed, that this expedient was put into his Head by the famous Sallmanaazor, a Native of the Island Formosa, who came from thence to London, above twenty Years ago, and in Conversation told my Friend, that in his Country when any young Person happened to be put to Death, the Executioner sold the Carcass to Persons of Quality, as a prime Dainty, and that, in his Time, the Body of a plump Girl of fifteen, who was crucified for an attempt to poison the Emperor, was sold to his Imperial Majesty's prime Minister of State, and other great Mandarins of the Court, in Joints from the Gibbet, at four hundred Crowns. Neither indeed can I deny, that if the same Use were made of several plump young Girls in this Town, who, without one single Groat to their Fortunes, cannot stir abroad without a Chair, and appear at a Play-house, and Assemblies in Foreign fineries, which they never will pay for; the Kingdom would not be the worse.

Some Persons of a desponding Spirit are in great concern about that vast Number of poor People, who are Aged, Diseased, or Maimed, and I have been desired to imploy my Thoughts what Course may be taken, to ease the Nation of so grievous an Incumbrance. But I am not in the least Pain upon that matter, because it is very well known, that they are every Day dying, and rotting, by cold and famine, and filth, and vermin, as fast as can be reasonably expected. And as to the younger Labourers, they are now in almost as hopeful a Condition. They cannot get Work, and consequently pine away for want of Nourishment, to a degree, that if at any Time they are accidentally hired to common Labour, they have not strength to perform it, and thus the Country and themselves are happily delivered from the Evils to come.

I have too long digressed, and therefore shall return to my Subject. I think the Advantages by the Proposal which I have made are obvious and many, as well as of the highest Importance.

For *First*, as I have already observed, it would greatly lessen the Number of Papists, with whom we are Yearly over-run, being the principal breeders of the Nation, as well as our most dangerous Enemies, and who stay at home on purpose with a Design to deliver the Kingdom to the Pretender, hoping to take their Advantage by the Absence of so many good Protestants, who have chosen rather to leave their Country, than stay at home, and pay Tithes against their Conscience, to an Episcopal Curate.

Secondly, The poorer Tenants will have something valuable of their own which by Law may be made lyable to Distress, and help to pay their Landlord's Rent, their Corn and Cattle being already seized, and Money a Thing unknown.

Thirdly, Whereas the Maintenance of an hundred thousand Children, from two Years old, and upwards, cannot be computed at less than Ten Shillings a Piece per Annum, the Nation's Stock will be thereby increased fifty thousand Pounds per Annum, besides the Profit of a new Dish, introduced to the Tables of all Gentlemen of Fortune in the Kingdom, who have any Refinement in Taste, and Money will circulate among our Slaves, the Goods being entirely of our own Growth and Manufacture.

Fourthly, The constant Breeders, besides the gain of eight Shillings Sterling per Annum, by the Sale of their Children, will be rid of the Charge of maintaining them after the first Year.

Fifthly, This Food would likewise bring great Custom to Taverns, where the Vintners will certainly be so prudent as to procure the best Receipts for dressing it to Perfection; and consequently have their Houses frequented by all the fine Gentlemen, who justly value themselves upon their Knowledge in good Eating; and a skilful Cook, who understands how to oblige his Guests, will contrive to make it as expensive as they please.

Sixthly, This would be a great Inducement to Marriage, which all wise Nations have either encouraged by Rewards, or enforced by Laws and Penalties. It would encrease the Care and Tenderness of Mothers towards their Children, when they were sure of a Settlement for Life, to the poor Babes, provided in some Sort by the Publick, to their annual Profit instead of Expense; we should soon see an honest Emulation among the married Women, which of them could bring the fattest Child to the Market. Men would become as fond of their Wives, during their Time of their Pregnancy, as they are now of their Mares in Foal, their Cows in Calf, or Sows when they are ready to farrow, nor offer to beat or kick them (as is too frequent a Practice) for fear of a Miscarriage.

Many other Advantages might be enumerated. For Instance, the Addition of some thousand Carcasses in our Exportation of Berel'd Beef: The Propagation of Swine's Flesh, and Improvement in Art of making good Bacon, so much wanted among us by the great Destruction of Pigs, too frequent at our Tables, which are no way comparable in Taste, or Magnificence to a well grown, fat yearling Child, which roasted whole will make a considerable

Figure at a Lord Mayor's Feast, or any other Publick Entertainment. But this, and many others, I omit, being studious of Brevity.

Supposing that one thousand Families in this City, would be constant Customers for Infant's Flesh, besides others who might have it at merry Meetings, particularly at Weddings and Christenings, I compute that Dublin would take off Annually about twenty thousand Carcasses, and the rest of the Kingdom (where probably they will be sold somewhat cheaper) the remaining eight Thousand.

I can think of no one Objection, that will possibly be raised against this Proposal, unless it should be urged, that the Number of People will be thereby much lessened in the Kingdom. This I freely own, and 'twas indeed one principal Design in offering it to the World. I desire the Reader will observe, that I calculate my Remedy for this one individual Kingdom of Ireland, and for no Other that ever was, is, or, I think, ever can be upon Earth. Therefore let no man talk to me of other Expedients: Of taxing our Absentees at five Shillings a Pound: Of using neither Cloaths, nor Household Furniture, except what is of our own Growth and Manufacture: Of utterly rejecting the Materials and Instruments that promote Foreign Luxury: Of curing the Expensiveness of Pride, Vanity, Idleness, and Gaming in our Women: Of introducing a Vein of Parcimony, Prudence and Temperance: Of learning to love our Country, wherein we differ even from Laplanders, and the Inhabitants of Topinamboo: Of quitting our Animosities, and Factions, nor act any longer like the Jews, who were murdering one another at the very Moment their City was taken: Of being a little cautious not to sell our Country and Consciences for nothing: Of teaching Landlords to have at least one Degree of Mercy towards their Tenants. Lastly, Of putting a Spirit of Honesty, Industry, and Skill into our Shop-keepers, who, if a Resolution could now be taken to buy only our Native Goods, would immediately unite to cheat and exact upon us in the Price, the Measure, and the Goodness, nor could ever yet be brought to make one fair Proposal of just Dealing, though often and earnestly invited to it.

Therefore I repeat, let no Man talk to me of these and the like Expedients, till he hath at least some Glimpse of Hope, that there will ever be some hearty and sincere Attempt to put them in Practice.

But as to my self, having been wearied out for many Years with offering vain, idle, visionary Thoughts, and at length utterly despairing of Success, I fortunately fell upon this Proposal, which as it is wholly new, so it hath something Solid and Real, of no Expence and little Trouble, full in our own Power, and whereby we can incur no Danger in disobliging England. For this kind of Commodity will not bear Exportation, the Flesh being of too tender a Consistence, to admit a long Continuance in Salt, although perhaps I cou'd name a Country, which wou'd be glad to eat up our whole Nation without it.

After all, I am not so violently bent upon my own Opinion, as to reject any offer, proposed by wise Men, which shall be found equally Innocent,

Cheap, Easy and Effectual. But before something of that Kind shall be advanced in Contradiction to my Scheme, and offering a better, I desire the Author or Authors, will be pleased maturely to consider two Points. *First*, as Things now stand, how they will be able to find Food and Raiment for a hundred Thousand useless Mouths and Backs. And *Secondly*, There being a round Million of Creatures in Human Figure, throughout this Kingdom, whose whole Subsistence put into a common Stock, would leave them in Debt two Millions of Pounds Sterling, adding those, who are Beggers by Profession, to the Bulk of Farmers, Cottagers and Labourers, with their Wives and Children, who are Beggers in Effect; I desire those Politicians, who dislike my Overture, and may perhaps be so bold to attempt an Answer, that they will first ask the Parents of these Mortals, Whether they would not at this Day think it a great Happiness to have been sold for Food at a Year Old, in the manner I prescribe, and thereby have avoided such a perpetual Scene of Misfortunes, as they have since gone through, by the Oppression of Landlords, the Impossibility of paying Rent without Money or Trade, the Want of common Sustenance, with neither House nor Cloaths to cover them from the Inclemencies of the Weather, and the most inevitable Prospect of intailing the like, or greater Miseries, upon their Breed for ever.

I profess in the Sincerity of my Heart, that I have not the least Personal Interest in endeavouring to promote this necessary Work, having no other Motive than the Publick Good of my Country, by advancing our Trade, providing for Infants, relieving the Poor, and giving some Pleasure to the Rich. I have no Children, by which I can propose to get a single Penny; the youngest being nine Years Old, and my Wife past Child-bearing.

ENVIRONMENTAL RESPONSIBILITY

The theme of overpopulation, along with that of pollution and re-source depletion, has long haunted development analysts. While we have pushed on making more of everything, including ourselves, we have also been unmaking the environment. In this sense, world development strategies may have been almost too successful. We may now be too good at using natural resources. We may now be too industrious, since our impact on the world's land, forests, rivers, lakes, oceans, and atmosphere has rapidly become severe. Having learned how to control disease epidemics as well, we have also deprived ourselves of one of the main ways in which, histori-cally, our numbers have been culled. The human population has grown as a consequence, and as the numbers of the living have out-stripped the current ways of providing for them, mass poverty has ensued, and that has only made environmental degradation worse and more widespread.

To the problem of overpopulation, Swift suggests a gruesome solution. The way to prevent the poor of Ireland littering the nation's streets and degrading the environment, he says, is to eat their babies.

This is considerably more radical than Crusoe's solution, at least in Atterbury's account of Crusoe. Both Swift and Atterbury, however, pose the same problem and in a similar way. In Swift's Ireland and on Crusoe's island there are just too many people, at least in terms of what can be sustained by the development policies their ruling classes use. The question of development policy is unstated in each case and deliberately so, since it is the point of the irony in each case, too. With such prodigious numbers, that is, with such unfortunate policies, charity becomes a problem. Atterbury's Crusoe is prepared to offer the fortunate Friday the garbage scraps his dog and cat don't want. Swift has another plan. Moreover, it is one he feels sure will advance trade, provide for the young, relieve the poor, and give pleasure to the rich. Could redistribution of each country's wealth and a more egalitarian approach to development be another, perhaps preferred solution? Swift and Atterbury don't say.

Though it is rarely posed in such stark, and in Swift's case, such disturbing terms, the whole process of world development does raise the question of whether economic growth is possible without severe ecological stress. If we try to protect the environment, however, will we undermine economic growth and stop all development? Indeed, may we not be developing ourselves to death right now, and should we not stop all growth-based development forthwith?

These are not questions that come readily to the classically inclined Marxist mind. While those who think in these analytic terms talk of transfers of value from wage-slaves to owners and managers, and of the need to explain the prevalence of contemporary alienation and exploitation, they have little to say about population growth, shortage of resources, or holes in the ozone layer. The classical Marxist description in the Communist Manifesto, for example, of capitalists restlessly scouring the globe, clearing whole continents for cultivation and conjuring whole populations out of the ground, gives a clear account of the environmental impact of capitalism on the march. It doesn't dwell on that impact, though. It prefers to privilege a concern for class conflict instead.

Questions about the limits to growth are not ones that come readily to the liberal mind, either. The global division of labor, plus comparative advantage, may make for production on a much expanded scale. They don't make for environmental responsibility, however. Liberal capitalist systems are predicated upon nonstop economic growth, and unless we assume that such growth is basically ecologically benign, nonstop growth is generally a cause for concern—not for liberals, though. In her review of "our common future" for the United Nations' World Commission on Environment and Development, for example, Gro Harlem Brundtland (1987:1) notes "ever increasing environmental decay, poverty, and hardship in an ever more polluted world among ever decreasing resources." At the same time she approves what she sees as a "new era of economic growth." It seems that growth is not a problem in environmental terms.

Not only is growth not a problem, but Brundtland welcomes it as a way of protecting the environment. Growth is necessary, she says, if we are to be able to provide for a world population twice the size of that today, which is the level at which the world's population is expected to stabilize. The negative effects of growth are best dealt with by allowing it to continue. "We have in the past," Brundtland says, "been concerned about the impacts of economic growth upon the environment. We are now forced to concern ourselves with the impacts of ecological stress—degradation of soils, water regimes, atmosphere, and forests—upon our economic prospects." Armed with such concern, we accuse the industrial world of having used up already "much of the planet's ecological capital." We attribute the plight of the African poor, for example, not only to national policies that gave "too little attention, too late, to the needs of smallholder agriculture and to . . . rapidly rising populations" but to a "global economic system that takes more out of a poor continent than it puts in." Is the solution a radical reversal of this extraction process, however? Is it a questioning of the sustainability of industrialism itself? Apparently not, for if Brundtland is to be believed, the solution requires more of the same (Brundtland 1987:5–6).

To the radical environmentalist—the deep green—this is liberal utopianism. The radical environmentalist is a conserver. She or he will depict the Brundtland argument as a defense of the market and of free enterprise and as such, as a defense of the affluence and greed of the machine-rich, resource-hungry global well-to-do. While liberals may gild their defense with a reformist concern for greater state control and greater concern for the "quality" of growth (Brundtland 1987:49), they have no desire, the radicals say, to question the wisdom of the growth approach itself, or to ask whether it really can meet the needs of the majority of earth's people, who are clearly not well-to-do. In what sense, they say, can a system like this, whose advocates readily concede that it provides well for one group of people and much less well for others, actually be said to "work" (Trainer 1985)?

To the radical environmentalist, conservation applies to the human population as well. It is thus that Abernethy (1994:85–86) argues that "economic expansion, especially if it is introduced from outside the society and is also broad-based, encourages the belief that formerly recognized limits can be discounted. . . . Extra births and consequent population growth . . . overshoot actual opportunity." It is noteworthy, she says, that Indian society was stable for two thousand years. It only became overpopulated in response to the sense that "times are good and getting better." When it appeared to the people that "wealth and opportunity" could grow "without effort and without limit," then they started reproducing more. If wealth and opportunity had become widespread, this may not have mattered, at least in the shorter term. One of the most overpopulated countries on earth is the Netherlands, but it is not usually regarded as overpopulated because it is developed. Because wealth and opportunity remain scarce, however, then it is the very effort to alleviate poverty, Abernethy argues, that spurs population growth. This is why we must welcome, she says, the fact that development is now seen as a problem as well as a solution.

This sounds uncomfortably like an argument by haves against have-nots. It does raise an important question, however, about the extent to which development is only ever "appropriate development," that is, a form of development that sends local signals about the most sustainable move to make next (Abernethy 1994:86–88).

The people to send such signals are not state makers, radical environmentalists say, since they are compromised by their commitment to markets and growth, or by their proximity to the capitalist class. The people to turn to are members of environmentally active social movements. They are not in it for short-term profits. They are thinking about the longer run.

In the long run we will be dead, of course, and it is our descendants and their descendants who will have to live with the consequences of what we do today (Lipietz 1992:54). It is on their behalf that we ask about liberal capitalism in terms of its sustainability.

What are we to make of a system like this that damages the environment as a matter of course and only attempts to repair it if there seems to be money in it (Lipietz 1992:55)? The hope seems to be that the world's major ecological systems are not ones that continue to cope and then collapse irretrievably. If liberal capitalism makes this assumption, as radical environmentalists say it does, then we must all hope that the planet's basic ecological systems do not pass in this way beyond repair. We must all hope that the liberal capitalist assumption is correct, for if it is not, then the last lesson our entire species will learn will be the meaning of environmental responsibility.

9

World Development: Making Margins

❖ **Pura Velasco (1994) "I Am a Global Commodity"**

Pura Velasco grew up in a rural community in the Philippines. She has worked as a healthcare worker in Saudi Arabia and as a domestic worker in Vienna and in Canada.

Q. Could you begin by telling me about the conditions in the Philippines that led to your decision to leave your home and go to another country to work as a domestic worker?

A. I came from a rural area. There was fighting between the military and the MPA—this is the underground movement of the revolutionary faction in the Philippines—and I was a single mother and it was very difficult for me to find a job. I decided to go to the city. The city—it's overcrowded and it's the same kind of situation with the unemployment and the poverty. Basically, this kind of situation drove me to go out and search for better opportunities outside of the country. Well, I thought there were better opportunities outside the country.

I went to Saudi Arabia as a clerk in a hospital. Again, in Saudi Arabia it was basically the same. I was faced with the issue of being discriminated against in connection with the other workers coming from the first world countries. We were badly treated, the salaries were not good and the living conditions were not good. We were treated like children, sometimes we were treated like animals. . . .

Q. You've mentioned that workers learn from the experience of exploitation. . . . It seems that there's a difference in how you viewed your work experience now from when you started. What led to the development of your analysis?

A. I would say that when I was still a student, before I got married, I had a middle class kind of consciousness. But from the time that I started working as a migrant worker in Saudi Arabia and in Vienna and here [Toronto], it sort of crystallized my thought that I am a worker and I really see the differences in class, race too, and sex.

Although I was educated and I was very active in the nationalist movement in my country, my understanding of class struggle was very limited. It was different in the sense that my experience was different from being working class. My background was middle class and I see it as a privilege being educated. But going to another country and servicing other people, it really crystallized my consciousness of who I am, of being a worker. I know that there really is a difference between someone who is middle class, someone who is a worker and someone who is rich. That's the reason I cannot be blinded. I know some people probably think I'm too idealistic, but I cannot be blinded because of my experience. When I first applied to work as a domestic worker for an ambassador [in Vienna], he asked me not to sit at the table in the kitchen to eat. I knew right away I was different and he was different. Before that, that was difficult for me to understand or see because before my experience was of being on the side of privilege. It is the experience of being a worker that has taught me, that has made me point to the fact of who I really am, it really showed me what identity I have. . . .

Q. When we first met, we met at a forum which you were involved in organizing around the 50th anniversary of the IMF, the World Bank and the Bretton Woods system. The event was protesting the IMF and World Bank Structural Adjustment Programs. Can you talk about the connection between these programs and your life?

A. As I said earlier, I was under no illusion when I made the decision to leave the country. I was the victim of the political and economic situation at home which was created by the structural adjustment policies of the International Monetary Fund and the World Bank. That was part of their manipulation, an individual's decision to leave her own family to move to another part of the world to take care of another family. I have no illusion about that. The connection is great. . . .

Q. It's clear from the economic restructuring policies of the World Bank and IMF, and the various trade agreements being negotiated in such fora as the General Agreement on Tariffs and Trade or the North American Free Trade Agreement, that transnational corporations are working towards an even more globalized economy and that such organizations and agreements are intended to facilitate the smooth operations of international business. What would you say this means in terms of organizing workers? Does organization have to be international in order to be effective? And in the case of Filipina migrant domestic workers is this organizing inherently international?

A. Yes, I would say that there is an international organizing that should happen. . . . You see, if the multinational corporations see their world as one, then the workers should also start to see the world as one. If the corporations are able to draw a big picture, the workers should also be taught how to paint the world as a big picture. Like connecting the struggle from the Philippines to what is happening here, not only with the struggle of Filipina women workers here, but . . . with all workers.

Q. The money made through the labour of migrant domestic workers and women who leave the Philippines to work as entertainers [an estimated 70,000 Filipinas go to Japan each year to work in the sex trade] is central to the Philippines debt repayment scheme which is being enforced by the IMF and World Bank. Does this make these women central to the economy and isn't this a strategically powerful position from which to organize?

A. Yeah, that's why we are having workshops on structural adjustment. Because it is important for workers to link the debt to what is happening in the Philippines and to what is happening here. And also to link the remittances of women who are sending money to their family back home and connect it with the money that is going out from the Philippines which is being used to service our debts to the IMF and World Bank. So that's the kind of work that we are doing, making the workers understand that kind of situation.

Some of the women fantasized about boycotting sending money to the Philippine government. We thought even of declaring a one day domestic workers' strike, for the women to stop working even just for an hour, just to show that we're doing this in protest of the IMF and the discrimination that domestic workers face, in protest of all the exploitation of poor people that is taking place in the whole world.

MAKING GENDERED MARGINS

When Pura was sent from the table to eat, a line was drawn, a border was policed, a margin was made. It was a painful moment for her. As a middle-class Filipina, Pura had had a middle-class education and middle-class experiences. As a domestic worker in Austria, however, a clear social perimeter excluded rather than included her. Her status changed.

World development does this. It changes people's status, and it creates in the process new hierarchies and new categories of inclusion and exclusion. This is a highly political process, since hierarchies of this sort are always about power—who supposedly has it, and who supposedly has not.

World development creates and helps sustain a number of important core-periphery relationships. The notion of states themselves as being arranged in this way is familiar to political economists from reformist Marxist analyses of global affairs. They tend to be less familiar, however, with core-periphery relationships of other kinds.

There are a number of significant edges and shores that do not correspond to the margins state makers try to privilege. Subsistence dwellers, for example, whether they are found in Manhattan's Central Park, the streets of Bombay, or the rain forests of Amazonia, live largely outside the world capitalist system. They sell their labor to no one. They accept no welfare payments. They don't vote. They don't shop. They are not preoccupied with appearing or being modern. They may wander, like some New York bag lady, down the middle of Wall Street. And yet like New York's bag ladies they live as far outside the politicoeconomic and politicocultural perimeters of what Wall Street means as do pigeons on a pavement. Like pigeons they may scavenge for the food that those who live in the system throw away. They may drink from public fountains and benefit, as do the birds, from the public utilities and public order that the system provides. But they, and all those like them, are fringe dwellers, of little seeming relevance to the world capitalist market at all.

They do help give the world capitalist market a shape though, albeit not in this case a statecentric one. They also provide developmental baselines. They make it easier to see how the various parts of the system work to sustain the integrity of the whole. And they tell very different stories about where the system came from and where it might be going to.

Those women in the world political economy who are not employed for a wage mostly live in private domains where they labor "informally" for families. Many do both. Women do have another alternative, however, and that is to work on the fringes of the capitalist world system. For example, a woman may be a street vendor, a microentrepreneur. As such she will not get her capital from the usual sources in the capitalist world system, and the money she makes will not be put into capitalist banks, either. Some of her trade goods might come from that system, but many will not. As such she also works for herself, so she will pay no wages to employees, nor taxes to the state. As far as the world's capitalists are concerned, she trades beyond their frontiers. She is part of the world political economy and she may well spend parts of her life, or even parts of her day, within the capitalist component of that political economy, and yet she is not part of it. She trades beyond its margins.

Women, as discussed already, take part in the capitalist world market at a disadvantage. We are faced in the case of gender with exploitation so systematic and on such a vast scale that we are well justified in talking, as some analysts do, of "gender imperialism." While developmental disparities are apparent in terms of the different fortunes of states (the mercantilist view) or the varying success of marketeers (the liberal view) or the competing interests of the classes that constitute world capitalism (the Marxist view), developmental disparities are also manifest in how well women do as compared to men.

The "sex-asymmetric" consequences of structural adjustment (Lim 1993:175) and the way that males constitute the ruling gender place a different slant on the world political economy in general and the meaning of "development" in particular. In gender terms, for example, development means the massive transfer of surplus value from one gender to another, a transfer not only apparent in unequal wage rates but in terms of the amount of work that females do that doesn't get paid for at all. It also includes the way that women who do make progress in terms of greater equality with men may get bashed physically by male partners for doing so. This places a rather different construction than the conventional one on the concept of *security*. After all, "assaults on women by their husbands or male partners are the world's most common form of violence," and the "disturbing . . . possibility" does exist, it seems, of a link between this and development (UNICEF 1995b:26).

The unpaid work that females do mostly happens in the home. Where there is a male householder in paid employ, his money is meant to provide for both. Where there's not, and the state makers don't provide "welfare" support, the female is meant to find work (at rates less than a male's) or find a way of making money informally—often on the margins. Having social services performed by women at home for an indirect price or for nothing at all shows up in greater profits for capitalists. Hence the trend toward a global division of labor where males are supposed to sell their labor for wages and females are supposed to be "housewives," consigned to the privatized domain of the family and designated as reproducers. The fact that capitalists also find females a useful source of cheap labor power has not reversed this trend. It has merely compounded the inequities and the iniquities. It is no accident, therefore, that those who defined the goals for the UN Decade of the Advancement of Women (1975–1985) saw unwaged work, and the need to get it recognized and paid for, as one of their primary goals.

In an NIC like South Korea, for example, four-fifths of the adult females do not appear in labor market statistics because they are ostensibly in homes making an "invisible" but highly significant contribution to the country's wealth-making activities. Indeed, it is possible to argue that Korea could not have joined the ranks of the newly developed, or joined them so quickly, if the males who dominate the country's wealth-making institutions had not used women's work so unfairly. If they had not, in other words, exploited them so much.

Even in Singapore, where females have had access to higher education in all the professions, and formal female employment has increased at a rate notably faster than that of males, the same unfairness is clearly apparent. Females more than males work in low-status, low-paying jobs. In every job they are paid less than males, regardless of educational skills. There is clear occupational segregation by sexes, and this persists, as does the social expectation that females have prime responsibility for home care. Singapore's "developmental" miracle, like Korea's, was only made possible, in other words, by overworking and underpaying the female half of its population.

❖ **Hinmatoo Yalkikt, Chief Joseph of the Nez Percé (1877) "Surrender Speech"**

Tell General Howard I know his heart. What he told me before I have in my heart. I am tired of fighting. Our chiefs are killed. Looking Glass is dead. It is the young men who say yes or no. He who led the young men is dead. It is cold and we have no blankets. The little children are freezing to death. My people, some of them have run away to the hills and have no blankets, no food; no one knows where they are—perhaps freezing to death. I want to have time to look for my children and see how many I can find. Maybe I shall find them among the dead. Hear me my chiefs. I am tired; my heart is sick and sad. From where the sun now stands, I will fight no more forever.

MARGINALIZING INDIGENOUS PEOPLES

The story of Chief Joseph and his people is a sad and stirring one. It is characteristic that when he finally surrendered, the chief's first thoughts were for his people and of his desire to find and help those who had fled. The language of social science talks of "developmental marginalization" and "indigenous peoples," and yet what pallid euphemisms these are for human beings who have names for each other and themselves, who are not concepts, and whose collective status as captive nations has been the cause of so much anguish and pain. "Internally colonized by settler peoples" does no justice to this process, and "claims for self-determination" sounds stupid beside the story such human beings tell of their attempts to get back some control over their cultures and their lives.

These are peoples without armies and usually without great wealth. What they do have, however, is the force of their own feelings, articulated as moral claims for return of land and other less-tangible cultural assets. The feelings they express are often those of desperation, since the issues they face may be matters of sheer survival (as borne out by their average longevity, infant mortality, incarceration, unemployment, school retention rates, and health and wealth profiles). They are feelings the language—any language—of world political economy is singularly ill-equipped to express.

Indigenous peoples would prefer to flourish rather than merely survive. They would claim the right not just to physical existence, but to the power to determine their own affairs and to exploit their resources as they see fit. These resources extend even as far as their bodily selves, since their genetic material can be of considerable value to biological engineers or pharmaceutical multinationals, who "bio-mine" indigenous peoples as part of their research.

Flourishing is problematic on the margins, wherever those margins might be. Analytic languages like liberalism or Marxism or mercantilism are of limited use when it comes to understanding the issues involved or prescribing appropriate change. Languages like these are of limited help in expressing the concerns of indigenous peoples. Indeed, they are part of the hegemonic discourse that helps oppress and exploit such peoples and that prevents them being heard.

Modern margins have mostly been made by one particular cultural tradition, that of the industrial capitalist West. This tradition values objectivity, rational thought, and the individual. Indigenous peoples, on the other hand, tend to value subjectivity, more holistic ways of thinking, and communalism. Their understanding of "development" reflects their values. They talk, for example, of ethno-development, not development per se, and in talking like this they are typically talking about the conservation of their culture. Ethno-development doesn't necessarily mean separate development, though. It may mean trying to move from the margins to become capitalist marketeers. That decision will depend upon who is winning the arguments within indigenous communities themselves about how best to fight "ethnocide" (Stavenhagen 1989:16). Some will want to stand alone regardless. Others will say, "If you can't beat 'em, join 'em," in a bid to play the capitalist game and with the profits implement programs that conserve their culture.

The difference between Western-style discourse and that of indigenous peoples is not only of significance to the latter, however. Indigenous peoples' knowledge and perspectives may be an important resource for those seeking alternative models of development; ones that are more sustainable—both socially and environmentally. Sustainability is something many Westerners are coming to realize they need themselves.

It is highly ironic that it is from some of those marginalized in the making of the capitalist industrial system that the clearest advice comes as to what to value and what to do if the world political economy itself is to survive.

❖ Ernst Schumacher (1973) "Buddhist Economics"

"Right Livelihood" is one of the requirements of the Buddha's Noble Eightfold Path. It is clear, therefore, that there must be such a thing as Buddhist Economics.

Buddhist countries, at the same time, have often stated that they wish to remain faithful to their heritage. So Burma: "The New Burma sees no conflict between religious values and economic progress. Spiritual health and material well-being are not enemies: they are natural allies."[1] Or: "We can blend successfully the religious and spiritual values of our heritage with the benefits of modern technology."[2] Or: "We Burmans have a sacred duty to conform both our dreams and our acts to our faith. This we shall ever do."[3]

All the same, such countries invariably assume that they can model their economic development plans in accordance with modern economics, and they call upon modern economists from so-called advanced countries to advise them, to formulate the policies to be pursued, and to construct the grand design for development, the Five-Year Plan or whatever it may be called. No one seems to think that a Buddhist way of life would call for Buddhist economics, just as the modern materialist way of life has brought forth modern economics.

Economists themselves, like most specialists, normally suffer from a kind of metaphysical blindness, assuming that theirs is a science of absolute and invariable truths, without any presuppositions. Some go as far as to claim that economic laws are as free from "metaphysics" or "values" as the law of gravitation. We need not, however, get involved in arguments of methodology. Instead, let us take some fundamentals and see what they look like when viewed by a modern economist and a Buddhist economist.

There is universal agreement that the fundamental source of wealth is human labour. Now, the modern economist has been brought up to consider labour or work as little more than a necessary evil. From the point of view of the employer, it is in any case simply an item of cost, to be reduced to a minimum if it cannot be eliminated altogether, say, by automation. From the point of view of the workman, it is a "disutility": to work is to make a sacrifice of one's leisure and comfort, and wages are a kind of compensation for the sacrifice. Hence the ideal from the point of view of the employer is to have output without employees, and the ideal from the point of view of the employee is to have income without employment.

The consequences of these attitudes both in theory and in practice are, of course, extremely far-reaching. If the ideal with regard to work is to get rid of it, every method that "reduces the work load" is a good thing. The most potent method, short of automation, is the so-called division of labour and the classical example is the pin factory eulogized in Adam Smith's *Wealth of Nations*. Here it is not a matter of ordinary specialisation, which mankind has practised from time immemorial, but of dividing up every complete process of production into minute parts, so that the final product can be produced at great speed without anyone having had to contribute more than a totally insignificant and, in most cases, unskilled movement of his limbs.

Work

The Buddhist point of view takes the function of work to be at least three-fold: to give a man [sic] a chance to utilise and develop his faculties; to enable him to overcome his ego-centredness by joining with other people in a common task; and to bring forth the goods and services needed for a becoming existence. Again, the consequences that flow from this view are endless. To organise work in such a manner that it becomes meaningless, boring, stultifying, or nerve-racking for the worker would be little short of criminal; it would indicate a greater concern with goods than with people, an evil lack of compassion and a soul-destroying degree of attachment to the most primitive side of this worldly existence. Equally, to strive for leisure as an alternative to work would be considered a complete misunderstanding of one of the basic truths of human existence, namely, that work and leisure are complementary parts of the same living process and cannot be separated without destroying the joy of work and the bliss of leisure.

From the Buddhist point of view, there are therefore two types of mechanization which must be clearly distinguished: one that enhances a man's skill and power and one that turns the work of man over to a mechanical slave, leaving man in a position of having to serve the slave. How to tell the one from the other? "The craftsman himself," says Ananda Coomaraswamy, a man equally competent to talk about the Modern West as the Ancient East, "The craftsman himself can always, if allowed to, draw the delicate distinction between the machine and the tool. The carpet loom is a tool, a contrivance for holding warp threads at a stretch for the pile to be woven round them by the craftsman's fingers; but the power loom is a machine, and its significance as a destroyer of culture lies in the fact that it does the essentially human part of the work."[4] It is clear, therefore, that Buddhist economics must be very different from the economics of modern materialism, since the Buddhist sees the essence of civilization not in a multiplication of wants but in the purification of human character. Character, at the same time, is formed primarily by a man's work. And work, properly conducted in conditions of human dignity and freedom, blesses those who do it and equally their products. The Indian philosopher and economist J C Kumarappa sums the matter up as follows:

If the nature of the work is properly appreciated and applied, it will stand in the same relation to the higher faculties as food is to the physical body. It nourishes and enlivens the higher man and urges him to produce the best he is capable of. It directs his free will along the proper course and disciplines the animal in him into progressive channels. It furnishes an excellent background for man to display his scale of values and develop his personality.[5]

If a man has no chance of obtaining work he is in a desperate position, not simply because he lacks an income but because he lacks this nourishing and enlivening factor of disciplined work which nothing can replace. A modern economist may engage in highly sophisticated calculations on whether full employment "pays" or whether it might be more "economic" to run an economy at less than full employment so as to ensure a greater mobility of labour, a better stability of wages, and so forth. His fundamental criterion of success is simply the total quantity of goods produced during a given period of time. "If the marginal urgency of goods is low," says Professor Galbraith in *The Affluent Society*, "then so is the urgency of employing the last man or the last million men in the labour force." And again: "If . . . we can afford some unemployment in the interest of stability—a proposition, incidentally, of impeccably conservative antecedents—then we can afford to give those who are unemployed the goods that enable them to sustain their accustomed standard of living."[6]

From a Buddhist point of view, this is standing the truth on its head by considering goods as more important than people and consumption as more important than creative activity. It means shifting the emphasis from the worker to the product of work, that is, from the human to the subhuman, a surrender to the forces of evil. The very start of Buddhist economic planning would be a planning for full employment, and the primary purpose of this would in fact be employment for everyone who needs an "outside" job: it would not be the maximization of employment nor the maximization of production. Women, on the whole, do not need an outside job [sic], and the large-scale employment of women in offices or factories would be considered a sign of serious economic failure. In particular, to let mothers of young children work in factories while the children run wild would be as uneconomic in the eyes of a Buddhist economist as the employment of a skilled worker as a soldier in the eyes of a modern economist.

While the materialist is mainly interested in goods, the Buddhist is mainly interested in liberation. But Buddhism is "The Middle Way" and therefore in no way antagonistic to physical well-being. It is not wealth that stands in the way of liberation but the attachment to wealth; not the enjoyment of pleasurable things but the craving for them. The keynote of Buddhist economics, therefore, is simplicity and nonviolence. From an economist's point of view, the marvel of the Buddhist way of life is the utter rationality of its pattern—amazingly small means leading to extra-ordinarily satisfactory result.

The Standard of Living

For the modern economist this is very difficult to understand. He is used to measuring the standard of living by the amount of annual consumption, assuming all the time that a man who consumes more is "better off" than a man who consumes less. A Buddhist economist would consider this approach excessively irrational: since consumption is merely a means to human well-being, the aim should be to obtain the maximum of well-being with the minimum of consumption. Thus, if the purpose of clothing is a certain amount of temperature comfort and an attractive appearance, the task is to attain this purpose with the smallest possible effort, that is, with the smallest annual destruction of cloth and with the help of designs that involve the smallest possible input of toil. The less toil there is, the more time and strength is left for artistic creativity. It would be highly uneconomic, for instance, to go in for complicated tailoring, like the modern West, when a much more beautiful effect can be achieved by the skilful draping of uncut material. It would be the height of folly to make material so that it should wear out quickly and the height of barbarity to make anything ugly, shabby or mean. What has just been said about clothing applies equally to all other human requirements. The ownership and the consumption of goods is a means to an end, and Buddhist economics is the systematic study of how to attain given ends with the minimum means.

Modern economics, on the other hand, considers consumption to be the sole end and purpose of all economic activity, taking the factors of production—land, labour, and capital—as the means. The former, in short, tries to maximize human satisfactions by the optimal pattern of consumption, while the latter tries to maximize consumption by the optimal pattern of productive effort. It is easy to see that the effort needed to sustain a way of life which seeks to attain the optimal pattern of consumption is likely to be much smaller than the effort needed to sustain a drive for maximum consumption. We need not be surprised, therefore, that the pressure and strain of living is very much less in, say, Burma than it is in the United States, in spite of the fact that the amount of labour-saving machinery used in the former country is only a minute fraction of the amount used in the latter.

The Pattern of Consumption

Simplicity and nonviolence are obviously closely related. The optimal pattern of consumption, producing a high degree of human satisfaction by means of a relatively low rate of consumption, allows people to live without great pressure and strain and to fulfil the primary injunction of Buddhist teaching: "Cease to do evil; try to do good." As physical resources are everywhere limited, people satisfying their needs by means of a modest use of resources are obviously less likely to be at each other's throats than people depending upon a high rate of use. Equally, people who live in highly self-sufficient local communities are less likely to get involved in large-scale violence than people whose existence depends on worldwide systems of trade.

From the point of view of Buddhist economics, therefore, production from local resources for local needs is the most rational way of economic life, while dependence on imports from afar and the consequent need to produce for export to unknown and distant peoples is highly uneconomic and justifiable only in exceptional cases and on a small scale. Just as the modern economist would admit that a high rate of consumption of transport services between a man's home and his place of work signifies a misfortune and not a high standard of life, so the Buddhist economist would hold that to satisfy human wants from far-away sources rather than from sources nearby signifies failure rather than success. The former might take statistics showing an increase in the number of ton/miles per head of the population carried by a country's transport system as proof of economic progress, while to the latter—the Buddhist economist—the same statistics would indicate a highly undesirable deterioration in the *pattern* of consumption.

Natural Resources

Another striking difference between modern economics and Buddhist economics arises over the use of natural resources. Bertrand de Jouvenel, the eminent French political philosopher, has characterised "Western man" in words which may be taken as a fair description of the modern economist:

> He tends to count nothing as an expenditure, other than human effort; he does not seem to mind how much mineral matter he wastes and, far worse, how much living matter he destroys. He does not seem to realise at all that human life is a dependent part of an ecosystem of many different forms of life. As the world is ruled from towns where men are cut off from any form of life other than human, the feeling of belonging to an ecosystem is not revived. This results in a harsh and improvident treatment of things upon which we ultimately depend, such as water and trees.[7]

The teaching of the Buddha, on the other hand, enjoins a reverent and nonviolent attitude not only to all sentient beings but also, with great emphasis, to trees. Every follower of the Buddha ought to plant a tree every few years and look after it until it is safely established, and the Buddhist economist can demonstrate without difficulty that the universal observance of this rule would result in a high rate of genuine economic development independent of any foreign aid. Much of the economic decay of Southeast

Asia (as of many other parts of the world) is undoubtedly due to a heedless and shameful neglect of trees.

Modern economics does not distinguish between renewable and non-renewable materials, as its very method is to equalize and quantify every-thing by means of a money price. Thus, taking various alternative fuels, like coal, oil, wood or water power: the only difference between them recognized by modern economics is relative cost per equivalent unit. The cheapest is automatically the one to be preferred, as to do otherwise would be irrational and "uneconomic." From a Buddhist point of view, of course, this will not do; the essential difference between nonrenewable fuels like coal and oil on the one hand and renewable fuels like wood and waterpower on the other cannot be simply overlooked. Nonrenewable goods must be used only if they are indispensable, and then only with the greatest care and the most meticu-lous concern for conservation. To use them heedlessly or extravagantly is an act of violence, and while complete nonviolence may not be attainable on this earth, there is nonetheless an ineluctable duty on man to aim at the ideal of nonviolence in all he does.

Just as a modern European economist would not consider it a great economic achievement if all European art treasures were sold to America at attractive prices, so the Buddhist economist would insist that a population basing its economic life on nonrenewable fuels is living parasitically, on capital instead of income. Such a way of life could have no permanence and could therefore be justified only as a purely temporary expedient. As the world's resources of nonrenewable fuels—coal, oil and natural gas—are exceedingly unevenly distributed over the globe and undoubtedly limited in quantity, it is clear that their exploitation at an ever increasing rate is an act of violence against nature which must almost inevitably lead to violence between men.

The Middle Way

This fact alone might give food for thought even to those people in Buddhist countries who care nothing for the religious and spiritual values of their heritage and ardently desire to embrace the materialism of modern econom-ics at the fastest possible speed. Before they dismiss Buddhist economics as nothing better than a nostalgic dream, they might wish to consider whether the path of economic development outlined by modern economics is likely to lead them to places where they really want to be. Towards the end of his courageous book *The Challenge of Man's Future,* Professor Harrison Brown of the California Institute of Technology gives the following appraisal:

> Thus we see that, just as industrial society is fundamentally unstable and subject to reversion to agrarian existence, so within it the condi-tions which offer individual freedom are unstable in their ability to

avoid the conditions which impose rigid organization and totalitarian control. Indeed, when we examine all of the foreseeable difficulties which threaten the survival of industrial civilization, it is difficult to see how the achievement of stability and the maintenance of individual liberty can be made compatible.[8]

Even if this were dismissed as a long-term view—and in the long term, as Keynes said, we are all dead—there is the immediate question of whether modernization, as currently practised without regard to religious spiritual values, is actually producing agreeable results. As far as the masses are concerned, the results appear to be disastrous—a collapse of the rural economy, a rising tide of unemployment in town and country, and the growth of a city proletariat without nourishment for either body or soul.

It is in the light of both immediate experience and long-term prospects that the study of Buddhist economics could be recommended even to those who believe that economic growth is more important than any spiritual or religious values. For it is not a question of choosing between "modern growth" and "traditional stagnation." It is a question of finding the right path of development, "The Middle Way" between materialist heedlessness and traditionalist immobility, in short, of finding "Right Livelihood."

That this can be done is not in doubt. But it requires much more than blind imitation of the materialist way of life of the so-called advanced countries.[9] It requires above all, the conscious and systematic development of a "Middle Way in Technology" as I have called it.[10] A technology more productive and powerful than the decayed technology of the ancient East, but at the same time nonviolent and immensely cheaper and simpler than the labour-saving technology of the modern West.

MAKING SPIRITUAL MARGINS

World development has many different dimensions, though perhaps the hardest to understand is the spiritual one. Questions of spirituality seem far away from the material world of political economy and the march of industrial market capitalism. And yet the very material nature of this march makes a spiritual statement. It says that human beings can now rely on themselves and their industrial production systems to supply their basic needs; that the greatest reward and the clearest measure of success in this respect is the chance and the capacity to consume the goods and services these productive systems provide; and that a sense of whatever it is that might seem divine to people has no essential part to play in making such provision.

The spiritual statement that capitalism makes is a particularly powerful one. This statement can be understood, though, not only by talking about the secular disenchantments wrought by modern science. These are familiar to most people today and I shall not rehearse them here. A good alternative is to let someone like Schumacher speak for himself.

Schumacher does something very unusual. He recasts political economy in Buddhist terms. He accepts as given the teachings of one of the world's greatest religious philosophies and he explores his idea of what these teachings mean in practical politicoeconomic terms. The results may seem, to those unfamiliar with such teachings, distinctly odd, and even bizarre. This is hardly surprising, since what Schumacher describes in this essay is in many respects the antithesis of what gets taken for granted today.

While Buddhism may be at odds with capitalism, those peoples who practice as Buddhists on the whole are not. Schumacher cites Burma in ways that make it sound like an exception here, but it seems generally to be the case that to have capitalism people must sublimate their Buddhism. In this they are not alone. Christian capitalists, for example, must likewise sublimate their commitment to Christianity. Though capitalism was developed in Christian Europe, the "greed is good" ethic of the capitalist entrepreneur is a far cry from the principle of brotherly love that Jesus Christ espoused. This is not to say that capitalists can't be Christians. Many are, and the Christian spirit has had an important historical influence upon capitalism, moderating its excesses by bringing to bear concepts like *charity* and *welfare*, and even—if Weber is right—providing the original impetus for capitalism as a whole.

Christianity is not capitalism, however, and the two are not, in spiritual terms, easy to reconcile; nor are Buddhism and capitalism. Where people want capitalism they tend, it seems, to lose their faith. This has profound existential consequences, which Marx talked about in terms of "alienation," and which reformist Marxists, like the so-called critical theorists of the Frankfurt school, have continued to talk about as one of the consequences of a capitalist mode of production (George 1994:150–155). Many of these consequences can be very depressing, and a wide range of New Age beliefs have sprung up to serve the needs of the distressed. Fundamentalists from the established religions have responded to this challenge in terms of spiritual rescue, too.

Most analysts of world political economy find all this hard to understand or discuss. As a dimension to world development, therefore, with the exception of the Marxists noted above, they largely leave it alone. It's easy to see why. Most analysts in the discipline find barely comprehensible a view of the world that would want to purify the human heart rather than make things. The Buddhist conclusion, for example, that to measure living standards in terms of annual rates of consumption you have to be fundamentally irrational, is a conclusion most analysts would find irrational in turn. Capitalists don't like Buddhists telling them that they are not rational enough, and that if they were more rational, they wouldn't be capitalists at all. Capitalism lies uneasily with revealed knowledge like Christianity or Islam, too. It is fundamentally at odds with the religious worldview.

What, then, are we to make of the margins this difference creates, both in our minds and in our "developing" world?

"'Listen' the saints say. 'He who desires true rest and happiness must raise his hope from things that perish and pass away and place it in the Word of God, so that, cleaving to that which abides forever, he may also together with it abide forever'" (Barthleme 1974). And yet fewer and fewer people seem to be listening like this. It is industrial market capitalism that abides instead. While the cathedrals and the temples are moved to the social margins to be turned into cultural curiosities—on the same tourist beat as museums and art galleries—in their stead are built office blocks and shopping malls. While people stop chanting the Kyrie, they start chanting other litanies, like "another dollar, another day." Values change. Instead of being measured in terms of their eternal worth, people are judged by what their labor power will bring in the marketplace. "Meaning [is] drained from work and assigned instead to remuneration. Unemployment obliterates the world of the unemployed . . . authentic self-determination is thwarted. The false consciousness created and catered to by mass culture perpetuates ignorance and powerlessness" (Barthelme 1974). Gods go, leaving god-sized holes.

This is marginalization of a pretty serious sort. It is not at all clear, though, how we should understand it in academic terms. Some attempts have been made but the field is still wide open (Robertson and Garrett 1991; Roberts 1995; Beyer 1993; Ray 1993; Meeks 1989). Where might we begin? What might prompt us to?

"Study of the tides of conflict and power in a system in which there is structural inequality" would be one good starting point, Barthelme suggests, in a reading not included here. With his tongue firmly in his cheek, he goes on to say that a "knowledge of European intellectual history since 1789 provides a useful background" and that "information theory offers interesting new possibilities." It's the remarks he makes that follow these that may be the most pertinent ones, however. "Passion is helpful," he concludes, "especially those types of passion which are non-licit. Doubt is a necessary precondition to meaningful action. Fear is the great mover, in the end" (Barthelme 1974).

NOTES

1. Pyidawtha, *The New Burma* (Economic and Social Board, Government of the Union of Burma, 1954), p. 10.
2. Ibid., p. 8.
3. Ibid., p. 128.
4. Ananda K. Coomaraswamy, *Art and Awadeshi* (Ganesh and Company, Madras), p. 30.
5. J. C. Kumarappa, *Economy of Permanence* (Sarva-Seva-Sangh-Publication, Rajghat, Kashi, 4th ed., 1958), p. 117.
6. J. K. Galbraith, *The Affluent Society* (Penguin, 1962), pp. 272–273.
7. Richard B. Gregg, *A Philosophy of Indian Economic Development* (Navajivan Publishing House, Ahmedabad, 1958), pp. 140–141.
8. Harrison Brown, *The Challenge of Man's Future* (Viking Press, New York, 1954), p. 225.
9. E. F. Schumacher, "Rural Industries," in *India at Midpassage* (Overseas Development Institute, London, 1964).
10. E. F. Schumacher, "Industrialisation Through Intermediate Technology," in *Minerals and Industries*, Vol. 1, no. 4 (Calcutta, 1964); Vijay Chebbi and George McRobie, *Dynamics of District Development* (SIET Institute, Hyderabad, 1964).

10

Postscript:
Thinking with a Clear Heart

❖ *Monty Python and the Holy Grail* (1974) "Arthur and Dennis"

Arthur and *Patsy* riding. They stop and look. We see a castle in the distance, and before it a peasant is working away on his knees trying to dig the earth with his bare hands and a twig. *Arthur* and *Patsy* ride up, and stop before the peasant.

Arthur: Old woman!
Dennis: (turning) Man.
Arthur: Man. I'm sorry. Old man, what knight lives in that castle?
Dennis: I'm thirty-seven.
Arthur: What?
Dennis: I'm only thirty-seven . . . I'm not old.
Arthur: Well—I can't just say: "Hey, Man!"
Dennis: You could say: "Dennis."
Arthur: I didn't know you were called Dennis.
Dennis: You didn't bother to find out, did you?
Arthur: I've said I'm sorry about the old woman, but from behind you looked . . .
Dennis: What I object to is that you automatically treat me as an inferior . . .
Arthur: Well . . . I *am* King.
Dennis: Oh, very nice. King, eh! I expect you've got a palace and fine clothes and courtiers and plenty of food. And how d'you get that? By exploiting the workers! By hanging onto outdated imperialistic dogma, which perpetuates the social and economic differences in our society! If there's *ever* going to be any progress . . .

An old woman appears.

Old woman: Dennis! Have you seen the cat's front legs? Oh! How d'you do?
Arthur: How d'you do, good lady . . . I am Arthur, King of the Britons . . . can you tell me who lives in that castle?
Old woman: King of the *who?*
Arthur: The Britons.

Old woman: Who are the Britons?
Arthur: All of us are . . . we are all Britons.

Dennis winks at the old woman.

. . . And I am your King . . .
Old woman: Oooooh! I didn't know we had a king. I thought we were an autonomous collective . . .
Dennis: You're fooling yourself. We're living in a dictatorship, a self-perpetuating autocracy in which the working classes . . .
Old woman: There you are, bringing class into it again . . .
Dennis: That's what it's all about . . . If only—
Arthur: Please, please, good people, I am in haste. What knight lives in that castle?
Old woman: No one lives there.
Arthur: Well, who is your lord?
Old woman: We don't have a lord.
Arthur: What?
Dennis: I told you, we're an anarcho-syndicalist commune, we take it in turns to act as a sort of executive officer for the week.
Arthur: Yes . . .
Dennis: . . . But all the decisions of that officer . . .
Arthur: Yes, I see.
Dennis: . . . must be approved at a bi-weekly meeting by a simple majority in the case of purely internal affairs.
Arthur: Be quiet.
Dennis: . . . but a two-thirds majority . . .
Arthur: Be quiet! I order you to shut up.
Old woman: Order, eh? Who does he think he is?
Arthur: I am your king.
Old woman: Well, I didn't vote for you.
Arthur: You don't vote for kings.
Old woman: Well, how did you become king, then?
Arthur: The Lady of the Lake, her arm clad in purest shimmering samite, held Excalibur aloft from the bosom of the waters to signify that by Divine Providence . . . I, Arthur, was to carry Excalibur . . . that is why I am your King. . . .
Dennis: Look, strange women lying on their backs in ponds handing over swords . . . that's no basis for a system of government. Supreme executive power derives from a mandate from the masses not from some farcical aquatic ceremony.
Arthur: Be quiet!
Dennis: You can't expect to wield supreme executive power just because some watery tart threw a sword at you.

Arthur: Shut up!
Dennis: I mean, if I went round saying I was an Emperor because some moistened bint had lobbed a scimitar at *me*, people would put me away.
Arthur: (Grabbing him by the collar) Shut up, will you. Shut up!
Dennis: Ah! *Now* . . . we see the violence inherent in the system.
Arthur: Shut up!

People (i.e. other peasants) are appearing and watching.

Dennis: (calling) Come and see the violence inherent in the system. Help, help, I'm being repressed!
Arthur: (aware that people are now coming out and watching) Bloody peasant! (pushes *Dennis* over into mud and prepares to ride off)
Dennis: Ooooooh! Did you hear that! What a give-away.
Arthur: Come on, Patsy.
They ride off.
Dennis: (in background as we pull out) Did you see him repressing me, then? That's what I've been on about . . .

THINKING WITH A CLEAR HEART

Authur and Dennis both speak English. However, the very same words mean completely different things to them. They speak entirely different analytical languages and so the mutual quality of their misunderstanding is complete. Their conceptions of human nature, the values they hold dear as a consequence, the societal implications of these values, do not compute. Authur is a king. He thinks about his place in the world (when he bothers to think about it at all) in terms of his divine right to rule. He takes his absolute authority for granted. Dennis is an anarcho-syndicalist, however. To him, Authur is a dictator who exploits and represses all those who provide him with his privileges and spoils.

As in the fictional world of Monty Python, so in the factional world of political economics; as Authur and Dennis see different versions of "reality," so too do those who talk about the world political economy. This is why a survey of the subject, if it is to make any claim to being comprehensive, must refer at every point to the various analytical languages in which the subject is described and explained.

In this book I have tried to show not only how the international political economy is becoming a world political economy, but also how the major analytical languages, worked out over the last two hundred years by those who have tried to understand world affairs in this way, might account for that transition. Even in good faith, these people disagree. And it's little wonder. The world political economy is a vast, tangled web of repeated human practices, advancing on a broad front, from one moment to the next. We do it as we try to understand it, and our understandings are part of what we try to do. We make different assumptions about human nature, and we take different positions on what to value as a consequence, and we act accordingly. The whole thing's a mess and it's a wonder we can make any sense of it at all.

I have not confined the attempt I've made here to understand the world political economy to academic analyses, either. We know about the world in ways other than the ways those conventional analyses promote and protect. By including readings of a nonacademic sort, I hope to have shown how valuable information about the subject can be found in unconventional places, and valuable insights, too, insights arguably not available from academic analyses.

The complexities of the world political economy are best addressed with a clear head, though too few realize this means having a clear heart as well. If we want to know how the world political economy works, in other words, we need to do as much as we can to clarify our thinking, our concepts, and the analytic languages we choose to use. We also need to do as much as we can to clarify our emotions, our values, and the understandings of human being we bring to bear. Clarification comes, that is, in both rational and nonrational forms. We not only have a neocortex in our heads (a "thinking" part), we also have a limbic system ("feeling" parts) as well. As a consequence we not only "know" about things analytically, we "know" things experientially, too.

It seems an obvious point to make but it's one with a heretic ring to it in such self-consciously scientific times. It's also a point well made in Velasco's story, for example, where she says how it was difficult for her to "understand and see" who she really was until she had experienced something other than the middle-class life she had led at home. She's not alone there.

My own efforts at clarification have taken me from Lodge's London to Enloe's banana plantations to Bastiat's sun-struck France. An odd journey, perhaps, but coming at the complexities of the world political economy in unconventional ways has confirmed for me my original hunch that the experiential does matter. Coming to terms with that fact while remaining academically credible is problematic. We face a huge challenge in this regard. It is a challenge worth facing, however, if only because it is here, I feel, that we also find our single biggest chance.

References

Abernethy, Virginia (1994) "Optimism and Overpopulation," *Atlantic Monthly,* December.

Albert, Mathias (1994) "Post-Modernization of the World Economy: The Philosophy and Economy of Structural Change." Paper presented at the annual meeting of the International Studies Association, Washington, D.C.

Amin, Samir (1993) "Replacing the International Monetary System?" *Monthly Review* 45:5.

—— (1994) "Can Environmental Problems Be Subject to Economic Calculations?" *Monthly Review* 45:4.

Anderson, Benedict (1992) "The New World Disorder," *New Left Review* 193.

amnonc@mercury.co.il (1995) "Why the World Needs Socialism," May 3.

Armstrong, Philip, et al. (1991) *Capitalism Since 1945.* Oxford: Basil Blackwell.

Ashley, Richard (1983) "Three Modes of Economism," *International Studies Quarterly* 27:4.

Atterbury, M. (1964) "Depression Hits Robinson Crusoe's Island." In Joyce Kornbluh, ed., *Rebel Voices.* Ann Arbor: University of Michigan.

"Background Briefing by Senior Administration Officials" (1994) Office of the Press Secretary, The White House, Washington, D.C., November 2.

Baker, R. (1995) "Riding the Rivers of Dirty Money," *Guardian Weekly,* June 18.

Ballance, Robert, et al. (1992) *The World's Pharmaceutical Industries.* Aldershot: Edward Elgar for UNIDO.

Barthelme, Donald (1974) "The Rise of Capitalism." In Donald Barthelme, *Sadness.* New York: Bantam.

Bastiat, Frédéric (1909) *Economic Sophisms,* trans. P. Stirling. London: T. Fisher Unwin.

Beckman, Peter, and Francine D'Amico, eds. (1994) *Women, Gender and World Politics: Perspectives, Policies and Prospects.* Westport: Bergin and Garvey.

Bello, Walden, and Stephanie Rosenfeld (1992) *Dragons in Distress: Asia's Miracle Economies in Crisis.* Harmondsworth: Penguin.

Bensusan-Butt, David (1980) "Learning Economics 1976." In David Bensusan-Butt, *On Economic Knowledge: A Sceptical Miscellany.* Canberra: A.N.U. Press.

Bernstein, Richard (1976) *The Restructuring of Social and Political Theory.* Oxford: Basil Blackwell.

Berthoud, Gérald (1992) "Market." In Wolfgang Sachs, ed., *The Development Dictionary: A Guide to Knowledge as Power.* London: Zed Press.

Beyer, Peter (1993) *Religion and Globalisation.* London: Sage.

Bina, Cyrus, and Behzad Yahgmaian (1991) "Post-war Global Accumulation and the Transnationalisation of Capital," *Capital and Class* 43.

Black, I. (1995) "World Leaders Pledge to Fight Poverty," *Guardian Weekly,* March 1.

Bollard, Alan, and David Mayes (1992) "Regionalism and the Pacific Rim," *Journal of Common Market Studies* 30:2.

Braverman, Harry (1974) *Labor and Monopoly Capital.* New York: Monthly Review Press.

Brown, Michael Barratt (1974) *The Economics of Imperialism.* Harmondsworth: Penguin.

Brundtland, Gro Harlem (1987) *Our Common Future.* Oxford: Oxford University Press.

———— (1995) "A Shameful Condition." In UNICEF, *The Progress of Nations.* New York: UNICEF.

Bukharin, Nikolai (1925) *Historical Materialism: A System of Sociology.* Moscow: International Publishers.

Burningham, David, ed. (1991) *Economics.* Sevenoaks: Hodder and Stoughton.

Button, Kenneth, and Werner Rothengatter (1993) "Global Environmental Degradation: The Role of Transport." In David Bannister and Kenneth Button, eds., *Transport, the Environment and Sustainable Development.* London: E. and F. Spon.

Caporaso, James (1987a) "International Political Economy: Fad or Field?" *International Studies Notes* 13:1.

———— (1987b) "The International Division of Labor: A Theoretical Overview." In James Caporaso, ed., *A Changing International Division of Labor.* Boulder: Lynne Rienner.

———— (1987c) "Labor in the Global Political Economy." In James Caporaso, ed., *A Changing International Division of Labor.* Boulder: Lynne Rienner.

Cardoso, Fernando (1972) "Dependency and Development in Latin America," *New Left Review,* July–August.

Chief Joseph (1877) "Surrender Speech." In Teresa McLuhan (1971), *Touch the Earth.*

Cline, William (1982) "Can the East Asian Model of Development Be Generalized?" *World Development* 10:2.

Cole, Kenneth, et al. (1991) *Why Economists Disagree: The Political Economy of Economics.* 2d ed. London: Longman.

Cox, Robert (1987) *Production, Power, and World Order: Social Forces in the Making of History.* New York: Columbia University Press.

———— (1991) "The Global Political Economy and Social Choice." In Daniel Drache and Meric Gertler, eds., *The New Era of Global Competition: State Policy and Market Power.* Montreal: McGill-Queen's University Press.

———— (1992) "Global Perestroika." In Ralph Miliband and Leo Panitch, eds., *Socialist Register.* London: Merlin Press.

Cypher, James (1993) "The Ideology of Economic Science in the Selling of NAFTA: The Political Economy of Elite Decision-Making," *Review of Radical Political Economics* 25:4.

Daly, Herman, ed. (1973) *Toward a Steady-State Economy.* San Francisco: W. H. Freeman.

Denzin, Norman, and Yvonne Lincoln, eds. (1994) *Handbook of Qualitative Research.* Thousand Oaks: Sage.

Dolan, Michael (1991) "The Political Economy of Global Restructuring and Its Impact on the Third World." Paper presented at the annual meeting of the International Studies Association, Vancouver.

Drucker, Peter (1988) "The Changed World Economy," In Charles Kegley and Eugene Wittkopf, eds., *The Global Agenda.* New York: Random House.

———— (1989) *The New Realities: In Government and Politics, in Economics and Business, in Society and World View.* New York: Harper and Row.

Eden, Lorraine (1993) "Bringing the Firm Back In: Multinationals in International Political Economy." In Lorraine Eden and Evan Potter, eds., *Multinationals in the Global Political Economy.* New York: St. Martin's Press.

Edwards, Chris (1985) *The Fragmented World: Competing Perspectives on Trade, Money and Crisis.* London: Methuen.

Elek, Andrew (1993) "Asia Pacific Economic Cooperation: Opportunities and Risks for a New Intitiative." Paper presented at a conference on Economic and Security Cooperation in the Asia-Pacific: Agenda for the 1990's, Canberra.

Enloe, Cynthia (1990) *Bananas, Beaches and Bases.* Berkeley: University of California Press.

Esteva, Gustavo (1992) "Development." In Wolfgang Sachs, ed., *The Development Dictionary: A Guide to Knowledge as Power.* London: Zed Press.

Fesharaki, Fereidun, et al. (1995) "Energy Outlook to 2010: Asia-Pacific Demand, Supply, and Climate Change Implications," *Asia Pacific Issues* 19 (April), (East-West Center).

Franklin, Michael (1988) *Rich Man's Farming: The Crisis in Agriculture.* London: Routledge.

Frederick, Howard (1993) *Global Communication and International Relations.* Belmont: Wadsworth.

Frieden, Jeffrey (1991) "Invested Interests: The Politics of National Economic Policies in a World of Global Finance," *International Organization* 45:4.

Friedman, Milton (1962) *Capitalism and Freedom.* Chicago: University of Chicago Press.

Fröbel, Folker, et al. (1978) "'The New International Division of Labor,'" *Social Science Information* 17:1.

Galloway, John (1991) "Competition Within and Between Global Industries." Paper presented at the fifteenth world congress of the International Political Science Association, Buenos Aires.

George, Jim (1994) *Discourses of World Politics.* Boulder: Lynne Rienner.

George, Susan (1986) *How the Other Half Dies.* Harmondsworth: Penguin.

——— (1988) *A Fate Worse Than Debt.* Harmondsworth: Penguin.

——— (1992) *The Debt Boomerang.* London: Pluto.

George, Susan, and Fabrizio Sabelli (1994) *Faith and Credit: The World Bank's Secular Empire.* Harmondsworth: Penguin.

Gill, Stephen (1990) "Intellectuals and Transnational Capital." In Ralph Miliband et al., eds., *The Socialist Register.* London: Merlin Press.

———, ed. (1993) *Gramsci, Historical Materialism and International Relations.* Cambridge: Cambridge University Press.

Gill, Stephen, and David Law (1988) *The Global Political Economy: Perspectives, Problems and Policies.* London: Harvester Wheatsheaf.

Gilpin, Robert (1974) "Three Models of the Future," *International Organisation* 29:1.

——— (1975) *U.S. Power and the Multinational Corporation: The Political Economy of Foreign Direct Investment.* New York: Basic Books.

——— (1987) *The Political Economy of International Relations.* Princeton: Princeton University Press.

Gomez, V., and M. Thea Sinclair (1991) "Integration in the Tourism Industry: A Case Study Approach." In M. Thea Sinclair and Michael Stabler, eds., *The Tourism Industry: An International Analysis.* Wallingford: C.A.B. International.

Green, Francis, and Bob Sutcliffe (1987) *The Profit System.* Harmondsworth: Penguin.

Grimwade, Nigel (1989) *International Trade: New Patterns of Trade, Production and Investment.* London: Routledge and Kegan Paul.

Grinspun, Ricardo, and Maxwell Cameron, eds. (1993) *The Political Economy of North American Free Trade.* London: Macmillan.

Gurtov, Mel (1994) *Global Politics in the Human Interest.* Boulder: Lynne Rienner.

Frank, Andre Gunder (1978) *Dependent Accumulation and Underdevelopment.* London: Macmillan.

Harris, K. (1995) "The Stupendous Seven—The New Masters of the Universe," *Media Studies Journal* 129 (Winter).

Harris, Nigel (1983) *Of Bread and Guns.* Harmondsworth: Penguin.

Hartsock, Nancy (1983) *Money, Sex and Power: Toward a Feminist Historical Materialism.* Boston: Northeastern University Press.

Hayek, Friedrich A. von (1988) *The Fatal Conceit: The Errors of Socialism.* London: Routledge and Kegan Paul.

Helleiner, Eric (1994) "From Bretton Woods to Global Finance: A World Turned Upside Down." In Geoffrey Stubbs and Richard Underhill, eds., *Political Economy and the Changing World Order.* London: Macmillan.

Hessler, Stephan (1994) "Regionalization of the World Economy: Fact or Fiction?" Paper presented at the annual meeting of the International Studies Association, Washington.

Hirschman, Albert (1985) "Against Parsimony: Three Easy Ways of Complicating Some Categories of Economic Discourse," *Economics and Philosophy* 1.

Hobson, John (1988) *Imperialism: A Study.* London: Unwin Hyman.

Holloway, John (1994) "Global Capital and the National State," *Capital and Class* 52.

Hull, Charles, ed. (1899) *The Economic Writings of Sir Wm Petty.* Vol. 1. Cambridge: University Press.

Hume, David (1955) *Writings on Economics.* First published in 1748. Ed. E. Rotwein. Edinburgh: Nelson.

Hymer, Stephen (1971) "Robinson Crusoe and the Secret of Primitive Accumulation," *Monthly Review* 23:4.

——— (1979) *The Multinational Corporation: A Radical Approach.* Cambridge: Cambridge University Press.

ILO (1994) *World Labour Report.* Geneva: International Labour Office.

Jenkins, Robin (1984) "Divisions Over the International Division of Labour," *Capital and Class* 22.

Jevons, William (1970) *The Theory of Political Economy.* Harmondsworth: Penguin.

Kahler, Miles (1993) "Trade and Domestic Differences." Paper presented at a conference on the State in Transition, La Trobe University.

Kapstein, Ethan (1992) *The Political Economy of National Security: A Global Perspective.* New York: McGraw-Hill.

Kautsky, Karl (1988) *The Materialist Conception of History.* New Haven: Yale University Press.

Keynes, John Maynard (1933) "National Self-Sufficiency," *The New Statesman and Nation,* July 8.

Kornbluth, Joyce, ed. (1964) *Rebel Voices: An IWW Anthology.* Ann Arbor: University of Michigan.

Krause, Keith (1992) *Arms and the State: Patterns of Military Production and Trade.* Cambridge: Cambridge University Press.

Krugman, Paul (1994) "The Myth of Asia's Miracle," *Foreign Affairs* 73:6.

Kwan, C. H. (1993) "The Asian Economies in the 1990's." In Tokyo Club Foundation for Global Studies, *The Economic Outlook Toward the Year 2000.* Tokyo: Nomura Research Institute.

Lambert, John (1991) "Europe: The Nation-State Dies Hard," *Capital and Class* 43.

Landes, David (1969) *The Unbound Prometheus: Technological Change and Industrial Development in Western Europe from 1750 to the Present.* London: Oxford University Press.

Lather, Patricia (1991) *Getting Smart: Feminist Research and Pedagogy Within the Postmodern.* New York: Routledge.

Leger, J. (1994) "Asia's Leading Companies," *Far Eastern Economic Review,* December 29–January 5.

Lenin, Vladimir (1973; written in 1916) *Imperialism, the Highest Stage of Capitalism.* Peking: Foreign Languages Press.

Levitsky, Melvyn (1992) "Progress in the International War Against Illicit Drugs." U.S. Department of State Dispatch, March 2.

Lim, Liu (1993) "The Feminization of Labour in the Asia-Pacific Rim Countries: From Contributing to Economic Dynamisn to Bearing the Brunt of Structural Adjustment." In Naohiro Ogawa et al., eds., *Human Resources in Development along the Asia-Pacific Rim.* Singapore: Oxford University Press.

Lipietz, Alain (1992) *Towards a New Economic Order: Postfordism, Ecology and Democracy.* Cambridge: Polity.

Lodge, David (1980) "My First Job," *London Review of Books,* September 4–17.

Lovering, John (1987) "The Atlantic Arms Economy: Towards a Military Regime of Accumulation?" *Capital and Class* 83.

Low, Patrick, ed. (1992) *International Trade and the Environment.* World Bank Discussion Paper no. 159.

Luxemburg, Rosa (1951) *The Accumulation of Capital.* First published in 1913. London: Routledge and Kegan Paul.

MacEwan, Arthur (1992) "Alternative to Free Trade: A Critique of the New Orthodoxy," *Monthly Review* 44:5.

Marx, Karl (1946) *Capital.* Vol. 1. First published in 1867. London: J. M. Dent.

Marx, Karl, and Friedrich Engels (1942) "The Communist Manifesto." In *Karl Marx: Selected Works.* Vol. 1. First published in 1848. London: Lawrence and Wishart.

McIntyre, Richard (1992) "The Political Economy of International Financial Reforms: A Class Analysis." In C. Polychroniou, ed., *Perspectives and Issues in International Political Economy.* Westport: Praeger.

McLuhan, Teresa (1971) *Touch the Earth: A Self-Portrait of Indian Existence.* New York: Outerbridge and Dienstfrey.

McMichael, Philip, and David Myhre (1991) "Global Regulation vs. the Nation-State: Agro-Food Systems and the New Politics of Capital," *Capital and Class* 43.

McVeagh, John (1981) *Tradefull Merchants: The Portrayal of the Capitalist in Literature.* London: Routledge and Kegan Paul.

Meeks, M. Douglas (1989) *God the Economist: The Doctrine and Political Economy.* Minneapolis: Fortress Press.

Mies, Maria (1986) *Patriarchy and Accumulation on a World Scale: Women in the International Division of Labor.* London: Zed Books.

——— (1988) *Women: The Last Colony.* London: Zed Books.

Moffitt, Michael (1984) *The World's Money: International Banking from Bretton Woods to the Brink of Insolvency.* London: Michael Joseph.

Monty Python and the Holy Grail (1974) London: Eyre Methuen.

Muller, Mike (1982) *The Health of Nations: A North-South Investigation.* London: Faber and Faber.

Murphy, Peter (1985) *Tourism: A Community Approach.* New York: Methuen.

Murray, P. (1993) "The European Community—Recasting the National State?," Paper presented at a conference on the State in Transition, La Trobe University.

Nandy, Ashis (1992) "State." In Wolfgang Sachs, ed., *The Development Dictionary: A Guide to Knowledge as Power.* London: Zed Press.

Neyer, Jürgen (1994) "Structural Changes in the World Economy and the New Shape of Conflicts." Paper presented at the annual ISA convention, Washington.

Overbeek, Henk (1994) "Global Restructuring and the Emerging Regional Migration Regime in Europe." Paper presented at the annual ISA convention, Washington.

Owen, Wilfred (1987) *Transportation and World Development.* Baltimore: Johns Hopkins University Press.

Pauly, Louis (1994) "Promoting a Global Economy: The Normative Role of the International Monetary Fund." In Richard Stubbs and Geoffrey Underhill, eds., *Political Economy and the Changing Global Order.* London: Macmillan.

Payer, Cheryl (1974) "The Lawyer's Typist: Variations on a Theme by Paul Samuelson," *Monthly Review* 25:10.

Peterson, V. Spike, and Anne Runyan (1993) *Global Gender Issues.* Boulder: Westview Press.

Petras, James (1993) "Cultural Imperialism in the Late 20th Century," *Journal of Contemporary Asia* 23:2.

Pettman, Jindy Jan (1994) "Women, Boundaries and Danger: Towards an International Political Economy of Sex." Paper presented at the annual ISA conference, Washington.

Pettman, Ralph (1991) *International Politics: Balance of Power, Balance of Productivity, Balance of Ideologies.* Boulder: Lynne Rienner.

Picciotto, Sol (1991) "The Internationalisation of the State," *Capital and Class* 43.

Polanyi, Karl (1957) *The Great Transformation: The Political and Economic Origins of Our Time.* First published in 1944. Boston: Beacon Press.

Potts, Lydia (1990) *The World Labour Market: A History of Migration.* London: Zed Books.

President's Commission on Organized Crime (1986) "America's Habit: Drug Abuse, Drug Trafficking, and Organized Crime." Report to the President and the Attorney General. Washington.

Radford, R. (1945) "The Economic Organisation of a P.O.W. Camp," *Economica,* New Series, 12:48.

Ranney, D. (1993) "NAFTA and the New Transnational Corporate Agenda," *Review of Radical Political Economics* 25:4.

Ray, Lawrence (1993) *Rethinking Critical Theory.* London: Sage.

Reynolds, Charles (1981) *Modes of Imperialism.* Oxford: Martin Robertson.

Ricardo, David (1971) *On the Principles of Political Economy, and Taxation.* First published 1817. Harmondsworth: Penguin.

Rich, Bruce (1994) *Mortgaging the Earth: The World Bank, Environmental Impoverishment, and the Crisis of Development.* Boston: Beacon Press.

Richter, Linda (1989) *The Politics of Tourism in Asia.* Honolulu: University of Hawaii Press.

Robert, Jean (1992) "Production." In Wolfgang Sachs, ed., *The Development Dictionary.* London: Zed Press.

Roberts, B. (1995) "1995 and the End of the Post–Cold War Era," *Washington Quarterly* 18:1.

Roberts, Richard, ed. (1995) *Religion and the Transformations of Capitalism.* London: Routledge.

Robertson, Roland, and William Garrett (1991) *Religion and Global Order.* New York: Paragon.

Rosaldo, Renato (1989) *Culture and Truth: The Remaking of Social Analysis.* Boston: Beacon Press.

Said, Edward (1978) *Orientalism.* New York: Pantheon.

Sampson, Anthony (1973) *The Sovereign State: The Secret History of ITT.* London: Hodder and Stoughton.

Sarup, Madan (1993) *An Introductory Guide to Post-Structuralism and Postmodernism.* 2d ed. Athens: University of Georgia Press.

Schlossstein, Steven (1991) *Asia's New Little Dragons: The Dynmaic Emergence of Indonesia, Thailand and Malaysia.* Chicago: Contemporary Books.

Schmitt, Hans (1979) "Mercantilism: A Modern Argument," *The Manchester School of Economic and Social Studies* 47.

Schumacher, Ernst (1973) "Buddhist Economics." In Herman Daly, ed., *Toward a Steady-State Economy.* San Francisco: W. H. Freeman.

Schumpeter, Joseph (1951) *Imperialism and Social Classes.* Oxford: Basil Blackwell.

Sen, Gita, and Caren Grown (1987) *Development, Crises and Alternative Visions: Third World Women's Perspectives.* New York: Monthly Review Press.

Sharma, Shalendra (1995) "Neo-Classical Political Economy and the Lessons from East Asia," *International Studies Notes* 20:2.

Sklar, Richard (1987) "Postimperialism: A Class Analysis of Multinational Corporate Expansion." In David Becker et al., *Postimperialism: International Capitalism and Development in the Late Twentieth Century.* Boulder: Lynne Rienner.

Smith, Adam (1892) *An Inquiry into the Nature and Causes of the Wealth of Nations.* First published in 1776. London: George Routledge and Sons.

Staniland, Martin (1985) *What Is Political Economy?* New Haven: Yale University Press.

Stavenhagen, Rodolfo (1989) "Effective Protection and Comprehensive Development of the Social and Economic Sectors in Indigenous Communities Through International Standard-Setting Activities." Paper prepared for a UN seminar on the effects of racism and racial discrimination on the social and economic relations between indigenous peoples and states, Geneva.

Steer, A. (1994) "Review: Bruce Rich, Mortgaging the Earth," *Finance and Development* 31:2.

Strange, Susan (1986) *Casino Capitalism.* Oxford: Oxford University Press.

——— (1988) *States and Markets.* London: Pinter.

——— (1991a) "Big Business and the State," *Millennium* 20:2.

——— (1991b) "An Eclectic Approach." In Craig Murphy and Roger Tooze, eds., *The New International Political Economy.* Boulder: Lynne Rienner.

Sweezy, Paul (1994) "The Triumph of Financial Capital," *Monthly Review* 46:2.

Swift, Jonathan (1932) *Satires and Personal Writings.* Oxford: Oxford University Press.

Sylvester, Christine (1990) "The Emperor's Theories and Transformations: Looking at the Field Through Feminist Lenses." In Dennis Pirages and Christine Sylvester, eds., *Transformations in the Global Political Economy.* New York: St. Martin's Press.

—— (1994) *Feminist Theory and International Relations in a Postmodern Era.* Cambridge: Cambridge University Press.

Tai, Hung-Chao, ed. (1989) *Confucianism and Economic Development: An Oriental Alternative?* Washington: Washington Institute Press.

Tawney, Richard (1930) "Forward." In Max Weber, *The Protestant Ethic and the Spirit of Capitalism.* London: Unwin.

Taylor, Ian (1994) "The Political Economy of Crime." In Mike Maguire et al., eds., *The Oxford Handbook of Criminology.* Oxford: Clarendon Press.

Thakur, Ramesh (1994) "NAFTA: Creating the North American Trading Bloc," *New Zealand International Review* 29:2.

Tickner, J. Ann (1992) *Gender in International Relations.* New York: Columbia University Press.

Trainer, Ted (1985) *Abandon Affluence!* London: Zed.

—— (1988) *Developed to Death: Rethinking Third World Development.* London: Marshall Pickering.

Tsuru, Shigeto (1993) *Japan's Capitalism: Creative Defeat and Beyond.* Cambridge: Cambridge University Press.

Tubiana, Lawrence (1989) "World Trade in Agricultural Products: From Global Regulation to Market Fragmentation." In David Goodman and Michael Redclift, eds., *The International Farm Crisis.* New York: St. Martin's Press.

UN (1989) *World Survey on the Role of Women in Development.* New York: United Nations.

UNCTAD (United Nations Committee on Trade, Aid and Development) (1994) *World Investment Report.* New York: United Nations.

UNDP (United Nations Development Programme) (1992) *Human Development Report.* Oxford: Oxford University Press.

—— (1993) *Human Development Report.* Oxford: Oxford University Press.

—— (1994) *Human Development Report.* Oxford: Oxford University Press.

UNICEF (United Nations Children's Fund) (1995a) *The Progress of Nations.* New York: UNICEF.

—— (1995b) *The State of the World's Children.* Oxford: Oxford University Press.

Velasco, Pura (1994) *I Am A Global Commodity: Women Domestic Workers, Economic Restructuring and International Solidarity.* Toronto: Cassette Culture.

Vickers, Jeanne (1991) *Women and the World Economic Crisis.* London: Zed Books.

Viner, Jacob (1948) "Power Versus Plenty as Objectives of Foreign Policy in the Seventeenth and Eighteenth Centuries," *World Politics* 1:1.

Vogel, Ezra (1991) *The Four Little Dragons.* Cambridge: Harvard University Press.

Von Werlhof, C. (1988) "The Proletarian Is Dead: Long Live the Housewife!" In Maria Mies et al., eds., *Women: The Last Colony.* London: Zed Books.

Wade, Robert (1992) "East Asia's Economic Success: Conflicting Perspectives, Partial Insights, Shaky Evidence," *World Politics* 44:2.

Walker, R.B.J. (1988) *One World/Many Worlds.* Boulder: Lynne Rienner.

Wallerstein, Immanuel (1979) *The Capitalist World-Economy.* Cambridge: Cambridge University Press.

Williams, Raymond (1983) *Keywords: A Vocabulary of Culture and Society.* London: Fontana Press.

Williams, S. (1986) "Arming the Third World: The Role of the Multinational Corporation." In Chris Dixon et al., eds., *Multinational Corporations and the Third World*. Boulder: Westview.

Wood, Ellen (1994) "From Opportunity to Imperative: The History of the Market," *Monthly Review* 46:3.

Woodall, P. (1994) "The Global Economy," *Economist*, October 1.

World Bank (1994a) *World Development Report: Infrastructure for Development*. Washington: World Bank.

——— (1994b) *Social Indicators of Development*. Washington: World Bank.

Wriston, Walter (1992) *The Twilight of Sovereignty: How the Information Revolution Is Transforming Our World*. New York: Charles Scribner's Sons.

Yergin, Daniel (1991) *The Prize: The Epic Quest for Oil, Money and Power*. New York: Simon and Schuster.

Index

About the Book

This innovative text offers a comprehensive survey of international political economy, but it is a survey with a difference. Built around a carefully selected set of nonacademic readings, it not only reviews the traditional analytic narratives and documents the transition from international to world political economy, but also critiques the rationalist bias of the discipline.

In pursuit of the clarity that rationalist discourse allows, posits Pettman, researchers too often eschew an indispensable source of knowledge about IPE. The subjective, the emotive, the personal, and the experiential are actively avoided. And the result as much blinds as illuminates.

Thus, Pettman encourages the student not only to stand back and "look" at IPE, but equally to move in close and "listen." *Understanding International Political Economy* (with readings for the fatigued!) introduces this important area of human knowledge in an exciting and provocative way, while demonstrating that information and insights are to be gained from the less, as well as the more, conventional accounts of what is involved.

Ralph Pettman holds the Foundation Chair of International Relations and International Political Economy at the Victoria University of Wellington, New Zealand. His numerous publications include *International Politics: Balance of Power, Balance of Productivity, Balance of Ideologies; Teaching for Human Rights;* and *State and Class: A Sociology of International Affairs.*